Nozima Akhrarkhodjaeva

THE INSTRUMENTALISATION OF MASS MEDIA IN ELECTORAL AUTHORITARIAN REGIMES

Evidence from Russia's Presidential
Election Campaigns of 2000 and 2008

ibidem-Verlag
Stuttgart

Bibliografische Information der Deutschen Nationalbibliothek
Die Deutsche Nationalbibliothek verzeichnet diese Publikation in der Deutschen Nationalbibliografie; detaillierte bibliografische Daten sind im Internet über http://dnb.d-nb.de abrufbar.

Bibliographic information published by the Deutsche Nationalbibliothek
Die Deutsche Nationalbibliothek lists this publication in the Deutsche Nationalbibliografie; detailed bibliographic data are available in the Internet at http://dnb.d-nb.de.

∞

Gedruckt auf alterungsbeständigem, säurefreien Papier
Printed on acid-free paper

ISSN: 1614-3515

ISBN-13: 978-3-8382-1013-1

© *ibidem*-Verlag
Stuttgart 2017

Alle Rechte vorbehalten

Das Werk einschließlich aller seiner Teile ist urheberrechtlich geschützt. Jede Verwertung außerhalb der engen Grenzen des Urheberrechtsgesetzes ist ohne Zustimmung des Verlages unzulässig und strafbar. Dies gilt insbesondere für Vervielfältigungen, Übersetzungen, Mikroverfilmungen und elektronische Speicherformen sowie die Einspeicherung und Verarbeitung in elektronischen Systemen.

All rights part of this publication may be reproduced, stored in or introduced into a retrieval system, or transmitted, in any form, or by any means (electronic, mechanical, photocopying, recording or otherwise) without the prior written permission of the publisher. Any person who does any unauthorized act in relation to this publication may be liable to criminal prosecution and civil claims for damages.

Printed in the EU

Contents

Introduction 1

1. **Hybrid regimes: types and measurements** 13
   1.1. Introduction 13
   1.2. The debate on hybrid regimes 15
   1.3. Types and concepts 19
   1.4. Regime typologies 25
   1.5. Issues of operationalisation 30
   1.6. Electoral authoritarian regimes 35
   1.7. Conclusions 42

2. **Electoral manipulations** 45
   2.1. Introduction 45
   2.2. Defining electoral manipulation 47
   2.3. Types of manipulation strategies 61
   2.4. Measuring electoral misconduct 65
   2.5. Electoral malpractice in competitive authoritarian regimes 73
   2.6. Conclusions 78

3. **Instrumentalisation of the media** 81
   3.1. Introduction 81
   3.2. Media effects debate 82
   3.3. Models of media effects: agenda setting, framing, priming 85
   3.4. Media bias 93
   3.5. Model: elections and the media in electoral autocracies 99
   3.6. Conclusions 125

4. **Strategies of media manipulation: The case of Russia** 129
   4.1. Introduction 129
   4.2. Research design 130
   4.3. Literature review 141
   4.4. Mechanisms of influence 147
   4.5. Journalists' reporting practices 171
   4.6. Trust in the media 179
   4.7. Conclusions 181

5. **Analysis of news content: presidential election campaigns 2000 and 2008** 187
   5.1. Introduction 187
   5.2. Research design 188
   5.3. Content analysis 191
   5.4. Presidential elections of 2000 207
   5.5. Presidential elections of 2008 223
   5.6. Discussion: drawing comparisons 234
   5.7. Conclusions 239

Conclusions 245

References 263

List of Tables

Introduction 1

1. **Hybrid regimes: types and measurements** 13
   Table 1.1. Number of "partly free" countries in the world, 1975-2010 18
   Table 1.2. Regime transitions in the Post-Soviet Eurasia, 1995-2010 18
   Table 1.3. Regime typologies: Dichotomous vs. Continuous 28
   Table 1.4. Regime typologies: trichotomous 29
   Table 1.5. The most recent and systematic typologies of hybrid regimes ... 32
   Table 1.6. Regime classification of post-Soviet States 33
   Table 1.7. Measuring regimes: Alternative indeces 34

2. **Electoral manipulations** 45
   Table 2.1. The chain of democratic choice by A. Schedler 56
   Table 2.2. Definitions of electoral fraud 59
   Table 2.3. Typologies of electoral manipulations 64
   Table 2.4. Types of electoral fraud 70
   Table 2.5. Mean scores for electoral malpractices across the regimes 75
   Table 2.6. Mean scores for electoral malpractices in competitive auth. regimes 76
   Table 2.7. Mean scores for electoral malpractices across the regimes 77

3. **Instrumentalisation of the media** 81
   Table 3.1. Typology of electoral malpractice 111
   Table 3.2. Ways of influencing the media 112
   Table 3.3. The effects of media manipulations on news content 114
   Table 3.4. Journalistic ethics and professionalism 117

4. **Strategies of media manipulation: The case of Russia** 129
   Table 4.1. List of parliamentary and presidential elections in Russia, 1995-2012 133
   Table 4.2. Owners and financiers of large media organizations, 2000 and 2008 156
   Table 4.3. Strategies of media control and manipulation, 2000-2008 162
   Table 4.4. Legal constraints on micro-level: number of legal charges, 2000-2008 166
   Table 4.5. Legal constraints placed on the media 169
   Table 4.6. Strategies of media control and manipulation on micro-level, 2000-2008 ... 170
   Table 4.7. Government control over the mass media 180
   Table 4.8. Objectivity of Russian mass media 180
   Table 4.9. Presidential treatment of candidates on central television and radio 181
   Table 4.10. Trust in the media 181
   Table 4.11. Constraints placed on the media: Year 2000 and prior 185
   Table 4.12. Constrains placed on the media: Year 2008 and after 186

5. **Analysis of news content: presidential election campaigns 2000 and 2008** 187
   Table 5.1. Effects of media manipulations on news content 189
   Table 5.2. Elections of 2000 and 2008 193
   Table 5.3. Percentage of media audience according to media outlets 195

Table 5.4. Popular online media in Russia, 2008 201
Table 5.5. Selected media outlets, Russia 202
Table 5.6. Names and brief description of the candidates 208
Table 5.7. Election results, 2000 210
Table 5.8. Topics most frequently appearing on TV news 216
Table 5.9. Topics and their frequencty by media outlet, 2000 217
Table 5.10. Names and brief description of the candidates, 2008 225
Table 5.11. Election results, 2008 226
Table 5.12. Topics and their frequency by media outlet, 2008 229
Table 5.13. Framing across media types and outlets 237
Table 5.14. Number of times each candidate was mentioned in the media, 2000 ... 238
Table 5.15. Number of times each candidate was mentioned in the media, 2008 ... 239
Table 5.16. Effects of media manipulations on news content 240

Conclusions 245
Table 6.1. Media manipulation in competitive vs. hegemonic regimes 252
Table 6.2. Content bias in competitive vs. hegemonic regimes 257

References 263

Introduction

Research focus

Elections are assumed to empower people against authoritarian rule, bring about democratically elected government, and most importantly, serve as an instrument by which citizens hold the government accountable. However, despite the fact that most political systems in the twenty-first century hold at least some sort of elections, the same type of rulers appear to remain and rule in the same authoritarian fashion. Many authors (Lindberg 2009; McCoy and Hartlyn 2008; Brownlee 2009) claim that repeated elections can lead to democratisation[1]. However, regardless of the regularity of elections in many authoritarian and semi-authoritarian regimes, incumbents use various tactics to manipulate voters' preferences or reduce the likelihood of opposition candidates being elected by changing electoral laws before election day (Birch 2011). One of the tools that leaders use to manipulate voters' preferences is the media. In democracies, the media's main task is to inform citizens, provide balanced coverage of political events, render political authorities accountable by monitoring their activities, and serve as a "marketplace" of ideas (Voltmer 2007; Dahl 1975). However, in states with weak democratic institutions, the situation is somewhat different.

---

[1] Lindberg's (2009: 41) research shows that "holding an increasing number of elections is by far the most important causal factor in increasing and spreading respect for civil liberties in Africa," Jason Brownlee also argues that "competitive elections increase the likelihood that democracy will succeed authoritarianism in the event of regime breakdown" (2009: 143).

Based on a case study of Russian media, I explore the role played by media in electoral authoritarian regimes in general, and in two sub-types specifically, i.e., competitive authoritarian and hegemonic authoritarian regimes, from a comparative perspective. I aim to determine how control of media access hinders the ability of the opposition to win elections and to discover the means by which the incumbent government uses its administrative resources to win elections. Furthermore, I explore the types of manipulation strategies that are used during electoral campaigns. One of the main arguments of the work is that in competitive authoritarian regimes, the media are among the main instruments used by the state to influence voters' choice and ensure regime stability.

Unlike fully authoritarian regimes, where democratic institutions either do not exist or exist only as a façade, in competitive authoritarian regimes, channels through which opposition can compete in executive elections do exist. In competitive authoritarian regimes, "democratic procedures are sufficiently meaningful for opposition groups to take them seriously as arenas through which they can contest for power (Levitsky and Way 2010: 7)." Rather than fully repressing the broadcasting media, competitive authoritarian regime governments prefer to use various strategies to influence reporting. Implementation of these strategies significantly reduces the opportunity for opposition forces to voice their views and opinions, let alone win elections. Mass media manipulation serves as an important instrument of regime stability. In other words, an incumbent manipulates broadcast media channels to win elections and legitimise his electoral success. As a result, in such regimes, the manipulation of media broadcasting is widespread.

The main goal of this work is to explore the role media play in competitive and hegemonic authoritarian regimes. I aim to find out how control of access to the media hinders opposition's chances to win elections and figure the strategies the incumbent government uses to manipulate media reporting. Furthermore, I am interested in types of manipulation strategies used during the electoral campaigns. One of the main arguments of the work is that media is one of the key instruments used by the state to influence voters' choice and thus to ensure regime stability in competitive authoritarian regimes.

Object of the study	The effects of media manipulation strategies that are used by the ruling elite on news media content in electoral authoritarian regimes.
Research questions	How do the media manipulation strategies that are employed by the ruling elite in electoral authoritarian regimes affect news content? The question has four principal components: 1) Types and extent of media manipulation strategies; 2) Mechanisms of influence; 3) Media's reaction to the influence; and 4) Effects of these manipulations on news content.
	What are the core differences in terms of media manipulation strategies and their effects on media content in competitive and hegemonic regimes?

Instrumentalisation of the media is best understood in the context of political and economic conditions. The principal issues discussed in this work involve the coping mechanisms of media companies, editors, and journalists in the changing political and economic environment; the interaction between the media, the state elite and the opposition; the financial and political considerations of the actors involved; the effects manipulation strategies have on news content or the information that the audience (i.e., voters) get; and finally, the effect that all these factors might have on election outcomes.

Placing relevant actors (i.e., the incumbent elite, opposition candidates, business elite, and the media) in their context to see how their actions are constrained by structural and institutional factors that are not of their own making reveals insightful details, which have not yet been studied. The principal goal of this work is to identify and map media manipulation strategies and to understand the effects that this manipulation has on news content in electoral authoritarian regimes. Further, differences in media coverage between competitive and hegemonic authoritarian regimes are established.

Importance, relevance, and contribution to theory

A large body of literature exists on hybrid regimes - (Zakaria 1997; Merkel 2004; O'Donnell 2008; Schedler 2002; Ottaway 2003; Howard and Roessler 2006; Brownlee 2009; Levitsky and Way 2010), media effects (Lasswell 1935; Lazarsfeld, Berelson and Gaudet 1944; Klapper 1960; McQuail 1992; Marcuse 1964; Herman and Chomski 1988), electoral malpractices (Mozaffar and Schedler 2002; Birch 2007; 2011; Schedler 2002; 2013), and media systems (Siebert et al. 1956; Hallin and Mncini 2004; 2011). Many scholars have acknowledged the important role of media outlets during the 'colour' revolutions that led to electoral change in several countries (McFaul 2005; Bunce and Wolchik 2006). There have even been studies of media systems in new democracies (Voltmer 2014) and studies of media effects on electoral outcomes in post-Soviet countries, mostly in relation to Russia (Enikolopov et al. 2011). However, systematic research on the role of the media in stabilising authoritarian rule in electoral autocracies has not yet been conducted. The key contributions of this work to the literature consist of the followings:

a) Bridging the literature on hybrid regime studies and electoral malpractices

Literature on hybrid regimes has expanded in recent decades. The debate revolves around the conceptualisation, classification, and operationalisation of such regimes. The categories proposed by scholars including Levitsky and Way (2010), Jason Brownlee (2009), Howard and Roessler (2006), and Schedler (2013) are well defined, and on a conceptual level, do not raise serious disagreements. However, the operationalisation and measurement criteria they use are problematic. On the one hand, scholars do not agree about how to assign a type to a case, and on the other, their measurement criteria are sometimes arbitrary. I argue that existing quantitative measurements are not always sufficient to characterise the difference between various types of hybrid regimes. Therefore, I propose to examine the qualitative characteristics of regimes to improve operationalisation.

My research shows that the difference between competitive and hegemonic regimes is more qualitative than previously understood and should be studied accordingly. The difference is subtle, and for the operationalisation of these two regime types, merely examining levels of contestation or the percentage of votes received by a single candidate is insufficient. Mozaffar and Schedler (2002: 5) argue that "electoral governance is a crucial variable in securing the credibility of elections in emerging democracies"; however, electoral governance has not been given enough attention in comparative democratisation studies. Using the literature on electoral manipulation / electoral fraud / electoral integrity might provide greater clarity regarding the concepts of electoral authoritarian regimes and their operationalisation. Using Birch's data set of electoral malpractice and the regime data sets of Howard and Roessler as well as of Levitsky and Way, I demonstrate that hegemonic and competitive regimes use different strategies to manipulate elections. Further research is needed to verify the results; however, based on this preliminary analysis, it can be argued that using data on electoral malpractice might solve the problem of drawing the boundaries between electoral authoritarian regime sub-types using quantitative approach.

b) Drawing a connection between the media and electoral outcomes in hybrid regimes

Various types of fraud/manipulations occur on and before election day; however, my research focuses on media manipulation strategies and their effect on news content — primarily because this area is an understudied but prominent part of electoral authoritarian regimes. My quantitative analysis shows that media manipulation is the most commonly used strategy in both sub-types of electoral authoritarianism, although the two use it to a different extent. In the qualitative part, I draw a comparison between the extent and types of media manipulation in competitive and hegemonic regimes.

Some argue that the media has the potential to shape the voter's vision and interpretation of political events, and in certain settings, to contribute to election outcomes through the effects that the media has on the audience. In non-democracies the media is used to manipulate public opinion. In authoritarian electoral regimes, where electoral outcomes depend not only on vote buying, repression, or nullifying the election results, governments are keen to use the media to construct positive views of the favoured candidate. To do so, various tools are used. The effects of these manipulations are mirrored in the media content. Apart from the ability to influence media decisions regarding agenda setting and event framing, the incumbent can force some media outlets to introduce certain content bias in the reporting and can force journalists and media organisations into self-censorship. These different media manipulation strategies and their effects on news content are detailed in this work.

c) Detailed and systematic comparative analysis of media instrumentalisation in Russia

There is an extensive body of literature on the Russian media and its role in Russian politics. Studies have been conducted on the effects of media on election results (Colton and McFaul 2003; White, Oates and McAllister 2005; Oates 2006; Enikolopov, Petrova and Zhuravskaya 2011), the Russian media and its evolution dynamics (Koltsova 2001; Koltsova 2006; Zasurskii 2004; Roudakova 2009); media system types in Russia (Becker 2004; Vartanova 2011), journalists and journalistic professionalism (Voltmer 2000; Pasti 2005), television viewers in Russia (Mickiewicz 2005), and the theme most closely related to this work, media instrumentalisation by the political elite (Lazitski 2013; Orttung and Walker 2014; Silitski 2009), the tightening of control over Russian television since Putin's rise to power and television content that aims at keeping the current regime in power (Lipman 2009; Lipman 2014; Gehlbach 2010; Burrett 2014), and on television content (Laruelle 2014; Rollberg 2014). Nonetheless, a detailed and systematic comparative analysis of media instrumentalisation in Russia across the two mentioned regime types is lacking. Some scholars including Walker and Orttung (2014), Silitski (2009), and Lazitsky (2013) have opened up the topic of media instrumentalisation. However, their work lacks the use of a systematic approach to studying the strategies that have been used by the ruling elite to influence the media. I aim to fill this gap by providing a systematic case study of media instrumentalisation and its effects on news content during presidential election campaigns.

d) Model illustrating the mechanisms of influence on media content

I develop a theoretical model (see the Figure 1) that aims to demonstrate the mechanisms that influence media content by placing pressure on news organisations and journalists; this model also depicts interactions between the actors. There is a constant information flow between the audience, the media, and political actors. The ruling elite attempts to influence media content by manipulating the legal framework; abusing state resources; coercion, etc. Journalists, in turn, calculate the risks associated with reporting on issues that are disapproved of by the state and act according to their best knowledge, their professional integrity and their own schema system. Some choose to report on issues that threaten the state's legitimacy or criticise the government or its policies, whereas others adjust to the demands of the ruling elite.

The model- illustrated in the Figure 1 presents a mechanism by which the media operates in electoral regimes. This model is derived from the theories of competitive authoritarianism, electoral authoritarianism, electoral malpractice, and political communication. As observed in this model, in electoral authoritarian regimes, both the opposition and the ruling elite have access to the media; however, access is skewed in favour of the incumbent. As Schedler (2013) also notes, the incumbent has access to legal and state resources through which he or she can manipulate the media.

When the majority of the population uses television news as the main source of information on political events and in absence of alternative views in the media, voter's opinions are partly shaped by the information that they receive from the television. The media cannot tell people "what to do or what to think" (Cohen 1963), however, by setting the agenda, it can implicitly direct the debates in certain directions; and/or, by using different frames, the media can present reality in a way that advantages one actor over another. By priming certain issues, the media can nudge the citizens to evaluate the performance of the government using the benchmarks that are most often discussed in the media. In countries where people have a degree of trust in the media, they are more vulnerable to media influence-. The ruling elite manipulates the media environment, pressures journalists, and restricts media freedom in a way that best suits their interests. How exactly this is done, the nature of the manipulations that are used, and how the effects of these manipulations are mirrored in the media content is explicated in the case study of the Russian presidential elections of 2000 and 2008. This comparative case study demonstrates the difference in functioning of competitive and hegemonic regimes.

Figure 1. A model of media effects in the electoral process

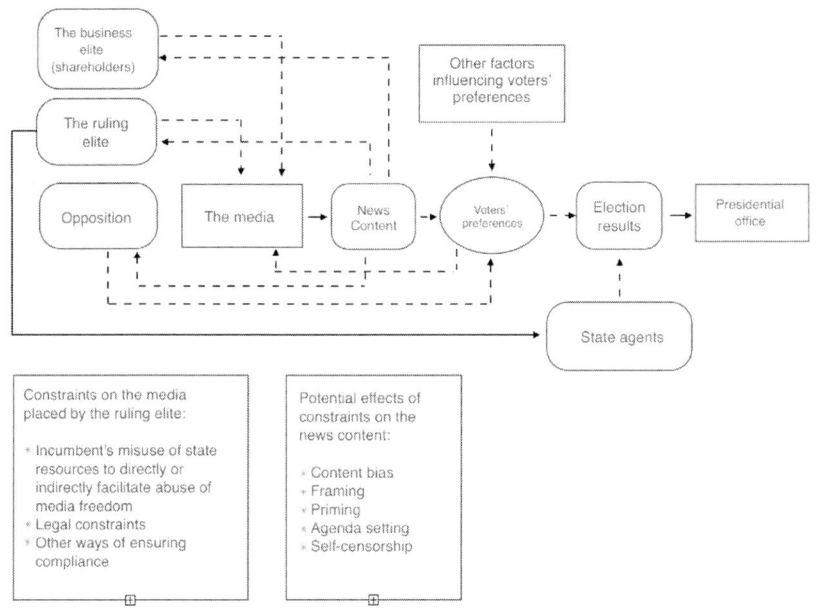

Methods

To explore the mechanisms of media manipulation employed by the ruling elite in competitive and hegemonic authoritarian regimes and the effects of these manipulations on news content, a longitudinal comparative in-depth case study design is employed. A case study approach provides valuable insights into the inner workings of a regime and the mechanisms that it uses to influence information flow within the country. This approach also helps to explain variation in candidate coverage during presidential election campaigns.

To map the media manipulation strategies that are employed by the incumbent government, general background information on media structure is gathered and examined using document analysis. This information is mostly based on media statistics and reports. To evaluate media freedom, different reports and data that are provided by Freedom House, Reporters Without Borders, and some other organisations are used. Statistical data on newspaper circulation, television channel coverage and Internet access are obtained from Internet World Stats, Annual Statistics (ex.: Rossiiskii Statisticheskii Ezhegodnik), some secondary sources, and information from the websites of various television channels and newspapers. I also look at legislation concerning the media to give a full picture of the strategies that are used by governments to curb media freedom. I use country reports prepared by Freedom House, Organisation for Security and Cooperation in Europe (OSCE), and official government sources as well as newspaper reports to study the legal framework.

To enrich the case study, interviews with eleven journalists and editors who are working in some of the most popular print and online media outlets the target audiences of which are intellectuals, academics, entrepreneurs, and politically active members of society, were conducted. Additionally, interviews conducted by other researchers have also been consulted. The main purpose of these interviews was to establish a link between the pressure (i.e., media manipulation strategies) exerted by the ruling elite on the media and its effect on media organisations and journalists.

Most importantly, employing coding and content analysis, I examine electoral campaigns to determine the extent of media coverage bias. This is done in two steps. First, using coding, news content is quantified to see whether the coverage of political affairs is skewed in favour of the incumbent. Second, using qualitative content analysis, I examine exactly how the candidates and their platforms are presented: the tone of coverage and framing are examined.

I also examine public opinion polls (polls related to trust in the media, the main source of political information, etc.) and the secondary literature to determine whether people consider the media a trustworthy news source.

Cases

A typical competitive authoritarian regime, which later turns into hegemonic regime is chosen to analyse the inner mechanisms of regime functioning. Choosing one country at two different times and two different political regimes helps to control for variables including culture, religion, historical background, and geographical location; at the same time, this selection helps to identify the differences between the inner workings of competitive and hegemonic regimes. Russia is taken as one of the most informative cases from among a broader universe of countries with competitive authoritarian regimes. Furthermore, elections that served as a point of change in regime dynamics are selected; i.e., presidential elections in Russia in 2000 and 2008[2].

Book outline

The book is divided into five chapters. *Chapter 1* discusses different regime typologies, covers an emerging debate on hybrid regimes, provides an overview of different types of hybrid regimes and the strategies that are used to conceptualise these regimes. The chapter also discusses the different types of regimes and regime typologies, brings forth a critical review of concepts, operationalisation and lays out scholarly work on electoral authoritarianism by carefully detailing and discussing the main characteristics and subtypes.

Chapter 2: One of the primary goals of the second chapter is to identify the patterns of electoral manipulation in electoral authoritarian regimes with a special focus on competitive authoritarian regimes to determine whether any particular type of electoral fraud predominates, i.e., is used to a greater extent in states with competitive regimes. The chapter also

---

[2] Details about case selection are given in Chapter 4.

discusses the variation in type and degree of electoral malpractices across the regimes.

Chapter 3 builds a theoretical framework through which the effects of media manipulation strategies on news content are analysed. The model demonstrates how the media are instrumentalised in competitive authoritarian regimes and is built on the relevant literature on a) hybrid regimes, b) electoral contests in competitive authoritarian regimes, c) media manipulation strategies that are employed by the ruling elite to ensure electoral stability, and d) the media and its effects on electoral outcomes.

Chapter 4 presents a comparative case study illustrating how media manipulation strategies function in competitive and hegemonic regimes. The chapter traces the development of the media landscape in Russia and highlights some of the most influential factors that have contributed to the growth of media instrumentalisation; the chapter also lists manipulation strategies that are used by the ruling elite to constrain the media and demonstrates how media instrumentalisation is executed.

Chapter 5 presents the results of content analysis and analyses news content to determine the presence and extent of content bias during the presidential election campaigns of 2000 (i.e., a competitive regime) and of 2008 (i.e., a hegemonic regime) in Russia. Conclusions follow.

1. Hybrid regimes: types and measurements

1.1. Introduction

Although the third wave of democratisation[3] led to the emergence of new democracies, not all autocracies democratised; instead, they followed distinct trajectories. Some of them transitioned to democracies, while many others either remained stable or became increasingly authoritarian, paving the way for research on hybrid regimes and new forms of authoritarianism. The proliferation of anocracies not only posed a challenge to existing dichotomous regime typologies (e.g., Przeworski et al. 2000) but also encouraged research on prospects of the democratisation of these regimes (e.g., Lindberg 2006; Brownlee 2007; Bunce and Wolchik 2011; Levitsky and Way 2010) and even triggered a debate among scholars studying conflicts (e.g., Sean Fox and Kristian Hoelscher 2011; Mansfield and Snyder 2002; 2005; for a critical review of Mansfield and Snyder's work, see Bogaards 2009). This chapter aims to give an overview of the emergent debate on hybrid regimes, and pursues several goals arranged and elaborated in the following six sections.

In the first section, following the recent scholarship on hybrid regimes, I argue that hybrid regimes have to be studied separately as distinct types of regimes. To support this argument, I present regime data from different sources that show that these regimes are present in approximately one-

---

[3] Samuel Huntington defines the period between 1974—the year marked by a revolutionary upheaval in Portugal, which led to democratic transition—and 1990 as the third wave of democratization. However, hybrid regimes existed long before this wave of transitions, which led to emergence and proliferation of a vigorous debate on hybrid regimes.

third of the world. In addition, for the case of post-Soviet states, I demonstrate that hybrids are not as unstable as claimed. Finally, I give some examples from the recent literature on hybrid regimes, demonstrating that internal dynamics and prospects of democratisation in these regimes are distinct from other regime types, whether democracies or closed autocracies. These examples all support the claim that hybrids should not be neglected or considered as temporary forms, but rather should be studied separately. Research should move beyond attempting to conceptualise and measure these new species; it should put more emphasis on studying the internal mechanism of these regimes in detail.

Second, an overview of different types of hybrid regimes and the strategies used to conceptualise these regimes are detailed. For the purpose of presenting conceptual debate, hybrids are divided into two groups, autocracies and democracies, "with adjectives." Further, classical subtypes and diminished subtypes of regimes are discussed; in addition, some conceptually confusing terms that have been used previously by scholars are critically assessed.

The third section is devoted to a discussion of different types of typologies. Here, three distinct types are detailed: dichotomous, continuous, and trichotomous typologies. The section argues that the latter, the trichotomous typology, is the most useful in studying regimes, as it is able to cover more cases.

In the next section, the operationalisation of concepts is discussed. Using post-Soviet cases, I show the existing disagreement in the literature as to which category cases are to be assigned. Disagreement is present not only in scholarly publications but also in regime data sets. I argue that concepts such as "competitive" and "hegemonic" authoritarian regimes are useful; however, confusion arises when scholars try to come up with measurements. This section critically evaluates the measurements and operationalisation of hybrid regimes. It outlines the importance of engaging with more detailed comparative case studies to draw clearer boundaries between sub-types of electoral authoritarianism and argues that in studying these categories of regimes, the literature on electoral fraud/manipulation/integrity can be of better use.

Finally, this chapter lays out scholarly work on electoral authoritarianism and carefully details and discusses its main characteristics and subtypes. The last section is devoted to concluding remarks.

1.2. The debate on hybrid regimes

The end of the Cold War marked the end of many authoritarian regimes across the world, while the remaining autocracies were forced to adopt representative institutions in the form of elections, multiple parties and legislative assemblies. It was argued that repetitive elections could lead to democratisation (Lindberg 2009; McCoy and Hartlyn 2008; Brownlee 2009). Regarding the example of African countries, Lindberg (2009: 41) claimed, "[…] holding an increasing number of elections is by far the most important causal factor in increasing and spreading respect for civil liberties […] [4]." Others argued, "competitive elections increase the likelihood that democracy will succeed authoritarianism in the event of regime breakdown" (Brownlee 2009: 143). Some research (Ruchan and Bernhard 2013) based on the evidence from Post-Communist Eurasia even showed that elections neither promote democracy nor stabilise the existing autocracies. Another interesting study on opposition coalitions and whether they promote democratisation by elections in electoral authoritarian regimes was conducted by Wahman (2013). He argues that even though an authoritarian leader can be overthrown as a result of

---

[4] However, the systematic re-examination of evidence from Africa conducted by M. Bogaards (2013) shows that out of 43 countries in Sub-Saharan Africa that hold multi-party elections, only five were democratised, but two of then later reverted to electoral authoritarianism. The results of this study do not confirm that there is a common trend towards democratization by elections in Africa; on the contrary, "the dominant trajectories are for free countries to remain free and for electoral autocracies to remain autocratic, while electoral democracies are vulnerable to reversal and breakdown (p. 3)."

opposition coordination, electoral turnover does not mean democratisation, and it is a lengthy process. A recent claim (Gandhi 2015) is that to make more sound arguments, the research on the role of elections in political change in authoritarian regimes should reconsider existing approaches and collect more systematic historical data on actors, their behaviour and the factors that serve as primary factors affecting the quality and the outcome of elections.

Overall, in the majority of cases, the process of democratisation has been somewhat dispiriting. Introduction of multiparty elections in many previously non-competitive regimes rarely led to establishment of liberal democracies, but rather gave rise to a variety of hybrid regimes that combine significant elements of both democratic competition and authoritarian rule. These regimes neither satisfied minimal conditions for democracies nor fit any of the classical authoritarian regime categories, such as "totalitarian," "authoritarian" (Linz 2000), "post-totalitarian" (Linz and Stepan 1996), "sultanistic" (Chehabi and Linz 1998) "single party regimes," "personalist," "monarchy," or "military dictatorships" (Geddes 1999; also see Brooker 2000[5]). They were frequently seen as regimes in transition to democracies and were treated as democratising. In the seminal work on regime transitions, O'Donnell and Schmitter (1986) studied the "transitions from certain authoritarian regimes toward an uncertain "something else." That "something else" is either the establishment of a democracy, a backslide to autocracy or, alternatively, the emergence of some unstable political realm.

> That "something" can be the installation of a political democracy or the restoration of a new, and possibly more severe, form of authoritarian rule. The outcome can also be simply confusion, that is, the rotation in power of successive government that fails to provide any enduring or predictable

---

[5] For a discussion of a full spectrum of non-democratic regimes, including hybrids and semi-competitive regimes, see Paul Brooker, *Non-Democratic Regimes: Theory, Government and Politics* (Saint Martin's Press, 2000), and a more recent, 3rd ed. Paul Brooker, *Non-Democratic Regimes* (Palgrave Macmillan, 2014).

solution to the problem of institutionalising political power. Transitions can also develop into widespread, violent confrontations, eventually giving way to revolutionary regimes which promote changes going far beyond the political realm (O'Donnell and Schmitter 1986: 1).

In sum, hybrid regimes were considered regimes in a state of transition or unstable regimes. However, in 2002, Thomas Carothers published an article in which he argued that the transition paradigm is out-dated and that it is time to move to a new generation of frameworks and models and come up with "a new paradigm of political change" to study a new landscape[6]. Since then, scholars have called for avoiding "democratizing bias" (Levitsky and Way 2002) or "transition bias" (Carothers 2002) and for studying hybrid regimes "in their own right, not only through the lenses of what they are not (autocracy or democracy)" (Hale 2011: 23). As Hale argued, these regimes are large in number, durable, and follow a distinctive logic in handling issues of governance, foreign policy, and the economy.

According to the Economist Intelligence Unit's Index of Democracy, of the 167 regimes included in the analysis, 86 could be classified as hybrid. This figure represents approximately 51.5% of all independent states, with exception of microstates. According to Freedom House, which classifies considers into "free," "partly free," and "not free," as of 2014, 59 countries (or roughly 30%) out of total 195 were classified as "partly free." Despite some claims that hybrids are not stable and are most likely to transition either to democracy or autocracy, the number of hybrid regimes across the

---

[6] Interestingly, although almost every work on hybrid regimes published after Carothers' article has blamed "transitologists" for creating a misleading paradigm and claimed that such works were in abundance, it seems that the confusion was not as widespread in the academic literature. Carothers himself refers mostly to governmental and non-governmental organizations, to democracy promoters in general and, to a much lesser extent, to the academic literature when criticising the "transition bias." A discussion of whether theories of Post-Communist regime transitions really dominated the academic debate or were a mere myth is presented in an article by Jordan Gans-Morse, "Searching for Transitologists: Contemporary Theories of Post-Communist Transitions and the Myth of a Dominant Paradigm," *Post-Soviet Affairs* 20, no. 4 (2004): 320-349.

globe does not seem to be declining. On the contrary, the number of countries ranked as "partly free" is increasing; see Table 1.1.

Table 1.1. Number of "partly free" countries in the world, 1975-2010

Years	Total countries	Free		Partly free		Not free	
		Number	%	Number	%	Number	%
1975	158	40	25	53	34	65	41
1980	162	51	31	51	31	60	37
1985	167	56	34	56	34	55	33
1990	165	65	40	50	30	50	30
1995	191	76	40	62	32	53	28
2000	192	86	45	58	30	48	25
2005	192	89	46	58	30	45	24
2010	194	87	45	60	31	47	24

Source: Freedom House, 2014

Table 1.2. Regime transitions in the Post-Soviet Eurasia, 1995-2010

	To electoral dem.	To comp. auth.	To hegemonic	To closed auth.	Total
From electoral dem.	31	1	0	0	32
From comp. auth.	1	34	3	0	38
From hegemonic	1	0	85	0	86
From closed auth.	0	0	1	18	19
Total	33	35	89	18	175

Source: Author's calculations based on Howard and Roessler's (2009) regime data set

Numerous case studies also point to the degree of hybrid regimes. For example, a comparative case study of Southeast Asian countries (Case

1996: 457) shows that "semidemocracy possesses some intrinsically stable characteristics." A study conducted by Wheatley and Zuercher (2008: 1) for the South Caucasus argues that hybrid regimes should not be "treated as a half-way stage in a process of transition […]." Using the sample of Post-Sovie Eurasian states drawn from Howard and Roessler's regime data set, one can see that hybrid regimes are quite durable. Table 1.2 shows number of transitions from one regime category to another in the Post-Soviet region between 1995 and 2010. As it can be seen not only most regimes in this region were predominantly hybrid but also that transitions from one regime to another were very rare: 7 in total. Interestingly, transitions from competitive and hegemonic regimes to electoral democracies were the result of the mass electoral protests, and after the protests in Georgia (2004), and Ukraine (2003), both countries moved to the category of electoral democracies. In the rest of the cases, competitive authoritarian regimes remained either stable or reverted to hegemonic authoritarianism (Belarus, Russia).

1.3. Types and concepts

The spread of hybrid regimes across the globe has raised a vigorous debate in the comparative politics literature, urging scholars to categorise and study such systems as distinct types of regimes. As a result, some scholars turned to "conceptual stretching" (Sartori 1970) — which occurs when, for instance, the concept of democracy is used to refer to a regime that does not fulfil the minimum requirements of democracy — by creating numerous types of "democracies with adjectives" (Collier and Levitsky 1997). Collier and Levitsky counted over 100 subtypes, some of the most confusing of them being "authoritarian democracy[7]" and "neopatrimonial

---

[7] Ex. John Peeler, *Building Democracy in Latin America*, (Boulder: Lynne Rienner Publishers, 2009); "Authoritarian democracy" — a term coined mostly when studying Latin American political systems, while "neopatrimonial democracy" was used by scholars of African politics.

democracy[8]." In this wave, Karl and Schmitter (1991) published an article clarifying "what democracy is ... and is not," outlining some of the essential characteristics of minimal democracy. Others engaged in "fallacy of electoralalism[9]," considering "the mere fact of elections—even ones from which specific parties or candidates are excluded, or in which substantial portions of the population cannot freely participate—as a sufficient condition for the existence of democracy (Karl and Schmitter 1991: 78)."

Since then, hybrid regimes have received different labels, such as "mixed," "grey zone," "grey area" or "hybrids" (Karl 1995; Carothers 2002; Bunce and Wolchik 2006)[10]. However, eventually, to capture the nature of hybrids, the literature introduced new concepts designed to examine these new species, with the most prominent of them being "competitive authoritarianism," "semi-authoritarianism," "delegative democracy," "illiberal democracy," and "defective democracy" — these subtypes of either authoritarianism or democracy were created using a "diminished" subtypes method as a strategy of conceptual innovation. Based on the logic of Collier and Levitsky (1997), in contrast to concepts such as "totalitarianism" or "military authoritarianism," classical types and subtypes of authoritarian regimes — "competitive authoritarianism" or "semi-authoritarianism" — are diminished subtypes of authoritarianism

---

[8] The problem with this sort of concept is not a mismatch with real cases, but rather confusion on a conceptual level. Political systems that are ruled in a neopatrimonial or authoritarian manner while elections are conducted in a way that somewhat resembles procedural democracies are not hard to find. However, it is important to make this analytical distinction between "how the incumbent is elected" and "how the state is governed." For a thorough discussion, see Guliyev Farid, "Personal Rule, Neopatrimonialism, and Regime Typologies: Integrating Dahlian and Weberian Approaches to Regime Studies," *Democratization* 18, no. 3 (2011): 575-601.

[9] The fallacy of electoralism is discussed in works of Terry Lynn Karl, "Dilemmas of Democratization in Latin America," *Comparative Politics* 23, no. 1 (1990): 1-21; Philippe Schmitter and Terry Lynn Karl, "What Democracy Is ... and Is Not," *Journal of Democracy* 2, no. 3 (1991): 75-88; Larry Diamond, "Is the Third Wave Over?" *Journal of Democracy* 7, no. 3 (1996): 20-37.

[10] For further discussion, see also Heidrun Zinecker, "Regime Hybridity in Developing Countries: Achievements and Limitations of New Research on Transitions," *International Studies Review*, 11, no. 2 (2009): 302-31.

because they are not full instances of the root definition of "authoritarianism" and lack some of the main characteristics of "full authoritarian" regimes[11]. Using this strategy, O'Donnell and Schmitter (1996) coined terms "dictablanca" and "democradura," or "liberalized autocracy" and "tutelary democracy," to refer to the regimes found in the "in-between" zone. The regimes in which "authoritarian rulers may tolerate or even promote liberalization in belief that by opening up certain spaces for individual and group action, they can relieve various pressures and obtain needed information and support without altering the structure of authority, that is, without becoming accountable to the citizenry for their actions or subjecting their claim to rule to fair and competitive elections" — were referred to as "liberalized autocracy," or "dictablanca." The regimes with limited political democracy were dubbed "democradura" and defined as the regimes in which democratisation has already begun but in which the advocates of the old regime have found new ways of restricting the freedom of individuals or groups who pose a potential threat to the incumbent. Although useful, these concepts did not spread well, but the logic behind them — dividing hybrid regimes into two general categories depending on whether the elections complied with the principles of minimal democracy or not — was used while mapping the terrain between autocracy and democracy. Similarly, Case (1996) distinguished between "semidemocracies" and "semiautocracies."

Scholars used two approaches in classifying hybrid regimes. First, the most widespread strategy involved adding adjectives to the concept of democracy, with the goal of sorting out between forms of democratic regimes containing some elements of autocracies and those that are not full liberal democracies. The second strategy involved adding adjectives to the concept of authoritarianism. These are the regimes that are not even minimally democratic, despite the fact that they hold elections; but at the

---

[11] Classical and diminished subtypes are further discussed later in this chapter in the section on regime typologies.

same time, they lack some of the key components of "full/closed authoritarian regimes."

"Democracy with adjectives[12]"

With regard to democracies with deficiencies, scholars have introduced an entirely new vocabulary of diminished subtypes of democracy (Collier and Levitsky 1997). Applying this method, Guillermo O'Donnell (1994) coined the term "delegative democracy," referring to regimes in which the president is elected through clean elections; however, too much power is concentrated in presidency. In delegative democracies, institutional constraints, which are supposed to keep officials accountable, are either non-existent or weak. Another concept is "illiberal democracy," which was devised by Fareed Zakaria (1997). This concept encompasses the regimes that are marked by free and fair elections but that have different defects in other areas, such as rule of law, separation of powers, protection of basic liberties, property rights, assembly, religion, and freedom of speech. A similar strategy was used by Wolfgang Merkel (2004) to delineate

---

[12] The term "democracy with adjectives" was coined by Collier and Levitsky to capture numerous subtypes of democracies that are not fully democratic. The authors argue that since the emergence of hybrid regimes, scholars have faced conceptual problems. On the one hand, they have tried to increase analytic differentiation to capture the various forms of new regimes; on the other, they have applied the concept of democracy to regimes that are not even minimally democratic, facing the threat of committing conceptual stretching. Examples could include concepts such as "military-dominated" or "protodemocracy." The authors argue that the scholars studying regimes use several strategies to create concepts. The first strategy is to use Sartori's approach of moving up and down the ladder of generality to cover more cases, for example, instead of using the concept of "democracy," using the "regime" concept. This strategy has been applied when creating classical regime types: authoritarianism, democracy, totalitarianism, etc. The second strategy is creating diminished subtypes, in other words, defining the concept of democracy and then specifying the attributes that are missing. Third is "precising the definition of democracy" by adding defining attributes to the concept of democracy. Their article critically reviews some other strategies, too. For a thorough review of the concepts used to describe different regimes, see David Collier and Steven Levitsky, "Democracy with Adjectives: Conceptual Innovation in Comparative Research," *World Politics* 49, no. 3 (1997): 430-451.

democratic regimes with defects in some of the fundamental components of democracy. His work is one of the most systematic attempts to create a typology of defective democracies. He distinguished between exclusive democracy, domain democracy, illiberal democracy, and delegative democracy.

Electoral democracy — a term used by Larry Diamond (1996) — describes a contemporary minimalist conception in which democracies "commonly acknowledge the need for minimal levels of civil freedom in order for competition and participation to be meaningful. Typically, however, they do not devote much attention to the basic freedoms involved, nor do they attempt to incorporate them into actual measures of democracy."

Less systematically applied and relatively unpopular concepts include "managed democracy" and "pseudodemocracy." The term pseudodemocracy was also introduced by Diamond (1996) to describe the regimes that "have legal opposition parties and perhaps many other constitutional features of electoral democracy, but fail to meet one of its crucial requirements: a sufficiently fair arena of contestation to allow the ruling party to be turned out of power." He also subdivided pseudodemocracies into "semidemocracies" (regimes that "approach electoral democracies in their pluralism, competitiveness, and civil liberties") and "hegemonic party systems" (regimes "in which an institutionalized ruling party makes extensive use of coercion, patronage, media control, and other tools to reduce opposition parties to decidedly 'second-class' status"). Diamond's definitions of pseudodemocracy and its subtypes closely reflect the concept of electoral authoritarianism and its subtypes; however, perhaps due to conceptual stretching (applying the concept of democracy to cases that are clearly authoritarian) or conceptual confusion (semidemocracy as a subtype of pseudodemocracy), the terms did not stick.

"Autocracy with adjectives"

The second strategy is used mainly to depict the species of hybrids that are not even minimally democratic. Ottaway (2003) proposed concept of "semi-authoritarianism" referring to "ambiguous systems that combine rhetorical acceptance of liberal democracy, the existence of some formal democratic institutions, and respect for a limited sphere of civil and political liberties with essentially illiberal or even authoritarian traits (2003: 3)." She characterised them as "political hybrids" allowing "little real competition for power, thus reducing government accountability (2003: 3)." Most recently, Schedler (2002; 2013) introduced the concept of "electoral authoritarianism" — a type of regime in which neither democracy is practiced, nor is open repression exercised. In electoral authoritarian regimes, multiparty elections are periodically organised to gain at least the façade of democratic legitimacy; however, these elections are held under tight authoritarian control. Elections are organised in a fashion in which incumbents attain some legitimacy to rule, but at the same time, any risk of losing the electoral competition is avoided. These are authoritarian regimes operating under the cover of democratic electoral institutions.

Moving down the "ladder of generality[13]," several scholars, such as Diamond (2002) and, later, Howard and Roessler (2006), followed by Brownlee (2006), subdivided electoral authoritarian regimes into hegemonic and competitive forms. The concept of "competitive authoritarianism" — a type of regime in which democratic institutions such as elections are considered to be the main way of obtaining political authority — was coined by Steven Levitsky and Lucan Way (2010: 5), and according to the authors, it is a diminished subtype of authoritarianism and

---

[13] Originally introduced by Sartori (1970) as a "ladder of abstraction," but later, for the sake of avoiding any confusion, renamed into "ladder of generality" by Collier and Levitsky (1997: 434), the term refers to a "pattern of inverse variation between the number of defining attributes and number of cases." The concept with fewer defining characteristics is higher on the ladder of generality, as it can encompass more cases, while the concept with more attributes applies to fewer cases and is hence lower on the ladder.

a type of regime in which elections are free but rarely fair and in which incumbents violate electoral procedures and rules so often that even minimum required democratic standards are not met. To win elections, incumbents use state resources, harass opposition, and deny the opposition sufficient media coverage. Although elections are rarely fair, competitive authoritarian regimes differ from other electoral authoritarian regimes in that democratic rules are not openly violated. Instead of repressing the opposition, more subtle strategies such as co-optation, bribery, compliant judiciaries, and "legal" harassments (ex., defamation lawsuits) are used. Nevertheless, despite the unfairness of electoral competition, elections are contested and the opposition forces may pose a significant challenge to incumbents. Democratic institutions are used not only to legitimise the existing authoritarian government but also to serve as a channel through which the opposition can voice its interests.

1.4. Regime typologies

As hybrid regimes are at the centre of this work, it is important to give a short overview of the existing typologies. I use hybrid regimes as an umbrella term for regimes that are neither purely democratic nor authoritarian. Many attempts have been made by scholars to devise new regime typologies that include intermediate categories between liberal democracies and autocracies. However, most of the proposed typologies, as Matthijs Bogaards (2009: 400) justly argues, are "rough sketches in which types are not fully defined, boundaries are not clearly specified and coding decisions seem arbitrary." In addition, not all of them have clear rules for operationalisation and cross-series data sets (e.g., Diamond 2002; Wigell 2008; Marlino 2009; Eckman 2009). I review the most systematic of recent approaches.

Dichotomous typologies

The study of hybrid regimes is relatively new; earlier works were concentrated mostly on studying features of either democracies or autocracies. Thus, the classical typologies were dichotomous, dividing regimes into two categories, autocracy and democracy, and studying them separately. Once the divide was made, scholars chose a side and studied the regime of their interest; this way, scholars such as Juan Linz (1964; 2000) and Chehabi and Linz (1998) who pioneered research on authoritarian, totalitarian, post-totalitarian, and sultanistic regimes, while Arend Lijphart (1999) studied types of democratic systems, delineating majoritarian and consensus types of institutional settings. Since Linz, the literature on authoritarian regimes proliferated and generated a great deal of knowledge. Based on dichotomous classifications new types of authoritarian regimes were identified and studied. For instance, Alvarez et al. (1996) recognised the existence of different types of authoritarian and democratic regimes, advancing dichotomous classification, at the core of which lies contestation. They differentiated between the regimes "that allow some, even if limited, regularised competition among conflicting visions and interests from those in which some values or interests enjoy a monopoly buttressed by a threat or the actual use of force" (1996: 4). Drawing on this work, Geddes (1999) later identified different sub-types of authoritarian regimes. She classified authoritarian regimes into military, single-party, and personalist regimes based on differences in their inner functioning, their responses to society and opponents, different ways of choosing the leaders and handling succession, and the decision-making procedures they use. She argued that in military regimes, power rests in the hands of a group of officers who rule and influence policies. In single-party regimes, a party dominates access to political office and exercises control over policies. In this type of regime, other parties can legally exist and even compete in elections; however, the power is with a dominant party. Personalist regimes resemble the sultanistic regimes discussed by Linz and Chehabi (1998), they are different from both single-party and military regimes, in that principal decisions are made by one person and an individual leader controls both the access to power and the exercise of power. The leader might have created the party or have a military background, but neither the party nor the military has the power to make independent decisions. The power emanates from the leader.

Continuous typologies

There are other methodological approaches to measuring and classifying the regimes, for example doing so using the continuum scale. An example of this approach would be Freedom House's Freedom in the World index, which rates countries on a seven-point scale, from democratic (1) to non-democratic (7). Polity IV's measurements, which rank countries from autocracies (-10) to democracies (10), would be another example. Table 1.3 maps some of the most influential works on regime studies.

For a long time, it was sufficient to separate regimes into two categories. However, as elections have been introduced and practiced in an increasing number of countries, the need for alternative typologies has risen. Controversies emerged around the concept of democracy and whether it is a dichotomous or continuous variable (for a discussion, see Collier and Adcock 1999, Elkins 2000, Munck and Verkuilen 2002; Bogaards 2009). Previous dichotomous and continuous typologies were heavily criticised for failing to account for the degree of election fairness in the case of dichotomous typologies and for having unspecified and arbitrary boundaries in the case of continuous typologies. If dichotomous typology is used, then hybrid regimes, composing around 30% of the regimes worldwide, would have to be allocated in the category they do not belong, and studied based on principal properties of either democracies or autocracy. This in turn would not allow us to study these regimes in more depth, thus, cultivating further the "transition bias." Regarding continuous typologies, the problem is mostly in arbitrariness of assigning a number to the type, and whether Freedom House and Polity IV scores can be used to differentiate between different types of regimes, if yes, then how well they do so (see Munck and Verkuilen 2002).

Table 1.3. Regime typologies: Dichotomous vs. Continuous

Dichotomous	
Authoritarianism	*Democracy*
Authoritarian regimes (Geddes 1999): — Military regimes — Single party regime — Personalist regime	Democracy
Non-democratic regimes (Linz) — Authoritarianism — Totalitarianism — Sultanism	

Continuous				
Polity IV				
Autocracy (-10 to -6)	Closed anocracy (-5 to 0)	Open anocracy (1 to 5)	Democracy (6 to 9)	Full-democracy (10)
Freedom House				
Not-Free (7-6)		Partially free (5-3)		Free (2-1)

Table 1.4. Regime typologies: trichotomous

Authors	Authoritarian regimes	Hybrids		Democratic regimes
Schedler 2013	Closed authoritarian	Electoral authoritarianism	Electoral democracy	Liberal democracy
Levitsky and Way 2010	Full authoritarianism	Competitive authoritarian	Democracy	
Brownlee 2009	Closed authoritarian	Electoral authoritarianism: - Hegemonic authoritarianism - Competitive authoritarianism	Democracy	
Howard and Roessler 2006	Closed authoritarian	Electoral authoritarianism: - Hegemonic authoritarianism - Competitive authoritarianism	Electoral democracy	Liberal democracy
Merkel 2004	Autocracy		Defective democracy: - Exclusive democracy - Domain democracy - Illiberal democracy - Delegative democracy	Embedded democracy
Others	Autocracy	Semi-authoritarianism (Ottaway 2003); Liberalized autocracy (Brumberg 2002); Sultanistic semi-authoritarianism (Guliyev 2005)	Delegative democracy (O'Donnell 1994)	Liberal democracy

Trichotomous typologies

In the light of these debates and as the the literature emphasising the role and importance of elections grew, new trichotomous typologies were introduced (see Table 1.4 above). Gasiorowski (1996) developed a database of political regimes using trichotomous regime-coding schemes, distinguishing between democracies, semi-democracies, and autocracies. This was shortly followed by Schedler's conceptualisation of regimes into authoritarian, democratic, and hybrid regimes. In trichotomous regime typologies hybrids are viewed as distinct regime types, neither autocracies nor democracies, and studied accordingly, thus solving the issue that dichotomous, and continuous typologies have. Although, this new regime typology solves some of the issues, operationalisation and classification of cases into regime categories still remain problematic. The next sub-section gives a critical assessment of issues concerning the operationalisation of hybrid regimes.

1.5. Issues of operationalisation

Some of the recent attempts to categorise hybrid regimes were made by Steven Levitsky and Lucan Way (2010); nevertheless, their categories of hybrid regimes include only competitive authoritarianism, thus lumping all other types of regimes into either democracy or autocracy. However, they admit that competitive authoritarianism is just one type of a larger group of hybrid regimes. In contrast to Levitsky and Way (2010), Jason Brownlee (2009) constructed a typology that divides the hybrid regime category into two, distinguishing between electoral democracy and electoral authoritarianism. Table 1.5 provides a short summary of the most recent typologies and their measurement criteria. The typologies, as such, are not problematic. The categories are well defined, and on a conceptual level, they do not raise serious disagreements. However, problems exist with the operationalisation and measurement criteria used by scholars. On the one hand, there is no agreement among scholars in regard to assigning a type to a case, and on the other, their measurement criteria are sometimes arbitrary. This section outlines some of the problematic issues and argues that existing methods are not sufficient to draw a clear boundary between hybrid regime subtypes.

As seen from Table 1.5, Brownlee used the Database of Political Institutions to categorise regimes. However, his typology fails the test of face validity. For example, Uzbekistan, which is usually referred to in the literature (Levitsky and Way 2010, Carothers 2002, McFaul 2005, Ottaway 2003, Fish 2006) as a case of outright authoritarianism, was coded as competitive authoritarian by Brownlee (see Table 1.6). If Brownlee's measurement criteria are used, then the difference between regimes such as Ukraine, Georgia and Uzbekistan simply disappears.

Roessler and Howard (2009; Howard and Roessler 2006) use a combination of Freedom House and Polity IV indicators as their measurement criteria. Their conceptualisation of regimes is clear and well defined. However, as they use Freedom House (FH) and Polity IV aggregates, the criticism of FH and Polity data sets by Gerardo Munck and Jay Verkuilen (2002) can be equally applied to Roessler and Howard's measurement.

To reiterate, their coding decisions seem to be arbitrary, and the authors do not clearly say why a regime should be called competitive authoritarian if the winner received less than 70% of the vote or seats in previous election, but if he/she received 70%, it should be coded as hegemonic authoritarianism. Using the method of "a rule of the thumb" is quite common. In identifying hegemonic regimes, Beatrice Magaloni (2006) used a 65% cut-off rule, among other criteria. For Brownlee (2009) the cut-off point is 75%. Regardless of the commonality of usage of these cut-off points, categorising the regimes based on arbitrarily established maximum percentage of votes received during the elections by the candidate will generate cases that, under a closer look, do not belong to the category. In other words, as Susan Hyde and Nikolay Marinov (2011) noted, "any threshold will be noisy and will aggregate different "types" of elections on either side of the threshold."

Table 1.5. The most recent and systematic typologies of hybrid regimes

Authors	Regime type	Measurement criteria
Howard and Roessler (2009); Time-frame: 1991-2006 (p. 112)	Liberal democracy	FH = 2 and Polity = 10
	Electoral democracy	FH ≤ 2 or Polity ≥ 6
	Competitive authoritarianism	FH ≥ 3 and Polity ≤ 5 and winner received < 70% of the vote or seats in previous election.
	Hegemonic authoritarianism	FH ≥ 3 and Polity ≤ 5 and winner received 70% of the vote or seats in previous election.
	Closed authoritarianism	No multicandidate national election for selection of executive.
Brownlee (2009); Time-frame: 1991-2004	Democracy	-
	Electoral authoritarian:	DPI index of legislative and executive electoral competitiveness = 5 – 7
	a. Competitive authoritarianism	DPI = 7 on one of the indices of legislative and executive electoral competitiveness
	b. Hegemonic authoritaria	DPI = 5 or 6 on one of the indices of legislative and executive electoral competitiveness
	Closed authoritarianism	DPI index of legislative and executive electoral competitiveness = 1 – 4
Levitsky and Way (2010) Time-frame: 1990-1995; 2008 (pp.365-368)	Democracy	1. The criteria for full authoritarianism are not met. 2. The criteria for competitive authoritarianism are not met. 3. There exists near-universal adult suffrage. 4. Basic civil liberties (speech, press, association) are systematically protected. 5. The authority of elected governments is not seriously restricted by unelected "tutelary" powers or major nonstate actors.
	Competitive authoritarianism	1. The criteria for full authoritarianism are not met. 2. There exists broad adult suffrage. 3. The authority of elected governments is not seriously restricted by unelected "tutelary" powers. 4. At least one of the following criteria is met: a. Unfair Elections. b. Violation of Civil Liberties. c. Uneven Playing Field.

	Full authoritarianism	1. National-level multiparty elections for the executive do not exist.
		Or
		2. At least one of the following indicators is present:
		  a. Major opposition parties and/or candidates are routinely excluded – either formally or effectively – competing in elections for the national executive.
		  b. Large-scale falsification of electoral results makes voting effectively meaningless.
		  c. Repression is so severe that major civic and opposition groups cannot operate in the public arena; thus, much of the opposition is underground, in prison, or in exile.

Table 1.6. Regime classification of post-Soviet States

Country/2001	Roessler and Howard (2009)	Diamond (2002)	Brownlee (2009)	Levitsky and Way (2010)
Armenia	Comp. auth.	Ambiguous	Electoral dem.	Comp. auth.
Azerbaijan	Hegemonic	Hegemonic	Comp. auth.	Full auth.
Belarus	Comp. auth.	Comp. auth.	Hegemonic	Comp. auth.
Georgia	Hegemonic	Ambiguous	Comp. auth.	Comp. auth.
Kazakhstan	Hegemonic	Hegemonic	Comp. auth.	Full auth.
Kyrgyzstan	Hegemonic	Hegemonic	Comp. auth.	Full auth.
Moldova	Electoral dem.	Electoral dem.	Electoral dem.	Comp. auth.
Russia	Electoral dem.	Comp. auth.	Electoral dem.	Comp. auth.
Tajikistan	Hegemonic	Hegemonic	Comp. auth.	Full auth.
Turkmenistan	Closed auth.	Closed auth.	Hegemonic	Full auth.
Ukraine	Electoral dem.	Ambiguous	Comp. auth.	Comp. auth.
Uzbekistan	Hegemonic	Hegemonic	Comp. auth.	Full auth.

Moreover, the authors classify Russia after 2000 as an electoral democracy, despite the fact that there is a growing stream of qualitative studies (Levitsky and Way 2010; Hassner 2008; Goode 2010) arguing that Russia became increasingly authoritarian since Vladimir Putin took over the presidency. Also, Ukraine is coded as an electoral democracy from the beginning of 1990s, which is against the literature on the positive effects of electoral protests on the regime in Ukraine. As can clearly be seen from Table 1.6, there is no agreement among scholars as to which category the post-Soviet states should be assigned. Alternative indices such as those of the Freedom House, Polity IV, and BTI, as well as Economist Democracy

Index, also differ in their categorisation and in the ratings of regimes (see Table 1.7).

Table 1.7. Measuring regimes: Alternative indeces

Country/2009-2010	Freedom House PR/CL	Polity IV	BTI	Economist Democracy index Overall/Electoral process and pluralism
Armenia	6/4	5	5	4.09/4.33
Azerbaijan	6/5	-7	3.92	3.15/2.17
Belarus	7/6	-7	4.08	3.34/2.58
Georgia	4/4	6	6.05	4.59/7.00
Kazakhstan	6/5	-6	4.17	3.30/1.33
Kyrgyzstan	6/5	1	4.40	4.31/5.75
Moldova	3/4	8	6.65	6.33/8.75
Russia	6/5	4	5.25	4.26/5.25
Tajikistan	6/5	-3	3.67	2.51/1.83
Turkmenistan	7/7	-9	2.78	1.72/0.00
Ukraine	3/2	7	7	6.30/9.17
Uzbekistan	7/7	-9	2.90	1.74/0.08

As this brief overview illustrates, existing quantitative measurements are not always sufficient to mark the difference between different types of hybrid regimes. I propose to look at qualitative characteristics of regimes for better operationalisation. The following section outlines the main characteristics of electoral authoritarian regimes and its competitive and hegemonic subtypes.

1.6. Electoral authoritarian regimes

The fairness of elections plays a crucial role in categorising political regimes. One can argue that two general strategies in classifying regimes are common. The first strategy is to delineate regime categories based on the access to power and a regime's formal institutional characteristics. For those who employ this strategy, the competitiveness of elections, voter turnout, universal suffrage, and the chances of the opposition to win elections are some of the most crucial characteristics in determining the regime type. For example, Levitsky and Way (2010) look at the competitiveness of elections and, more specifically, whether any violation of civil liberties can be observed and, if so, its extent, whether elections are fair, and if the playing field is sufficiently even. Another example would be Schedler's (2013) work, in which he emphasises the role of elections and institutions of representation in defining the regime and its dynamics. For him, the defining characteristic of electoral authoritarian regimes is a presence of "inclusive multiparty elections at the national level," which are constantly undermined via "severe and systematic manipulation (p.55)." Freedom House also concentrates mostly on freedom, competitiveness, and fairness of elections while assessing "freedom in the world."

The second strategy used by scholars gives more weight to the control of power and influence in the classification of regimes. Regime studies of this sort were carried out by Barbara Geddes (1999), Houchang Chehabi and Juan Linz (1998), Wahman, Teorell and Hadenius (2013), Geddes, Wright and Frantz (2012). Geddes, Wright and Frantz (2014) define a regime as "basic informal and formal rules that determine what interests are represented in the authoritarian leadership group and whether these interests can constrain the dictator (p.314)." In her earlier works, Geddes (1999) classifies authoritarian regimes based on the principle of who has the power; in other words, the regimes were classified based on the group from which the leader can be selected and who and/or which group influences policy decisions. Chehabi and Linz (1998) look at the structure of power, the economy, and the conception of politics by the ruler. Wahman, Teorell and Hadenius (2013: 20) focus on the institutional setup of the regime and the modes of accessing and maintaining power. However, what all these classifications have in common is that as a first step, they divide regimes into main categories based on the competitiveness of elections and then delineate sub-categories. In other words, election quality is assessed, and once it is established that elections were not competitive and hence not democratic based on assessment of institutions and higher echelons of power, the types of authoritarian rule are identified. Both proponents of classic dichotomous regime typologies and those advocating the importance of hybrid regimes, acknowledge the importance of electoral competition in determining the regime type.

To classify regimes into democracies and non-democracies, Robert Dahl's (1997) definition and principal characteristics of "polyarchy" are widely used. To briefly recall the essential components of procedural democracy, in democracies, elections are sufficiently free and fair, i.e., no fraud or voter intimidation that might effect the outcome of the elections is observed; political parties campaign on relatively even grounds; opposition is not subjected to harassment or repression and is not denied access to the broadcast media. In essence, for a regime to be considered a procedural democracy, citizens must have an opportunity to "formulate" their preferences, share them with each other, and have them "weighted equally" in government decision making. To follow the principal components of Robert Dahl's (1997: 2-3) much-praised formulation of democracy, to be considered a polyarchy, a country's citizens should have:

— Freedom to form and join organisations
— Freedom of expression
— Right to vote
— Right of political leaders to compete for support
— Alternative sources of information
— Free and fair elections

— Institutions for making government policies depend on votes and other expressions of preferences

The rules of a procedural democracy described by Dahl are clear; however, the ways of breaking them, especially in non-democratic regimes, are numerous, as Aristotle once stated in his well-known work Nicomachean Ethics, "for men are good in but one way, but bad in many." This is not to say that the elections are perfectly democratic in democracies, as this activity involves mass mobilisation and coordination of thousands of tasks and people, some errors such as "defective ballots, incomplete and inaccurate voter rolls, exclusion of registered voters, inaccuracies in counting, tabulation and recording votes, and human mistakes" (Mozaffar and Schedler 2002: 6) are inevitable. However, the magnitude of deficiencies, human mistakes and coordination problems do not have a systematic impact on the outcome of elections. Thus, the advocates of continuous regime typologies and those who find the category of hybrid regimes useful classify non-democratic regimes based on the extent of fraud present during the elections. As Schedler (2013) noted, hybrid regimes themselves can be seen as divided into electoral democracy and electoral authoritarianism. The former fulfils the list of criteria outlined by Robert Dahl (1997) to be called a democracy or a poliarchy, whereas in the latter, democratic institutions are present; however, the elections do not comply with the standards.

The presence of multiparty elections is one of the main characteristics that distinguishes electoral authoritarian regimes from closed autocracies. Currently, elections are practiced not only in democracies but also in a majority of autocracies; however, as Schedler (2013) highlights, elections in some systems are likely to matter more than in others. On some occasions, elections are a mere *façade*; in others, they might define the internal dynamics of regimes. For instance, in closed authoritarian regimes, elections either do not play any role or simply do not transpire. In contrast, the main characteristics of electoral authoritarian regimes are regularly held elections, universal suffrage, the subjugation of the head of government to electoral confirmation, and the presence of multiparty competitions. Schedler (2013: 2) described these regimes as follows:

> Electoral authoritarian regimes establish the institutions of liberal democracy on paper, yet subvert then in practice through severe, widespread, and systematic manipulation. They play the game of multiparty elections, as they hold regular elections for the chief executive and a national legislative assembly. These elections are broadly inclusive (they are held under universal suffrage), minimally pluralistic (opposition parties are permitted to run), minimally competitive (parties and candidates outside the ruling coalition, while denied victory, are allowed to win votes and seats), and minimally open (dissidence is not subject to massive, but often to selective and intermittent repression).

Electoral autocracies are further divided into hegemonic and competitive forms, regime subtypes that will be carefully discussed in the following section. The difference between the two, as Brownlee (2009: 518) argued, is in "the opposition's strength to challenge the incumbent"; similarly, Levitsky and Way (2010) argued that the distinction is in the opposition's chances to win elections.

Competitive authoritarianism

The concept of competitive authoritarianism was introduced by Levitsky and Way; they define it as follows:

> Competitive authoritarian regimes are civilian regimes in which formal democratic institutions exist and are widely viewed as the primary means of gaining power, but in which incumbents' abuse of the state places them at a significant advantage vis-a-vis their opponents. Such regimes are competitive in that opposition parties use democratic institutions to contest seriously for power, but they are not democratic because the playing field is heavily skewed in favour of incumbents. Competition is thus real but unfair (2010: 5).

For a regime to be considered competitive authoritarian, one of the following principles of democracy should be broken: 1) free elections; 2) broad protection of civil liberties; or 3) a reasonably level playing field. The principal characteristic that differentiates competitive authoritarianism from other regime types is an uneven playing field between incumbents and opposition. As emphasis is placed on the fairness of elections, the phenomena of an uneven playing field echoes the literature on electoral fraud/manipulation, with the only distinction being what Levitsky and Way referred to as an "uneven playing field": media manipulation, the manipulation of the legal system, and the access to state resources. A level playing field is one of the principle criterion of free and fair elections. The authors also justly argue that fairness of elections should not be assessed only based on observations of the election day. For example, skewed access to media and finance has a significant effect on elections, but these effects are difficult to account for on the day of elections. Another example could be the ownership of media companies by government's cronies, it might not be recognised as a violation of civil liberties but does have an effect on media content. Scholarship of electoral integrity also emphasises the importance of in-between election time for assessing overall fairness of elections.

An uneven playing field, as argued by Levitsky and Way, is "[a]mong the most effective, but the least analyzed, means of autocratic survival (2010: 57)." While repression or electoral fraud can be obvious to outside observers, an uneven playing field is less evident; however, it has a severe effect on electoral competition. An uneven playing field is defined as "one in which incumbent abuse of the state generates such disparities in access to resources, media, or state institutions that opposition parties' ability to organize and compete for national office is seriously impaired (2010: 57)." An uneven playing field is one of the main characteristics of competitive authoritarian regimes. The authors (Levitsky and Way, 2010: 9-12) distinguished three main aspects of the political playing field: access to media; access to resources; and access to the law.

Uneven access to resources is formed when the incumbent uses the state resources for his own advantage. Such resource disparities can hinder the opposition's chances to win elections. These discrepancies can be created in several ways. One is using state resources for partisan interests. Another way is monopolising access to private-sector finance by exploiting state control over credit and state contracts, licenses and other resources. As a result, the companies that benefit from distributed state resources (i.e., state contracts, licenses, etc.) make donations to the governing party.

Access to the law is uneven when technically independent arbiters such as judiciaries, electoral commissions, and others are in favour of incumbents, as they are manipulated via blackmail, bribery, and intimidation.

Uneven access to media is created by restricting the opposition's access to the media that reach a majority of the population. Levitsky and Way distinguish several ways in which opposition is denied access to the media. Some include biased and partisan coverage, disparities in the access to broadcast media, indirect links between the governing party and the owners of independent media outlets, and control over the state-owned media.

Hegemonic authoritarianism

Although scholarship on hybrid regimes often uses the concept of electoral authoritarianism, the difference between hegemonic and competitive regimes and the difference between hegemonic and closed regimes are not well defined. For example, Schedler describes electoral authoritarian regimes as those in which elections are minimally contested, open, and pluralistic. Hegemonic regimes are regimes in which the opposition does not stand a chance of winning elections, but as a subtype of electoral authoritarian regime, it should have minimally contested, minimally open, and minimally pluralistic elections.

When classifying hybrids, Howard and Roessler (2006) use quite different definitions; for them, the mere existence of ballots, election days, and voting processes is enough to call the regime hegemonic.

> Hegemonic authoritarian regimes do hold regular elections as part of their system of governance, but in addition to widespread violations of political,

civil, and human rights, the elections are not actually competitive. Because no other party, except the ruling one, is allowed to effectively compete (i.e., the opposition is completely shut out from access to state-owned media coverage, banned from holding political rallies, or forced into exile or in jail), the dominant candidate or party wins overwhelmingly to a de facto one-party state (p.367).

Brownlee's definition does not add more clarity. In his work, the difference between competitive and hegemonic regimes is quantitative; he looks at the level of competition in the Democratic Performance Index (DPI) of legislative and executive electoral competitiveness, and those cases that score 7, he classifies as competitive, and those that score 5 or 6 on the same dimension are considered hegemonic regimes. In other words, if the largest party received less than 75% of votes during elections, Brownlee would consider it a competitive election, and if multiple parties won seats but the largest party received more than 75% of the seats or multiple parties are legal and only one won seats, the regime would be coded as hegemonic. If one is to apply the measurements and definitions provided by either Howard and Roessler (2006) or Brownlee (2009), their classifications of regimes would negate those of Levitsky and Way (2010). For example, Levitsky and Way would classify Russia beginning from 2008 as full authoritarian, while Brownlee, Howard and Roessler would classify it as either a competitive authoritarian or an electoral democratic regime. Moreover, the case of Uzbekistan would be hegemonic authoritarian in both typologies, even though it does not fit Schedler's definition of electoral authoritarianism; as it is by no means minimally contested, minimally open, or pluralistic. After the last Uzbekistan's presidential elections in 2007, the OSCE election observation mission reported that "[w]hile there were four candidates, including one woman and one candidate nominated by an initiative group of voters, the voters were nonetheless left without a real choice as all contestants publicly endorsed the policies of the incumbent president, Mr. Islam Karimov. Legal and administrative obstacles prevented political movements representing alternative views from registering as political parties or initiative groups, thereby precluding them from fielding presidential candidates" (OSCE December, 2007).

There is a significant difference between the regime in Russia since 2008 — classified as full authoritarian by Levitsky and Way — and the regime in Uzbekistan, and this, in turn, points at measurement errors in the coding of competitive authoritarianism *per se*. These errors have also been critically addressed in more recent articles by Bardall (2015) and Helle (2015). Some clarity is also needed in conceptualisation. Levitsky and Way (2010) show how competitive authoritarian regimes are different from full autocracies and democracies. However, they do not discuss competitive regimes in the context of other hybrid regimes, nor do they show the existing specific differences among them, which adds confusion to regime classification by making regimes as different as Russia in 2008 and Uzbekistan fall into the same category of full authoritarian regimes.

1.7. Conclusions

To sum up, this chapter a) gave an overview of existing literature on hybrid regimes, b) argued that these regimes are stable and should be studied as a separate category, c) presented various regime typologies, d) discussed approaches used for classifying regimes, and e) outlined some of the most problematic issues related to both, conceptualisation and operationalisation of hybrid regimes, which are also addressed in this book. The research conducted in this work aims at showing that the difference between competitive and hegemonic regimes is more qualitative, subtle, and for the operationalisation of these two regimes, merely examining levels of contestation or a percentage of votes received by a single candidate is not sufficient. Elections and their competitiveness are at the centre of electoral authoritarian regimes. Both Schedler (2013) and Levitsky and Way (2010) pay much attention to electoral fraud and even certain types of electoral manipulations in defining the characteristics of these regimes. As Mozaffar and Schedler (2002: 5) argue, "electoral governance is a crucial variable in securing the credibility of elections in emerging democracies"; however, electoral governance is widely neglected in comparative democratization studies. In line with this thought, I argue that using the literature on electoral manipulation / electoral fraud / electoral integrity provides more clarity to the concepts and their operationalisation while studying and measuring electoral authoritarian regimes. Thus, I agree with Yonatan Morse (2012), who argues that "identifying electoral authoritarian regimes requires paying greater attention to the actual quality of elections rather than observing mere procedures."

Sub-types of electoral authoritarian regimes are somewhat difficult to differentiate; it is not entirely clear where the boundaries should be drawn, on both a conceptual level and a measurement level. As Morse (2012: 163) notes, "[r]esearch cannot be too distant from actual cases, leading to conceptual ambiguity, nor too close to specific cases, thus failing to generate comparative leverage. Closer engagement with detailed and confined comparisons will generate more conceptual clarity and will in turn form the basis for sounder theory building and comparative analysis."

Many argue that regime type should not be determined by examining only the outcomes of elections and the irregularities that occur on the election day as a large part of electoral manipulations take place between elections. Thus, using the literature on electoral malpractice/fraud to better define regime boundaries can be effective as the literature on electoral malpractice mostly looks at fraud committed throughout the entire electoral process. This work is concerned specifically with electoral authoritarian regimes. Thus, the role of elections in electoral authoritarian regimes and the literature of electoral malpractice are further discussed in the following section.

2. Electoral manipulations

2.1. Introduction

The expansion of electoral authoritarian regimes set in motion a whole new set of election manipulation strategies used by the state elite to win the contest in mostly free—as most of electoral autocracies allow universal suffrage — and sometimes even seemingly fair elections. The leaders come up with a great number of various practices to win elections. Hence, the question of electoral fraud was raised in various academic and non-academic circles. The topic was popularised, and several articles have been published in *The Economist* and *Foreign Policy* magazines. For instance, *The Economist* (3 March 2012) [14] counts five different strategies of vote manipulation. Among them are gerrymandering, biased media coverage, changing/adapting the laws governing political parties in favour of the incumbent, vote-buying, ballot box stuffing. Paul Collier, in his article in *Foreign Policy*, "The Dictator's Handbook," outlines at least seven different non-democratic practices used by an incumbent government to win elections. Among them are creating tame opposition parties, controlling the laws governing political parties, and changing the institutional design.

---

[14] See *The Economist*, "Weighing the votes: A brief guide to electoral fraud for the busy despot." Retrieved from http://www.economist.com/node/21548946.

In recent years, the issue of electoral fraud has received acclaim in the academic circles[15] as well. For instance, Allina-Pisano (2010) argued that leaders might also use administrative resources to rewrite existing social contracts during the pre-election campaign to gain popular support. Sarah Birch (2007) argued that malpractice is more likely during elections held in single-member districts; in other words, electoral system design might also influence the level of electoral misconduct.

Although the strategies used to manipulate election outcomes are as old as the elections themselves, not much has been written on electoral fraud prior to the 2000s. Fabrice Lehoucq[16] (2003), based on the results of his meta-analysis, argues that there is only a handful of works written on electoral fraud; and the majority was conducted by entomologists and historians, and only a few by social scientists. However, interest in the topic has been growing in recent years. Some of the most systematic research in the area was conducted by Sarah Birch, Alberto Simpser, Daniela Donno, Pippa Norris, Andreas Schedler, etc. These works are presented and discussed in details in this chapter.

The chapter pursues two main goals. First, it aims to detail and discuss some of the most relevant works in the field, attempting to bridge the literature on electoral fraud and electoral authoritarianism. One of the primary goals of this chapter is to identify the patterns of electoral manipulation in electoral authoritarian regimes, with a special focus on competitive authoritarian regimes, to determine whether any particular

---

[15] For instance, a recent article published by Netina Tan (2013) looks at the manipulation of a majoritarian electoral system for ensuring a legislative supermajority in Singapore; more generally on types of electoral fraud in authoritarian regimes, see Calingaert, "Election Rigging and How to Fight It," *Journal of Democracy* 17, no. 3 (2006): 138-151; for earlier works on the topic, see McDonald, "Electoral Fraud and Regime Controls in Latin," *The Western Political Quarterly* 25, no. 1 (1972): 81-93.

[16] Lehoucq (2003) provides an insightful review of research on electoral fraud. He argues that only a few works focus of electoral fraud, its magnitude, and causes. His review focuses mostly on ballot rigging. Another systematic overview of material written on electoral fraud has been carried out by Carolien van Ham (2014). Her work presents an evaluation of different data sets on electoral integrity.

type of electoral fraud prevails, i.e., used to a greater extent in the states with competitive regimes. To do so, after careful explications of the definitions and types of electoral fraud, a set of criteria for evaluating data sets of electoral malpractice is constructed, and the existing data sets are examined. Using the data set, which optimally suits the purposes of this work, patterns of electoral manipulation across the regime types are identified. Having identified general patterns of electoral fraud, as a second objective, the chapter argues that data sets on electoral fraud can be used to differentiate between competitive and hegemonic authoritarian regimes. Analysis of the data shows that in the latter case, strategies used by the ruling elite are less disguised. Fraud is mostly committed on election day, during tabulation and counting, and through electoral administration. In contrast, in competitive authoritarian regimes, the fraud is subtler and is, for example, manifested in the media coverage of political events.

The chapter is divided into five sections following the introduction. The second and third sections are devoted to discussion of the definitions and types of manipulation strategies proposed by scholars and election monitors. A thorough discussion of the concepts and their theoretical underpinnings is used to identify the most suitable concept and definition of fraud for this study. In the fourth section, cross-national data sets measuring electoral fraud are presented; and are scrutinised against the criteria outlined in the same section. Section five is dedicated to outlining the patterns of electoral fraud in electoral authoritarian regimes and is followed by a section containing some concluding remarks.

2.2. Defining electoral manipulation

In reviewing the concept of electoral fraud, some authors (e.g., van Ham 2014) make a distinction between positive and negative terms. Positive terms include free and fair elections, clean elections, democratic elections, election quality, and electoral integrity. Negative concepts are flawed elections, electoral malpractice, electoral misconduct, electoral manipulation, fraud, corruption, and election rigging.

Van Ham notes that the key distinction between negative and positive definitions is that negative ones accentuate the "intentionality." The example of a negative definition would be the one proposed by Schedler (2013). He defines electoral fraud as a "purposeful enterprise" (p.259), "the manipulation of electoral administration for partisan advantage at any stage of the electoral process (before, during, and after election day)" (p.197). Similarly, Birch defines electoral malpractice as "poor electoral conduct characterized by the intention either to distort democratic electoral process to make it serve electoral ends other than those of democracy, or to maintain an alternative electoral economy, based on non-democratic institutions" (2011: 26). Another example of a negative definition would be by Vickery and Schein (2012), who draws a line between electoral fraud and electoral malpractice based on actors' intentions. For them, electoral fraud is "a deliberate wrong-doing" (p.9), whereas malpractice is a consequence of "carelessness or neglect" (p.10). Van Ham claims that this focus on intentional actions causes conceptual as well as measurement problems as it would be "difficult to distinguish intentional actions from organizational incapacity." Moreover, not only intentional but also non-intentional irregularities (e.g., inaccurate voter registration) can have significant consequences for election integrity. However, it is worth noting that in most of the works on the topic, the distinction between positive and negative definitions in terms of intentionality is analytical rather than practical; i.e., although it is sometimes mentioned by some scholars that fraud is a "purposeful enterprise," for benchmarking, mostly universal/democratic/legal or other principles according to which elections should be conducted are used.

Following Pippa Norris, I consider that within the framework of the current project, it is more practical to group the works in the field of electoral studies based on their points of reference (i.e., theories, norms, rules, etc.) when judging whether fraud occurred. As mentioned above, several approaches have been used for benchmarking, and these studies can be roughly grouped based on the aspects considered to be of the highest importance by an author in assessing the election quality. One group of scholars proposes using universal principles/international standards as a yardstick for assessing the quality of elections. A second camp uses democratic principles as a benchmark. The administrative aspects of the electoral process are the focus of a third group of researchers, and a fourth group claims that the legal framework provides the most effective and transparent standards for evaluating elections.

Legal aspects

One way to define an instance of electoral manipulation is to look at the legal aspects of elections. This way, any action that breaks the law concerning elections would be considered an electoral fraud; conversely, even if the action seems morally objectionable, it is not considered fraud unless the law is breached. Legalistic conception helps draw a line between legally acceptable and unacceptable activities. For example, Lehoucq's (2003: 235) conceptualisation of electoral fraud is mostly legalistic; he argues that "in addition to being concealed and potentially affecting election results, an act is fraudulent if it breaks the law." According to his logic, even if citizens vote against their own interests because of political pressure, those exerting the pressure cannot be accused of fraudulent actions unless the law is broken[17]. Another example of such an approach can be seen in the report by Nikolai Vulchanov and Anders Eriksson (2010: 3), prepared for European Commission for Democracy through Law. They propose assessing the quality of elections by putting special emphasis on transparency, which "relates to written law, sub-legal acts of the election

---

[17] He uses an example of peasants and landlords to illustrate the point. Lehoucq (2003) argues that "landlords are not guilty of electoral fraud when all their retainers vote for their party." He states: "Even if we can demonstrate that retainers voted against their own interests, we cannot call this fraudulent unless a law has been broken."

administration at all levels and its performance during the election process[18]." They define electoral fraud as "an intentional deception made for personal gain or to damage another individual. In a general election context, fraud could be any action running contrary to the legal framework that intends to provide undue gains to specific electoral contestants" (p.4). Basically, to identify fraud, they propose analysing the legal framework of the election administration to determine whether it matches the performance during the electoral process.

There are certain advantages to this approach; for example, it is not always fruitful to use the same standards/requirements in every case, regardless of its idiosyncrasies, as in case with international standards. Thus, one might assume that the domestic laws and regulations are adopted to fit the specificities of a given country. For instance, Innocent Chukwuma[19], an unofficial election observer notes that postal and proxy ballots have the potential for massive abuse in Nigeria. The same remarks have been made by Jamaican MP and election monitor Lisa Hanna; however, in Britain, the issue does not raise too many questions. Another example would be an endorsement received by the new candidate from the incumbent. Although this practice might be widespread in the United States, in the Russian[20] or Mexican[21] context, it can be quite controversial.

---

[18] See a report based on the comments by Nikolai Vulchanov and Anders Erikssonm, Report on Figure Based Management of Possible Election Fraud. Adopted by the Council for Democratic Election at its 35th meeting (Venice, 16 December 2010) and by the Venice Commission at its 85th Plenary Session (Venice, 17-18 December 2010).

[19] During the 2008 Russian presidential election, Dmitry Medvedev's popularity as a candidate for president was significantly influenced by Putin's endorsement of his candidacy.

[20] See Michael Alvarez, Thad E. Hall, and Susan D. Hyde, *Election Fraud: Detecting and Deterring Electoral Manipulation*. Washington, DC: Brookings Institution Press, (2008).

Thus, one might argue that assessing electoral misconduct based on the legal framework of the specific country can help avoid such issues. Additionally, as Norris (2014: 35) notes, "a legalistic approach is grounded in the interpretation of specific legal provisions, and this is attractive as a practical and concrete yardstick for election management bodies seeking to stamp put blatantly illegal acts, such as forging voter cards, vote buying, or ballot stuffing." However, it must be argued that in non-democratic countries, the judiciary is not always independent of the incumbent government; hence, both creating the legal framework and interpreting the laws might be biased in favour of the incumbent. Furthermore, the possibility of a mismatch between democratic norms and legal provisions cannot be entirely dismissed. An action might be legal but may not correspond democratic or international norms of electoral conduct.

Moreover, although some claim that "a legalistic conception of fraud permits assessing the location of the boundaries between acceptable and unacceptable political activity," this approach has some serious limitations. First, using this approach might be reasonable when dealing with countries with relatively fair political institutions and a legal framework that ensures fair competition during the elections. However, more often than not in non-democratic countries, the laws are bent under a dictator's whim or to serve partisan interests. As Ziblatt (2009: 4) rightly argues, "electoral manipulations might at times not violate formal law but may violate democratic norms of freedom and fairness." Second, as the laws are not universally identical across countries, assessing election fairness based on

---

[21] See Fabrice Lehoucq, "Electoral Fraud: Causes, Types, and Consequences," *Annual Review of Political Science* 6 (2003), 233-256; for a case study of Costa Rica, see Fabrice Lehoucq and Ivan Molina, *Stuffing the Ballot Box: Fraud, Electoral Reform, and Democratization in Costa Rica*, Cambridge: Cambridge University Press (2002). For further discussion of this approach, see Vickery Chad and Erica Shein, "Assessing Electoral Fraud in New Democracies: Refining the Vocabulary," International Foundation for Electoral Systems (IFES) White Papers, May 2012; and Pippa Norris, *Why Electoral Integrity Matters*. New York: Cambridge University Press 2014.

the legal framework makes comparisons and the creation of data sets of electoral fraud nearly impossible.

Taking into consideration some of the above-mentioned concerns, Vickery Chad and Erica Shein (2012) propose using a definition of electoral fraud that would combine the inclusive [22] (i.e., democratic norms and international standards) and the restrictive [23] (i.e., legal aspects) approaches. In other words, they offer a middle-range definition of electoral fraud, combining legal aspects and universal principles. They define electoral fraud as "a deliberate wrong-doing by election officials or other electoral stakeholders, which distorts the individual or collective will of the voters" (p.9) and distinguish it from electoral malpractice, arguing that if the law was breached by an election administrator unintentionally, the action should be considered malpractice and not fraud (p.10). According to the authors, "[i]f election administrators knowingly and intentionally remove or omit indelible ink from targeted precinct election material kits to allow multiple voting for one party or candidate, then they have likely committed fraud and should be prosecuted accordingly (2012: 5)." But, "if poorly-trained polling station officials neglect to apply indelible ink to the fingers of voters, as per the requirements of the electoral process, and thereby unknowingly open the process to abuse, they may have only committed malpractice (p.5)." However, this slight change in defining the concept does not solve the problem of the legal approach, but adds further confusion as to how to determine whether the action was intentional or unintentional.

---

[22] In the category of inclusive approaches, Chad and Schein (2012) include the works that "situate their definitions normatively, finding that electoral wrongdoing violates domestic norms or internationally accepted standards for free and fair elections (p. 3)."

[23] However, in the second category, "approaches that focus only or mostly on the letter of the law (i.e., fraud can be identified by whether it violates existing domestic legal provisions) (Chad and Shein 2012: 5)" are assigned.

Administrative aspects

Another way of defining electoral fraud is assessing administrative aspects of elections, i.e., administration and conduct of elections, including voter registration, voter education, legal framework, election management, access to and design of the ballot, campaign regulation, polling, counting and tabulating the vote, resolving election related disputes, election result implementation and post-election procedures (Elklit and Reynolds 2002). Norris (2014: 36) frames problems related to electoral administration as "electoral maladministration" and states that it mostly refers to "more routine flaws and unintended mishaps by election officials." She further explains that "these problems may be caused by managerial failures, inefficiency, incompetence, long lines at polling stations, inaccurate or dated electoral registers, the lack of security link, the insufficient provision of ballot papers, the misplacement of ballot boxes, the breakdown or technical inaccuracy of electronic voting machines, or mathematical errors during the vote count."

Elklit and Reynolds (2002; 2005a) advance the idea that it is necessary to study the administration of elections mainly for two reasons: 1) "elections are complicated process, particularly when it comes to administration," and there is no guarantee that things will run smoothly; and 2) the quality of election administration is closely related to "the development of political legitimacy and democratic consolidation in new democracies." Similarly, Pastor (2007) argues that administrative issues of the electoral process should be taken seriously, especially in transitioning democracies. He insists that "in a poor, relatively uneducated developing country, the boundary line separating political manipulation and technical incapacity is rarely surveyed, and elections can fail for one or both reasons" (p.2).

Several works have covered the issues related to managing the elections on election day and the problems associated with it. For instance, Alvarez and Hall (2006) look at the voting equipment, voting procedures, voter registration and, in general, the election system "built around polling place voting on a single day" to analyse the complexities and flaws occurring in such systems. Alvarez, Atkenson and Hall (2006) also published a book on a similar topic, analysing and presenting potential challenges that might transpire during the elections and proposing techniques that would make the election process more accurate and better managed. Others, such as Spencer and Markovits (2010), examine the inner-workings of polls and measure "how variations in the voting process may contribute to the formation of a line during an election."

Although this approach is of great help when trying to improve the overall performance of electoral management, it has its drawbacks when it comes to the general evaluation of freedom and fairness of elections. For example, Birch (2012) and Schedler (2013) do not consider these types of electoral maladministration to be a type of electoral fraud for the simple reason that fraud was not the primary intention and, thus, can be regarded as a human factor or marginal error. In addition, malpractice committed by actors other than electoral officials is not the primary interest of research on administrative malpractice. As a result, fraud such as the disenfranchisement of certain group of citizens or the exclusion of opposition parties, is not covered and cannot be stretched to be part of election maladministration (Norris 2014).

Overall, the approach is useful in fixing problems related to election management, but the fixes as well as the problems are case specific as the elections are not administered according to the same rules in every country. For instance, in the United States, the rules governing the administration of elections vary from state to state.

Democratic norms

Another approach to assess election quality and define the concept of electoral fraud is to use the concept of a procedural democracy, which has been discussed in the previous chapter (section 1.6.), as a foundation. This approach is widely used by political science scholars. Some of the most recent works using this approach were Schedler (2013), Birch (2011), Donno (2014), Simpser (2013). Despite some differences in conceptualisation and operationalisation, their works put democratic norms at the centre of election assessment. For instance, Donno defines a free election as the one "in which parties are able to campaign openly and without hindrance, voters are free to vote their preferences, and official results accurately reflect the votes cast. A fair election is one in which all parties and candidates are subject to the same procedures for registering and appearing on the ballot, and all compete on a level playing field. Electoral misconduct can be defined as any action that violates these standards (52)". Schedler's definition of electoral fraud is shorter, but his approach is more systematic. He argues that "[e]lectoral fraud is the manipulation of electoral administration for partisan advantage at any stage of the electoral process (before, during, and after election day) (p.197)." He first gives a clear definition of democratic elections, outlines its main components, and then provides a list of potential violations of these norms. For Birch, electoral malpractice is "poor electoral conduct characterised by the intention either to distort a democratic electoral process to make it serve electoral ends other than those of democracy…" (p.26). Both Schedler and Birch emphasise the importance of actors and their intention in their definition of electoral fraud.

A slightly different approach is used by Simpser (2013), who proposes using two different definitions of electoral manipulation. One is conceptual and the other is operational. For the conceptual definition, he takes Schedler's "chain of democratic choice," which is based on Dahl's (1997) definition of poliarchy, whereas his operational definition consists of a list of electoral manipulations that he compiled (see Table 2.4). However, the spectre of manipulations that he includes only partially covers the electoral cycle. For example, the list does not mention uneven playing field or possible manipulations that take place before and after the elections affecting the results.

Table 2.1. The chain of democratic choice by A. Schedler

Dimensions of electoral choice	Normative premises of democratic choice	Strategies of electoral manipulation
Object of choice	*Empowerment:* Democratic elections involve the delegation of decision-making authority.	*Reserved positions:* limiting the scope of elective offices *Reserved domains:* limiting the jurisdiction of elective offices
Range of choice	*Freedom of supply:* Citizens must be free to form, join, and support conflicting parties, candidates, and policies	*Exclusion of opposition actors:* restricting access to electoral arena *Fragmentation of opposition actors:* disorganising electoral dissidence *Subversion:* simulating and controlling opposition parties
Formation of preferences	*Freedom of demand:* Citizens must be able to learn about available alternatives through alternative sources of information.	*Repression:* restricting political and civil liberties *Unfairness:* restricting access to media and money
Agents of choice	*Inclusion:* Democracy assigns equal rights of participation to all full members of the political community.	*Formal disenfranchisement:* legal suffrage restrictions *Informal disenfranchisement:* practical suffrage restrictions
Expression of preferences	*Insulation:* Citizens must be free to express their electoral preferences.	*Coercion:* voter intimidation *Corruption:* vote buying
Aggregation of preferences	*Integrity:* One person, one vote. The democratic ideal of equality demands weighting votes equally.	*Redistributive institutions of electoral governance:* biased rules of electoral competition and organization *Redistributive practices of electoral governance:* electoral fraud and impunity
Consequences of choice	*Decisiveness:* Elections without consequences do not qualify as democratic.	*Tutelage:* preventing elected officers from exercising their constitutional powers *Reversion:* preventing victors from taking office or elected officers from concluding their constitutional terms

Source: Schedler, 2013: 84

Schedler (2013) proposes a rather systematic conceptualisation of electoral manipulations. He discerns manipulation strategies based on the rules or "the links of the democratic chain" they aim to break. Based on Dahl's definition of democracy, he distinguishes seven more concrete ground rules—empowerment, freedom of supply, freedom of demand, inclusion, insulation, integrity, decisiveness—and strategies that autocrats use at each stage to control election outcomes—disempowerment, supply-side restrictions, demand-side restrictions, exclusive suffrage, external interference, redistributive electoral governance (Table 2.1).

International standards[24]

Norris (2014) makes a distinction between democratic values and international standards, claiming that the concept of democracy is too vague and there is no consensus "on a single understanding of democratic principles and values that could provide a common or universal standard for evaluation the quality of elections around the world (38)." Based on this argument, she proposes using international standards as a benchmark, also stating that international law has the capacity to impose "legitimate," "authoritative," and "binding obligations" on the international community. Some (Davis-Roberts and Carrol 2009) argue that in addition to being authoritative, as it relies on states' acknowledged legal commitments, public international law provides a more objective and transparent basis for election observation.

Moreover, Norris proposes using the concept of 'electoral integrity', as opposed to electoral fraud or malpractice, defining it as a concept that "emphasizes shared international principles and standards of elections, applying universally to all countries worldwide throughout all stages in the electoral cycle, including during the pre-electoral period, the campaign, on polling day, and its aftermath" (p.21). She claims that the concept of

---

[24] Norris derives international standards for elections from "multilateral agreements, international conventions, treaties, and international law" (2014: 39).

electoral integrity and the approach it employs is much broader than the frameworks based on domestic law, electoral administration, or democratic principles. Furthermore, she argues that "the most legitimate and authoritative standards of electoral integrity are derived from multilateral agreements, international conventions, treaties, and international law" (p.39).

However, international standards regarding elections are derived from the basic democratic principles, human rights, and rule of law. As the Declaration of Principles for International Election Observations commemorated by the United Nations [25] on October 27, 2005, states: "International election observation expresses the interest of the international community in the achievement of democratic elections, as part of democratic development, including respect for human rights and the rule of law" (p.1). According to this declaration, "[g]enuine democratic elections are an expression of sovereignty, which belongs to the people of a country, the free expression of whose will provides the basis for the authority and legitimacy of government. The rights of citizens to vote and to be elected at periodic, genuine democratic elections are internationally recognized human rights" (p.2). The principles outlined in this declaration have also been endorsed by number of international organizations, including Council of Europe, European Commission, African Union, Asian Network for Free Elections (ANFREL), Electoral Reform International Services, IFES, International IDEA, Organization for Security and Cooperation in Europe, Office of Democratic Institutions and Human Rights (OSCE/ODIHR), United Nations Secretariat, among others. As seen from their statement, international organisations also use democratic principles as a yardstick against which the fairness of elections is measured. To reiterate, the core principles of free and fair elections are rooted in the

---

[25] Similar values are outlined by the European Commission for Democracy Through Law (2002). "Code of good practice in electoral matters. Guidelines and explanatory report," adopted by the Venice Commission at its 52nd session (Venice, 18-19 October 2002).

concept of democracy; thus, the distinction between these two approaches (i.e., democratic principles and international standards) to conducting elections is not fundamentally different.

As seen from this discussion, every approach has its merits and drawbacks. When choosing a definition of electoral fraud, one should consider the specificities of the field as well as the question to be addressed using that definition. As this work is focused on the kinds and extent of electoral fraud in certain types of regimes, it is appropriate to define electoral fraud using an approach that employs democratic principles for benchmarking. In addition, although the scholars might focus on different aspects of elections in measuring the fairness/integrity, the basic principles are derived from the concept of democracy, to illustrate this point, Table 2.2 summarises the definitions of electoral fraud proposed in some of the most prominent publications on the subject. Of these definitions, those provided by Schedler and Birch use democratic principles for benchmarking. Both definitions emphasise the idea of intentionality and use a list of criteria defining democratic regimes. Further in this work when concepts as electoral fraud/manipulation/malpractice are employed they are defined using these two definitions.

Table 2.2. Definitions of electoral fraud

Author	Concept	Definition	Data set
Birch (2011)	Electoral malpractice	"Electoral malpractice represents a particularization of the electoral process that draws it closer to the alternative electoral models [...]. Electoral malpractice is not simply poor electoral conduct, it is poor electoral conduct of a certain type: poor electoral conduct characterized by the intention either to distort a democratic electoral process in order to make it serve electoral ends other than those of democracy, or to maintain an alternative electoral economy, based on non-democratic institutions" (p.26).	Yes
Hyde and Marinov (2012)	Electoral competition	"The institution of contested elections can be thought of as a structure of the game and the electoral outcome as the realization of a random variable. Where the realization is at least in some doubt, competitiveness can exist. Where the outcome is certain, the structure prohibits competition and elections cannot be competitive" (p.4).	Yes

Author	Concept	Definition	Data set
Schedler (2013)	Electoral manipulation	"Electoral fraud is the manipulation of electoral administration for partisan advantage at any stage of the electoral process (before, during, and after election day)" (p.197).	
Donno (2013)	Electoral misconduct	"A free election is one in which parties are able to campaign openly and without hinderance, voters are free to vote their preferences, and official results accurately reflect the votes cast. A fair election is one in which all parties and candidates are subject to the same procedures for registering and appearing on the ballot, and all compete on a level playing field. Electoral misconduct can be defined as any action that violates these standards" (p.52).	Yes
Simpser (2014)	Electoral manipulation	Conceptual definition: Electoral fraud is any deviation from the principle specification of what constitutes democratic elections. Principle components of democratic election are borrowed from Schedler's "chain of democratic choice" (pp.34-35). Operational definition: Electoral manipulation is any action covered by the list provided on Table 2.4 (p.38).	Yes
Norris (2014); Norris, Frank and Martinez i Coma (2014)	Electoral integrity	"Emphasizes shared international principles and standards of elections, applying universally to all countries worldwide throughout all stages in the electoral cycle, including during the pre-electoral period, the campaign, on polling day, and its aftermath. Conversely, electoral "malpractice" violate international standards of electoral integrity […]"(p. 39).	Yes
Kelley (2012)	Election quality	"The State Department's assessment of whether the election represents the will of thee voters, is free and fair, or in other ways frankly endorses the outcome, based on the entire content of the State Department report" (p. 188).	Yes
Elklit and Reynolds (2005)	Election quality	"[W]hether the rules, as written, are applied fairly and without partisan bias" (p. 151).	-
Lehoucq (2003)	Electoral fraud	"[I]n addition to being concealed and potentially affecting election results, an act is fraudulent if it breaks the law" (p. 235).	-
Ziblat (2009)	Electoral fraud	"Electoral fraud can consist of a range of illegal and legal actions that violate democratic norms by inflating or deflating vote totals for one candidate or party, including actions such as violence, coercion, "influence," vote buying, or procedural manipulations" (p. 4).	

Author	Concept	Definition	Data set
Vickery and Schein (2012)	Electoral fraud	Electoral fraud is a deliberate wrong-doing by election officials or other electoral stakeholders, which distorts the individual or collective will of the voters (p. 9).	-
	Electoral malpractice	Electoral malpractice is the breach by an election professional of his or her relevant duty of care, resulting from carelessness or neglect (p. 10).	
Rafael Lopez-Pinter (2010)	Electoral fraud	"Electoral fraud can be defined as any purposeful action taken to tamper with electoral activities and election-related materials in order to affect the results of an election, which may interfere with or thwart the will of the voters" (p. 9).	-
Vulchanov and Eriksson (2010)	Electoral fraud	"In the broadest sense, a fraud is an intentional deception made for personal gain or to damage another individual. In a general election context, fraud could be any action running contrary to the legal framework that intends to provide undue gains to specific electoral contestants" (p. 4).	-

2.3. Types of manipulation strategies

Most of the authors whose proposed definitions of electoral fraud were discussed in the previous section also lay out a map of possible types of fraud. This section is aimed at elaborating on these indicators. Generally, the approaches used when creating different sets of fraud indicators can be divided into two groups. One can be considered theory driven, whereas the other is a data-driven approach. The former accumulates indicators derived from the concept, whereas the latter looks at the electoral process and, based on observations, creates and expands the list of indicators. Similarly, Van Ham mentions that process-based and concept-based approaches are used to conceptualise electoral fraud. She claims that those using the concept-based approach define election integrity based on "ideal democratic standards," whereas the process-based approach stresses the electoral process itself, before, during, and on election day. She states that an example of such a process-based conceptualisation would be the work by Mozaffar and Schedler (2002), who stress a systematic examination of electoral governance. Electoral governance[26] is defined as "the wider set of activities that creates and maintains the broad institutional framework in which voting and electoral competition take place" (2002: 7).

In the theory-driven approach, electoral fraud is defined as a deviation from the main principles of democratic elections. In the data-driven approach, the concept is defined based on empirical observations before, during, and after election day. However, the latter approach might not be the most useful in studying electoral autocracies, or even in classifying regimes; although, it can prove to be of use in improving the quality of elections, the electoral process, as well as electoral governance[27]. Using the data-driven approach might certainly help identify a larger amount of inaccuracies along with manipulations, which might be useful in improving the quality of elections that are already democratic. However, it is worth mentioning that in practice, as Dahl (1971) notes, no election attains the ideal type. As has been briefly discussed in the previous chapter, elections require the mobilisation of vast resources and coordination of numerous tasks; thus, some inaccuracies — considering the human factor — are inevitable. In addition, using the data-driven approach would mean lumping together deliberate manipulations and unintentional inaccuracies, i.e., human mistakes. This, in turn, might complicate the process of drawing boundaries between minimal procedural democracies and electoral autocracies.

Depending on the purpose of a research and the research question, both approaches can be of value. In this work, because I am also looking for a better way of drawing a dividing line between competitive and hegemonic authoritarian regimes, it is worthwhile to examine the types of

---

[26] Mozaffar and Schedler divide this set of activities, arguing that electoral governance operates on three levels: rule making—"designing the basic rules of the electoral game"; rule application—"implementing these rules to organize the electoral game"; and rule adjudication—"resolving disputes arising within the game" (p.7).

[27] See Shaheen Mozaffar and Andreas Schedler, "The Comparative Study of Electoral Governance - Introduction," *International Political Science Review* 23, no. 1 (2002): 5-27.

electoral fraud that are also mentioned in the political regime literature. An outline of various electoral fraud typologies advanced by different scholars is given in Table 2.2. As seen, they are quite varied but share some principle components. All of the works listed in this table, except for Elklit and Reynolds (2005) and Schedler (2013) also present cross-national data sets on electoral fraud. As has been discussed earlier, scholars use different approaches for conceptualising electoral fraud. Similarly, their analytical frameworks vary, as do the lists of electoral malpractice included in their studies. For identifying patterns of electoral fraud in competitive authoritarian regimes and determining whether the argument by Levitsky and Way (2010) about the main manipulation strategies used in competitive regimes holds true, it is vital to choose the typology of malpractice, which covers a wide range of fraud, including the types outlined by Levitsky and Way. Based on the analytical framework used for creating each set of possible manipulation strategies, several typologies seem to be appropriate for the purposes of this study. However, not all of them provide a suitable data set for further analysis. For the purposes of the current study, a typology provided by Sarah Birch seems to be the most optimal.

Birch distinguishes the following practices: deficiencies in the legal framework governing the elections; control over the electoral authorities; banning or rejecting a significant number of major contestants in violation of the law; obstruction of opportunities for public inspection of voter registration; refusal of citizenry registration; inadequate polling arrangements; presence of significant irregularities during the voting process; not processing a dispute about the results of an election in a timely, comprehensive and impartial manner; not allowing international observers to inspect the elections; controlling the electoral administration; circulating too few voting slips; media bias in coverage of the electoral campaign; ignoring established campaign resources; intimidating voters; intimidating candidates, activists, etc. All these practices can be considered a type of electoral malpractice. Birch (2011) defines malpractice as follows:

[...] a particular type of violation: specifically, a violation that serves to substitute personal or partisan gain on the part of a restricted number of political actors for popular control by all. In this sense, electoral malpractice represents a particularization of the electoral process that draws it closer to the alternative electoral models [...]. Electoral malpractice is not simply poor electoral conduct, it is poor electoral conduct of a certain type: poor electoral conduct characterized by the intention either to distort a democratic electoral process to make it serve electoral ends other than those of democracy, or to maintain an alternative electoral economy, based on non-democratic institutions (2011: 26).

In this sense, there is a difference between electoral malpractice and "mispractice," which might involve electoral deficiencies resulting not from an intent to rig the elections, but rather, from incompetence, resource insufficiency, human error, or *force majeure* situations. Based on this definition of electoral malpractice, Birch has classified possible electoral malpractice conducted on election day as well as those before the actual election. She distinguishes three types of electoral malpractice: 1) manipulation of electoral design; 2) manipulation of vote choice; 3) and manipulation of the voting act. She also makes a distinction between legitimate forms of manipulation and illegitimate forms. For example, the main goal of an electoral campaign is to manipulate citizens' vote choices and is considered a legitimate form of vote manipulation. In contrast, restricting access to media, creating tame parties, controlling opposition, voter intimidation, and vote buying are illegitimate (see Table 2.3).

Table 2.3. Typologies of electoral manipulations

	Legitimate	Illigitimate
Manipulation of institutional design	Ex.: Choice of overall electoral system	Ex.: Gerrymandering
Manipulation of vote choice	Ex.: Legal campaign activity	Ex.: Vote buying
Manipulation of the voting act	No legitimate forms	Ex.: Ballot box stuffing

Source: Birch, 2011: 27

Levitsky and Way use the concept of uneven playing field, Schedler, as summarised in Table 2.2 refers to similar practices/strategies as the repertoire of electoral manipulations, whereas Birch employs the concept of electoral malpractice. However, all three refer to essentially similar strategies used by incumbents to stay in power, with the only exception being that Birch and Schedler cover a much broader area of manipulation practiced to a different extent across regimes. In contrast, Levitsky and Way mainly focus on strategies that are widespread in competitive authoritarian regimes. The broader area of manipulations can help show whether some types are used in certain regime types more often than in the others. The concept of "electoral manipulations" is primarily used in this work and is defined as any act intentionally violating main principles of democratic elections, at any stage of electoral process, i.e., before, during, and after the elections. Later in the text, concepts such as "electoral misconduct," "electoral malpractice," and "electoral fraud" are used interchangeably referring to the same act.

2.4. Measuring electoral misconduct

A data set appropriate for the purposes of this work should meet the following criteria: 1) it should use an ordinal scale for coding because binary classifications are not suitable for identifying the patterns of electoral manipulations across the regime types; 2) to make comparisons possible, the data should have a relatively large scope; 3) information on which data are built should be derived from various sources to avoid bias; and 4) most importantly, it should cover a wide spectre of electoral fraud, including the indicators outlined by Levitsky and Way as the main indicators of competitive authoritarian regimes. In this section, I provide a short review and assess, based on the listed criteria, each data set to identify the one that optimally suits the purposes of this work.

In regard to data measuring electoral misconduct/fraud, several works stand out. Most of the data sets used by scholars for regime studies include a variable that measures the quality of elections. Standard data sets on democracy, such as Freedom House (FH) and Polity IV, have some components that closely relate to the quality of electoral process. Polity contains a variable measuring the competitiveness of executive recruitment, and it also looks at political competition, opposition, and so on; however, it does not have any details on a broader spectre of the types of electoral fraud and their extent. Another commonly used democracy data set, Freedom in the World, contains two subcomponents: political rights, which is aimed at evaluating the electoral process, political pluralism and participation, and the functioning of government. However, data on these components is available only from 2006, and as in the case of Polity, the data on the electoral process is not sufficiently detailed.

The World Bank Political Institutions Database (DPI), which provides comparative indicators of electoral results, legislature, cabinet and political ideology covering 172 countries for the period 1975-2012, also looks at the electoral results and contains a variable "Fraud." This variable evaluates whether "vote fraud or candidate intimidation were serious enough to affect the outcome of elections" (Beck et al. 2012: 17). However, the coding is dichotomous and tricky. The countries where "opposition parties are officially and constitutionally banned, where irregularities are not mentioned (although may still exist)" are coded as "0," and countries, where "opposition is officially legal but suppressed anyway" are coded as "1." The variable cannot be used separately from other indicators. In addition, like FH and Polity, DPI does not contain a detailed evaluation of different dimensions of the electoral process.

Another data set, which assesses the fairness of elections was introduced by Lindberg. His data set provides information on the fairness of elections in Africa between 1989 and 2003. The most relevant variables include the participation of real opposition in the election, occurrence of violence on election day or during the campaign period, and whether the elections were essentially judged free and fair. Two major problems in applying the data for the purposes of the current work would be its regional scope and the limited number of indicators of electoral fraud.

Some other cross-national measurements of electoral misconduct that might fit some of the outlined requirements are those proposed by Hyde and Marinov (NELDA), Norris (PEI), Birch (IEM), Donno (EDEN), Simpser (CNMEM), and Kelly (QED). Elklit and Reynolds (2005) and Bland et al. (2013)[28] also advance an analytical framework for measuring the quality of elections and claim to have a better measurement scheme for electoral misconduct. Regrettably, their works currently have only pilot implementations[29]. Table 2.4 provides a short summary of the main facts regarding the data sets and outlines some of the weaknesses of each.

The National Elections Across Democracy and Autocracy (NELDA): This data set, created by Hyde and Marinov (2012), is arguably one of the most comprehensive works. It covers both presidential and parliamentary national elections in 157 states worldwide[30], for the period between 1945 and 2006, and contains data for 2600 election events. The sources used by the authors are plentiful. Their assessment of elections is based on election reports by various organizations, news articles, data handbooks, and case studies when necessary, which minimises potential bias. For each election, 58 variables assessing the quality of the election are coded, ensuring a detailed and thorough analysis of every election.

The data are systematic, detailed, and comprehensive. However, their conceptual framework is based on Przeworski's minimalist definition of democracy. As mentioned in the previous section, the accent is on three

---

[28] The Electoral Administration Systems Index (EASI) is compiled based on information gathered from expert surveys. It looks at three electoral dimensions: participation, competition, and integrity of the process. The dimensions are further divided according to the electoral cycle: pre-election, during the election, post-election period (2013: 365).

[29] For a similar work, see Myagkov, Ordershook and Shakin, "Fraud or Fairytales: Russia and Ukraine's Electoral Experience," *Post-Soviet Affairs* 21, no. 2 (2005): 91-131.

[30] Excluding micro states with a population less than 500,000. In addition, Western countries (almost all members of the OECD) are not included in the data set.

main conditions that are also outlined by Przeworski et al. (2000), i.e., whether 1) opposition is allowed; 2) multiple parties are legal; and 3) more than one candidate competes. Przeworski et al. uses these criteria for building a dichotomous classification of political regimes. Similarly, Hyde and Marinov's data set uses binary classification of elections, differentiating between competitive and non-competitive. These basic criteria are helpful in drawing a line between competitive and not-competitive elections, but it loses value when information about the extent of fraud is needed. In addition, the NELDA's coding system is binary; therefore, the variables assessing the elections in detail cannot be used for identifying the degree of fraud, which is necessary in studying electoral authoritarian regimes.

Perceptions of Electoral Integrity (PEI): Norris's data set is built on expert surveys and covers a large spectre of malpractice that can transpire throughout the electoral process, which she divides into eleven steps. The variables included in the series are derived from universally accepted norms and values according to which democratic elections should be conducted. In total, 49 measures of electoral integrity are included in the data set. All items are coded on a 0-5 ordinal scale, from the most negative to the most positive evaluation. The data set covers all independent nation-states with a

Enforcement of Democratic Electoral Norms (EDEN): This database, introduced by Donno, covers both presidential and parliamentary national election events in 119 states, over a period of 17 years (1990-2007). The coding of electoral misconduct is built on observer reports and international news articles. The elections are coded as "flawed" if there were any of the types of electoral misconduct mentioned in Table 2.5, within the following categories: 1) restrictions on freedom of movement, expression, or association; 2) creation of a biased playing field; and 3) ballot fraud. This data set is not useful for the purposes of my work as it does not contain detailed information on the presence (as in Donno's coding, to be considered flawed it is enough for one type of fraud to transpire) and intensity (due to the binary coding system) of different types of the misconduct.

A Cross-national Measure of Electoral Manipulation (CNMEM): Another database measuring electoral fraud has been introduced by Simpser (2014). His data set covers the period between 1990 and 2007 and provides data for 874 executive and legislative elections in states that have a population of at least 1 million and where more than one party is allowed to compete during the elections. He uses three different categories for measuring electoral manipulation, and every type of misconduct from the list (provided on Table 2.5) is ranked as either "small and insignificant," "intermediate," or "widespread." For obtaining relevant information on electoral conduct, multiple sources have been consulted, including reference works on elections (Europa Yearbook and Dieter Nohlen's handbooks of elections), the reports of international election observers (NDI, the Carter Center, OSCE/ODIHR), reports by NGOs (International IDEA and IFES), and journalistic articles. Simpser makes interesting findings regarding the patterns of electoral misconduct. His research shows that pre-election manipulations are higher than election day manipulations in all the regions of the world except the post-Soviet region. Another interesting finding is that manipulations are more frequent during executive elections rather than legislative elections.

Unfortunately, the types of electoral fraud that are mentioned by Levitsky and Way as principal indicators when defining competitive authoritarian regimes are not included in Simpser's list of misconduct. Important components such as media coverage, misuse of state resources, or faulty legal framework are not included.

Quality of Elections Data (QED): This data set, introduced by Kelley, has quite a large scope, providing data for 1206 election events, between 1978 and 2004, in 172 states across the world. The major drawback of this data set is its reliance on a single source (i.e., "Country Reports on Human Rights Practices," by the US State Department) for the information.

Index of Electoral Malpractice (IEM): Along with a typology of electoral malpractice, Birch has created a new cross-national data set of malpractice observed during parliamentary and presidential elections in countries that made an initial transition from authoritarianism. The data covers countries of Latin America, Eastern Europe and the former Soviet Union, and Sub-Saharan Africa, from 1995 to 2006, in total providing information on electoral malpractice during 136 elections. The data set accounts for fourteen different types of electoral malpractice: 1) legal framework; 2) electoral authority independence; 3) contestation; 4) voter registration; 5) polling arrangements; 6) voting; 7) counting, tabulation, reporting; 8) dispute adjudication; 9) observer access; 10) media coverage; 11) misuse of state resources; 12) vote buying; 13) voter intimidation/obstruction; and 14) candidate intimidation/obstruction. IEM not only covers the election but also looks at the pre-election period. International standards and democratic norms are taken as a benchmark against which the degree of electoral malpractice is measured.

Table 2.4. Types of electoral fraud

Author	Concept	Indicators of fraud	
Birch (2011)	Electoral malpractice	- Legal framework - Electoral authority independence - Contestation - Voter registration - Polling arrangements - Voting Counting, tabulation, reporting	- Dispute adjudication - Observer access - Media coverage - Misuse of state resources - Vote buying - Voter intimidation obstruction Candidate intimidation/obstruction
Schedler (2013)	Electoral manipulation	- Reserved positions - Reserved domains - Exclusion of opposition actors - Fragmentation of opposition actors - Subversion - Repression Unfairness	- Formal disenfranchisement - Coercion - Corruption - Biased rules of electoral competition and organization - Electoral fraud and impunity - Tutelage - Reversion

Electoral manipulations

Author	Concept	Indicators of fraud	
Donno (2013)	Electoral misconduct	*Restrictions on freedom of movement, expression, or association:* - Existence of harsh or arbitrary burdens on opposition parties' ability to register and/or appear on the ballot - Intimidation of opposition parties, candidates, or supporters - Restrictions on opposition party campaign activity *Creation of a biased playing field:* - Restrictions on the media's ability to report on the campaign - Imbalance in media reporting and access - De facto or *de jure* bias within institutions that organise and arbitrate elections - Misuse of state resources to help the incumbent's or ruling party's campaign	*Ballot fraud:* - Intimidation of voters on election day - Systematic omission of voters from registration lists - Violation of the secret ballot - Multiple voting - Ballot box tampering or stuffing - Destruction or alteration of ballots - Faulty counting or tabulation of ballots - Certification of fraudulent results
Kelley (2012)		*Pre-election administration* - Problems in voter lists/registration - Complaints about electoral commission conduct - Voter information and procedural problems - Technical/procedural difficulties *Election day administration* - Informational insufficiencies and confusion - Administrative insufficiencies - Problems in voter lists - Complaints about electoral commission on election day *Legal problems* - Deficiencies in legal framework - Limits to scope and jurisdiction of elective offices Unreasonable limits of who can run for office	*Pre-election cheating* - Improper use of public funds - Restrictions on freedom to campaign - Restrictions on media - Intimidation *Election day cheating* - Vote processing and tabulation tampering - Voter fraud - Intimidation on election day *Pre-election violence* - Physical violence and unrest before election day *Election day violence* Physical violence and unrest of election day
Hyde & Marinov (2012)	Electoral competition	- Whether opposition is allowed - Multiple parties are legal	More than one candidate competes

Author	Concept	Indicators of fraud	
Norris (2014) and Norris, Frank and Martinez i Coma (2014) and Norris, Frank and Martinez i Coma (2014)	Electoral integrity	Pre-election 1. *Electoral laws* - electoral laws were unfair to smaller parties - electoral laws restricted citizens' rights 2. *Electoral procedures* - elections were well managed - information about voting procedures was widely available - election officials were fair - elections were conducted in accordance with the law 3. *District boundaries* - boundaries discriminated against some parties - boundaries favoured incumbents - boundaries were impartial 4. *Voter registration* - some citizens were not listed in the register - the electoral register was inaccurate - some ineligible electors were registered 5. *Registration process for parties and candidates to get on the ballot* - some opposition candidates were prevented from running - women had equal opportunities to run for office - ethnic and national minorities had equal opportunities to run for office - only top party leaders selected candidates - some parties/candidates were restricted from holding campaign rallies Campaign 6. *Media's coverage of these elections* - Newspapers provided balanced election news - TV new favoured the governing party - parties/candidates had fair access to political broadcasts and advertising - journalists provided fair coverage of the elections social media were used to expose electoral fraud	7. *Campaign finance* - parties/candidates had equitable access to public donations - parties/candidates publish transparent financial accounts - rich people buy election - some state resources were improperly used for campaigning Election Day 8. *When voting* - some voters were threatened with violence at the polls - some fraudulent votes were cast - the process of voting was easy - voters were offered a genuine choice at the ballot box - postal ballots were available - special voting facilities were available for the disabled - national citizens living abroad could vote - some form of Internet voting was available Post-election 9. *After the polls closed* - ballot boxes were secure - the results were announced without undue delay - votes were counted fairly - international election monitors were restricted 10. *Official results announced* - parties/candidates challenged the results - the election led to peaceful protests - the election triggered violent protests - any disputes were resolved through legal channels 11. *Electoral authorities administering elections* - the election authorities were impartial - the authorities distributed information to citizens - the authorities allowed public scrutiny of their performance the election authorities performed well	

Author	Concept	Indicators of fraud	
Simpser (2014)	Electoral manipulation	- Stuffing ballot boxes (or destroying ballots) - Falsifying results or otherwise tampering with the vote count - Tampering with voter registration lists - Vote buying before the election - Vote buying during the election Creating obstacles to voter registration	- Creating obstacles to candidate registration - Intimidating voters before the election - Intimidating voters during the election - Intimidating candidates - Voting multiple times Voting by those who are ineligible, such as minors
Elklit and Reynolds (2005)		- Legal framework - Electoral management - Constituency and polling district demarcation - Voter education - Voter registration Access to and design of ballot paper. Party and candidate nomination and registration	- Campaign regulation - Polling - Counting and tabulation the vote - Resolving election related complaints. Verification of final results and certification Post-election procedures

The data set is coded on a 1-5 ordinal scale, where "1" is the most positive and "5" is the most negative. It covers a large spectre of malpractice and uses a systematic approach for conceptualising electoral malpractice, choosing the indicators, and coding. The only limitation of this data set is its scope. Regardless of this limitation the data set is the most suitable for measuring unevenness of the playing field in electoral authoritarian regimes. The types of electoral fraud measured by Birch closely corresponds to concept of uneven playing field advanced by Levitsky and Way; additionally, the data set covers 136 cases, the number of cases small albeit enough for the purposes of illustration. Data set by Pippa Norris could also be used, however, it covers only the period between 2012 and 2014.

2.5. Electoral malpractice in competitive authoritarian regimes

As discussed in earlier sections, the rules can be broken in many different ways, and the list of electoral manipulations can be endless; however, the question is whether there are any patterns. Is any combination of strategies applied more often than the others? Is there any correlation between the type of regime in place and the kind of electoral manipulation employed? Do the incumbents operating in competitive authoritarian regime settings use the same strategies as those in hegemonic autocracies? Is there a difference in the magnitude of manipulation or in the kind of manipulation? Schedler's analysis of manipulation strategies in different regime types shows that media manipulation seems to be present among any other type of electoral manipulations employed because, when successful, it provides a chance to cover up other manipulations (2013: 200). Thus, I argue that media plays a particularly interesting and significant role in competitive authoritarian regimes. To illustrate the significance and extent of media manipulations employed in competitive authoritarian regimes, I check the variation in the degree of electoral malpractice across the regimes. I group the countries by regime type to determine which types of electoral malpractice prevail in competitive authoritarian regimes. Two main objectives are behind this analysis:

1) To establish whether manipulation/skewing of the playing field is a distinguishing characteristic of competitive authoritarian regimes and is pertinent to this type of regime. If a skewed level playing field in competitive authoritarian regimes is the main characteristic that distinguishes competitive authoritarian regimes from hegemonic or closed authoritarian regimes as Levitsky and Way (2010) claim, then we should see that the degree of malpractice associated with the playing field (e.g., media coverage, misuse of state resources, and legal framework) is higher than the degree of other types of malpractice.

2) To identify the most important arrow in the quiver of electoral malpractice—the one that offers the highest chance to win elections without losing the legitimacy, and thus is mostly used in competitive authoritarian regimes.

Regime data: I use Howard and Roessler's regime data; then, I check the results using Levitsky and Way's classification to answer the second question. If any pattern exists, then it should be visible regardless of the regime data set used. I use descriptive statistics (frequencies) to calculate the mean scores. *Electoral malpractice data:* I use the data set compiled by Birch, which was presented and discussed in the previous section.

The results are presented in Table 2.6. The higher the number is, the higher the degree of malpractice (1 being the lowest degree of malpractice, and 5 being the highest degree of malpractice). As seen from this table, "media coverage" and "misuse of state resources" have the highest mean scores. This observation is in line with the theory. Seemingly, a skewed playing field is the most-used practice in competitive authoritarian regimes. However, "legal framework" does not have the expected higher score.

Table 2.5. Mean scores for electoral malpractices across the regimes

Regime types and number of observations/Types of electoral malpractices	LD (N=5)	ED (N=70)	CA (N=22)	HA (N=31)
Media coverage	1.60	2.43	3.55	3.87
Misuse of state resources	2.00	2.64	3.30	3.21
Counting, tabulation, reporting	1.00	2.12	3.05	3.93
Voter registration	1.25	2.52	2.94	
Dispute adjudication	1.75	2.06	2.93	3.50
Voting	2.00	2.03	2.90	2.97
Legal framework	1.75	2.29	2.88	3.07
Candidate intimidation/Obstruction	1.00	1.81	2.75	3.14
Polling arrangements	1.75	2.03	2.63	2.62
Electoral authority independence	1.25	1.66	2.57	3.53
Voter intimidation/Obstruction	1.00	1.67	2.55	3.19
Observer access	1.40	1.46	2.14	2.83
Contestation	1.50	1.49	1.89	2.97
Vote Buying	1.20	1.29	1.86	1.64

Note: *Based on Howard and Roessler's regime data
**LD – Liberal democracy; ED – Electoral democracy; CA – Competitive authoritarianism; HA – Hegemonic authoritarianism.

Table 2.6. Mean scores for electoral malpractices in competitive authoritarian regimes

Regime types and number of observations/Types of electoral malpractices	CA (N=37)
Media coverage	2.88
Misuse of state resources	2.82
Voter registration	2.59
Counting, tabulation, reporting	2.56
Legal framework	2.55
Dispute adjudication	2.44
Voting	2.24
Polling arrangements	2.19
Candidate intimidation/Obstruction	2.18
Voter intimidation/Obstruction	2.09
Electoral authority independence	2.07
Contestation	2.04
Observer Access	1.88
Vote Buying	1.44

Note: *Based on Levitsky and Way (2010) data
**CA – Competitive authoritarianism

To determine whether the results were biased by the regime categorisations, as a test, I use Levitsky and Way's categorisation to group the malpractice. As their data are not complete and covers only the period from 1990 to 1995 and 2008, I added only those cases that match Birch's cases, ending up with 37 cases. As presented in Table 2.7, the initial results were confirmed when Levitsky and Way's categorisation was used. The results are slightly different when only competitive authoritarian regimes based on Levitsky and Way's categorisation are taken. However, mean scores are calculated and compared, again, media coverage has the highest score, followed by misuse of state resources. This pattern once again outlines the importance of media in competitive authoritarian regimes. The analyses show that media manipulation is widespread and employed most frequently, both in competitive and hegemonic authoritarian regimes. However, in competitive authoritarian regimes, media manipulations occupy the most prominent place, followed closely by misuse of state resources, then by the incumbent, and counting, tabulation, reporting.

Table 2.7. Mean scores for electoral malpractices across the regimes

Regime types and number of observations/Types of electoral malpractices	HA	Regime types and number of observations/Types of electoral malpractices	CA
Counting, tabulation, reporting	3.93	Media coverage	3.55
Media coverage	3.87	Misuse of State Resources	3.30
Electoral authority independence	3.53	Counting, tabulation, reporting	3.05
Dispute adjudication	3.50	Voter registration	2.94
Voter registration	3.22	Dispute adjudication	2.93
Misuse of state resources	3.21	Voting	2.90
Voter intimidation obstruction	3.19	Legal framework	2.88
Candidate intimidation/Obstruction	3.14	Candidate intimidation/Obstruction	2.75
Legal framework	3.07	Polling arrangements	2.63
Voting	2.97	Electoral authority independence	2.57
Contestation	2.97	Voter intimidation obstruction	2.55
Observer access	2.83	Observer access	2.14
Polling arrangements	2.62	Contestation	1.89
Vote buying	1.64	Vote buying	1.86

Note: * CA — Competitive authoritarianism, number of cases: 22; HA — Hegemonic authoritarianism, number of cases: 31.
** Based on Haward and Roessler's regime data and Birch's electoral malpractice data.

Interestingly, when the most-used practices in competitive and hegemonic regimes are compared (Table 2.8), the results show that a battery of the most often used manipulation techniques is slightly different in hegemonic regimes. In these regimes, apart from media coverage, problems are most often detected during counting, tabulation, and reporting of the results as well as in the independence of the electoral authority. According to the analysis, in competitive regimes, subtler, less detectable ways of affecting the outcomes of elections are used. The regime aims at taking precautionary measures before election day. They do so by a) manipulating the media to gain voters' support; b) adjusting the legal framework to create a partisan advantage; and c) misusing state resources or, to use Leonard Wantchekon's (2003) terminology, abusing the 'incumbency advantage'. Using Birch's typology of malpractice, it can be argued that the manipulation of the voting act is more widespread in hegemonic regimes, whereas competitive regimes prefer manipulation of institutional design and vote choice. The differences are visible, and further research could make use of electoral fraud data sets to draw better justified and more clean boundaries between these two sub-types of electoral authoritarian regimes.

2.6. Conclusions

Elections in authoritarian regimes have raised a multitude of questions, some of them being related to the electoral process itself. This chapter has presented recent studies of elections or, to be more precise, electoral fraud persistent across regimes. Although the literature on democracies is abundant, the field of electoral integrity is relatively new. Nevertheless, scholars have come up with various concepts and definitions of electoral malpractice. The definitions of fraud vary depending on the principles used as a benchmark for detecting it. Some use democratic principles, whereas others prefer international standards or argue that the legal framework should serve as a yardstick for delineating fraud. Examining the administration of elections has also been proposed as a possible benchmark. At the core, the basic standards against which the fraud is measured are derived essentially from the democratic principles. As discussed earlier in this chapter, every definition and approach to defining the concept has its pros and cons. However, for the purposes of this study, which is concerned with the kinds and extent of fraud in particular regimes, it is fitting to define electoral fraud using the approach that employs democratic principles for benchmarking. The definition used here is a combination of Schedler's and Birch's definitions of electoral fraud and electoral misconduct. Both put emphasis on the intentionally of misconduct and use basic democratic principles of electoral conduct throughout the whole period of the electoral process. Although "manipulation" is primarily used in the text, concepts such as "electoral misconduct," "fraud," and "malpractice" are sometimes used interchangeably to depict the same phenomena as the concept of "electoral manipulation."

A detailed presentation and discussion of different concepts, definitions, and data sets revealed that Birch's data set of electoral malpractice is the most suitable to measure the extent of different kinds of manipulation strategies across the regimes. However, Schedler's definition is by far the most systematic and theoretically grounded.

The analyses conducted using Birch's data set of electoral malpractice and Howard and Roessler's as well as Levitsky and Way's regime data sets show that hegemonic and competitive regimes use different strategies to manipulate elections. Further research is needed to verify the results, but, based on this preliminary analysis, it can be argued that using data on electoral malpractice might solve the problem of drawing the boundaries between sub-types of electoral authoritarian regimes. As argued in the first chapter, regime studies face a significant challenge of the operationalisation of hybrid regimes. As elections are principal in electoral authoritarian regimes, the distinction between sub-types can be achieved by either looking at the degree of electoral fraud or by looking at the battery of manipulations. The results of this analysis show that competitive regimes mostly use disguised strategies of manipulations, whereas hegemonic regimes not only manipulate elections more often but also use more overt practices in doing so.

Another important finding of the analysis is that the principal tool used in competitive authoritarian regimes to manipulate election results is through media manipulations. The results remain the same when different regime data sets are used for analysis. Thus, although many different types of fraud have been listed, my research focuses only on media coverage — primarily because it is an understudied but prominent part of competitive authoritarian regimes. As previously mentioned, media manipulation is the strategy used most often in both sub-types of electoral authoritarianism, but to a different extent. This study draws a qualitative comparison between the extent and types of media manipulations in competitive and hegemonic regimes. In further discussion of electoral fraud, I use the concept of 'manipulation' because it better captures the mechanisms of influence on the media. The next chapter a) presents literature on media effects; b) discusses the role of the media; c) proposes a model locating the media in the chain of the electoral process as well as demonstrating the mechanisms of the media's functioning in electoral authoritarian regimes; and d) touches upon the impact of the socio-political and economic environment on media freedom and pluralism.

3. Instrumentalisation of the media

3.1. Introduction

The media were named as one of the crucial factors contributing to the outbreak and success of electoral protests (McFaul 2005; Bunce and Wolchik 2006). However, despite the evidence, common sense, and relatively ubiquitous belief that the media's role is significant in the modern world, the direct effects of media on individuals' and communities' opinions and behaviour remain uncertain. The debate on the effects of the media on audiences and their preferences is long-lasting, but much is still undefined. There is a growing consensus that, depending on various conditions, the effect of the media can be more or less significant, and that the media cannot be considered a primary or sufficient reason to cause any effect, especially considering how difficult it is to assess these effects. All these nuances must be outlined and taken into account when studying the role of the media in non-democratic political regimes, and this is precisely the main goal of this chapter.

The chapter is also aimed at presenting a model according to which — as is argued in this work — the media are instrumentalised in electoral authoritarian regimes. However, before proceeding to the model, the chapter outlines and details some of the crucial elements of the model and relevant debates in media research. The chapter is divided into five sections. First, I outline the debate on media effects, which is further elaborated in the second section, where some of the most prominent models of media effects theory — such as agenda setting, framing, and priming — are explicated. The following section presents and discusses types of media bias and the difference between bias in countries with severe violations of media pluralism and countries where media freedom and pluralism is at minimum risk. The fifth section details the role of the media during the elections and presents a model of media functioning in electoral authoritarian regimes (the general logic and mechanisms are similar in both competitive and hegemonic regimes. However the extent of manipulations and sometimes the types of manipulations may vary). It is also aimed at presenting some principal features of media outlets and discusses how different types of media can be susceptible to manipulations. And in the last — sixth — section, the conclusions follow.

3.2. Media effects debate

The debate on the effects of the media on attitudes has continued for several decades[31]. Its history dates back to the beginning of the 20th century, when the media were successfully used by Nazis as a propaganda machine. This phenomenon led scholars to believe that the media have strong direct effects. The theory was advanced by Payne Fund researchers (Blumer, 1933; Blumer and Hauser, 1933; Peterson and Thurstone, 1933) who studied the effects of films on children in 1930s as well as Harold Lasswell (1935), who

---

[31] A detailed discussion of 'media effects research' has been presented in several publications, e.g., a debate between Lance Bennett and Shanto Iyengar, 'A New Era of Minimal Effects? The Changing Foundations of Political Communication,' *Journal of Communication* 58 (2008) 707-731; and Lance R. Holbert, Kelly Garrett and Laurel Gleason, 'A New Era of Minimal Effects? A response to Bennett and Iyengar,' *Journal of Communication* 60 (2010): 15-34; see also Russell Neuman and Lauren Guggenheim, 'The Evolution of Media Effects Theory: A Six-Stage Model of Communicative Research,' *Communication Theory* 21 (2011) 169-196. For a broad introduction to the topic, see Brian McNair, *An Introduction to Political Communication*. London: Routledge, Taylor and Francis Group (2007); William P. Eveland, "A mix of attributes' approach to the study of media effects and new communication technologies,' *Journal of Communication* 53, no. 3 (2003): 395-410. A detailed discussion is also provided in the edited volume by Jennings Bryant and Mary Beth Oliver, *Media Effects. Advances in Theory and Research*, 3rd ed. New York and London: Routledge (2009). The history of 'media effects research' is also discussed by Melvin L. DeFleur and Sandra Ball-Rokeach, *Theories of Mass Communication*, 5th ed., New York and London: Longman (1989); Elisabeth Noelle-Neumann, 'The effect of media on media effects research,' *Journal of Communication* 33, no. 3 (1983): 157-165.

argued that the political messages sent through the media have a significant impact on the audiences. The audience was considered to consist of passive and atomised individuals without access to alternative sources of information ("hypodermic needle model"). Later, in 1944, Paul Lazarsfeld, Bernard Berelson, and Hazel Gaudet's study showed that people were more influenced by personal contacts than radio or newspapers. Based on this empirical data, Katz and Lazarsfeld (1955) developed the 'two-step flow theory,' which asserts that information from the media is passed on to the audience through the opinion leader, who adds his or her own interpretation of the media information. Later, the paradigm was revisited and it was argued that the effects of the media are limited in general and depend significantly on the context, i.e., the audience and social and cultural factors. In 1960, Joseph Klapper claimed that the media do not have a direct effect on the audience but rather reinforces the individual's prior dispositions and existing attitudes.

Similarly, Denis McQuail (2010) divides the history of media effects research into four phases. The first phase he calls the "all-powerful media" phase, which lasted from the beginning of the 20th century until the 1930s. The media was believed to have a powerful influence on opinions and beliefs and was even capable of changing habits and behaviour. However, this belief was not supported by scientific research but rather by the popularity that the media was enjoying at the time and the effective use of media propaganda in the interwar period by dictatorial regimes. Putting the effects of the media under scrutiny marked the second phase of media effects research, which continued until the early 1960s. During this phase, McQuail (2010: 456) argues "[m]ore account was taken of the intervening effects of social and demographic variables, such as age, education and sex, and also of social psychological factors, such as predispositions and prior attitudes, personality type, persuadability, degree of interest and motivation, trust in the source, etc." This in turn diminished the significance of the media effects to a minimum. The third phase — "powerful media was rediscovered" — marked the revitalised interest in media effects research. Some (Lang and Lang 1981) argued that the evidence gathered by previous research did not prove insignificance of the media factor. McQuail states that one of the reasons for the renewal of the debate was the introduction of television – a medium that attracted a much larger part of population than any other media form before – in the market in 1950s and 1960s. At the beginning of the 1970s, McQuail (2010: 459) defines the fourth phase as "negotiated media influence." The dominant view of at the time was the media are "having their most significant effects by constructing meanings. The media tend to offer a "preferred" view of social reality (one that purports to be widely accepted and reliable)."

Current research on media effects combines elements from both significant and minimal media effects perspectives. One group of scholars argue that the media have significant effects as it constructs the social reality (McQuail 1992; Marcuse 1964; Herman and Chomski 1988). Others argue that media report issues in which the audience is interested. For example, Daya Kishan Thussu (2009) argues that growing commercialism and dependence on advertisement and public ratings influence the news agenda and editorial priorities. To attract larger audiences, the media may cover issues reflecting the interests of the audience. However, it would be more accurate to say that the influence is not one directional but rather interactive. As Voltmer (20013: 59) expresses it, "…media influences interact with, and are moderated by, other trends in society, sometimes acting as catalysts through which events or developments are set in motion, sometimes acting as amplifiers of already existing forces, sometimes reinforcing the status quo" (Voltmer 2013: 59).

To summarise, despite a long-lasting debate revolving around media effects research, it is still difficult to establish a link between the media and its audience using quantitative research, even more so when a large number of factors – such as the audience (social status, age, education level, demographics, income level and etc.), political system, level of pluralism in the country, and other variables – should be taken into consideration. This study does not intend to prove or disprove the significance of the effects that media might have on the audience. It rather aims at showing the extent to which media is instrumentalised and the mechanisms with which media manipulation is used to shape public opinion. Despite the absence of reliable research, which would present direct evidence of the impact that the media have on attitudes, it is hard to argue with a theory that even if the media do not compel people to think in certain ways, it still gives its audience information for further processing. It also has the capability of stressing some issues over others, presenting information in a certain manner, and highlighting the points of interest. This theory of media effects has been dubbed "agenda setting," which followed after a decades-long debate over the media's strong vs. minimal effects.

3.3. Models of media effects: agenda setting, framing, priming

Kaid and Johnston (1991) proposed the idea that political reality is composed of three main aspects: 1) objective political reality, which refers to actual political events occurring day to day — for example, elections, meetings, talks, or any event that actually takes place in political arena; 2) subjective reality, which is the reality of events as seen by the audience or how people see and interpret the reality; and 3) constructed reality, which is the reality constructed by the media through a certain representation, framing of the events, or the reality as seen by journalists and reporters. Constructed reality is important in shaping the subjective reality of the audience (Street 2001; McNair 2007; Kaid and Johnston 1991; Konig et al. 2009; Stroemberg 2004). The media sets the agenda for the political debate (Voltmer 2013; Lawrence 2000). Interpreting and passing along information about the events occurring in political domain to the audience and facilitating subjective perceptions of the audience puts the media in the centre of the political communication process.

In an earlier publication, McCombs and Shaw (1972) note that in the modern world "[t]he information in the mass media becomes the only contact many have with politics. The pledges, promises, and rhetoric encapsulated in news stories, columns, and editorials constitute much of the information upon which a voting decision has to be made" (p.176). Today, we can add to this list countless blogs, websites, and social platforms where people can access information and share their opinions, although it must be noted that, in most of the world, online media is still the privilege of a few. On average, people do not actively seek out, evaluate, and compare information concerning politics based on various sources, but rather rely on available sources, which they consider trustworthy.

As the majority of communication scholars note, reports by the media on political events are neither neutral nor impartial (McNair 2007; Kaid and Johnston 1991; Domke et al. 1997; Street 2001; Entman 2007). Subjectivities, biases and value judgments are abundant in the media coverage of happenings in the political arena. Even when the event is described in a neutral tone, the framing of the event, i.e., the way it is defined and constructed, is subjective. The same piece of news, when framed differently, can have different effects on the audience (Nelson et al. 1997; Brewer 2003; Entman 2007; Jasperson et al. 1998). Some claim that the media do not just reflect but often shape the social reality (Parenti 1993; Schlesinger 1978). Agenda setting or identifying the events worth covering; priming, i.e., influencing individuals' evaluation of the event by activating certain mental constructs (Entman 2007); and framing have been recognised by scholars as the most well-known ways in which the media construct reality, affect the audience's perception of reality and as a result influence some socio-political processes. Thus, even though the direct effects of the media on the audience's behaviour are hard to measure, agenda setting, framing, and generally the way any information is presented and delivered by the media to audiences is crucial[32], especially if apart from the media, people do not have many sources of information. The following section gives an overview of the recent research in political communication. It outlines some of the main terms, defines and discusses their importance and influence, and presents the literature on agenda setting, framing, and priming.

Agenda setting

Agenda setting or making certain issues more salient is often cited as an idea that was first introduced by Bernard Cohen. However, some (Baran and Davis 2010) claim that similar ideas were advanced by Lang and Lang (1966) and even earlier by Walter Lippmann (1922). Lang and Lang argued that '[t]he mass media force attention to certain issues. They build up public images of political figures. They are constantly presenting objects suggesting what individuals in the mass should think about, know about, have feelings about' (468). In 1963, amidst the debate on media effects, Bernard Cohen published a book in which he claimed that the press

> ...may not be successful in telling its readers what to think, but it is stunningly successful in telling its readers what to think about. And it follows from this that the world looks different to different people, depending not only on their personal interests, but also on the map that is drawn for them by the writers, editors, and publishers of the papers they read (p.13).

Later, in 1972, Cohen's ideas were tested by Maxwell McCombs and Donald Shaw. They observed that "normally the better educated and most politically interested (and those least likely to change political beliefs), actively seek information; but most seem to acquire it, if at all, without

---

[32] On the relationship between framing, agenda setting, and priming effects, see Dietram A. Scheufele and David Tewksbury, 'Framing, agenda setting, and priming: The evolution of three media effects models,' Journal of Communication 57, no. 1 (2007): 9-20. There is also a special issue of the Journal of Communication dedicated solely to theoretical explanations of these concepts; see *Journal of Communication* 57, no. 1 (2007): 1-141.

much effort." These voters are most susceptible to media influence. Based on interviews conducted with undecided voters and media materials gathered during the 1968 presidential elections in the USA, the authors checked if the media had a significant impact on voters' identification of the major issues of the campaign. They conclude that "the data suggest a very strong relationship between the emphasis placed on different campaign issues by the media and the judgments of voters as to the salience and importance of various campaign topics" (p.181)[33]. In 1982, Iyengar, Peters and Kinder published an article that tested a popular claim that "the problems that media decide are important become so in the minds of the public" (p.849). Their experiments show that television news programs affect the viewers' perceptions of the importance of any particular issue. This is later referred to as priming. Their study demonstrates that the issues covered in the evening news have greater weight in viewer's evaluations of the presidential performance. If problems related to the economy of the country are the main focus of the news, then the audience is more likely to evaluate the president's performance based on his achievements in the sphere of economy, while granting the problems in other areas only secondary importance.

The research on agenda setting has expanded since and has pushed the paradigm of media effects further. If McCombs and his colleagues (McCombs and Shaw 1972; Shaw and McCombs 1977; McCombs and Weaver 1985; McCombs, Shaw and Weaver 1997) revitalised the debate on

---

[33] Some might argue that it is possibly not the media that sets the agenda but rather the audience, and the media merely satisfies the demand by highlighting some topics over the others. However, this criticism does not discard the power of the media to form public opinion when it comes to political events but simply shows that there is an interdependency between the media and its audience. For a study on the relationship between the public agenda and the mass media agenda, see Jan Kleinnijenhuis and Edwald Rietberg, "Parties, Media, the Public and the Economy: Patterns of Societal Agenda-Setting," *European Journal of Political Research: Official Journal of the European Consortium for Political Research*, 28, no. 1 (1995): 95-118. They test whether agenda-setting is top-down (set by the media) or bottom-up (a response to public demand) process.

media effects, attributing at least some significance to the media, Entman went further, arguing (1989) that "the media make a significant contribution to what people think — to their political preferences and evaluations — precisely by affecting what they think about." He criticises the whole literature on agenda setting, which is rooted in Bernard Cohen's oft quoted statement that the media "may not be not be successful in telling its readers what to think, but it is [...] successful in telling its readers what to think about," arguing that even if being restated many times by many scholars, the statement is not well grounded. This idea is based on two simple assumptions. The first is "selectivity," an assumption that the audience selects the information they like and discards what they do not like. The second is "inattention," which holds that the audience pays so little attention to the media that it cannot possibly have any influence. Both assumptions lay a foundation in thinking that the media only reinforces existing preferences but does not help form new attitudes or change old ones (p.348). Entman himself proposes to use an "interdependence model," which links agenda setting scholarship to research by cognitive psychologists on information-processing models. His model rests upon the assumption that the formation of public opinion is the result of "an interaction between media messages and what audiences make of them." He advances the following statement:

> The way to control attitudes is to provide a partial selection of information for a person to think about, or process. The only way to influence what people think is precisely to shape what they think about. No matter what the message, whether conveyed through media or in person, control over others' thinking can never be complete. Influence can be exerted through selection of information, but conclusions cannot be dictated. If the media (or anyone) can affect what people think about — the information they process — the media can affect their attitudes (p.349).

The author suggests thinking about the media as "contributing to — but not controlling — the structure of publicly available information that shapes the way people can and do think politically" (p.367). The media do not have the capacity to force people to think in certain ways, but media messages interact with people's cognitive structures, or "schemas" — a composition of beliefs, values, attitudes, and preferences — alongside the rules helping to link different messages and ideas. Information is rejected if it openly contradicts this schema; however, this action would be more applicable in cases of open and deliberate propaganda, as media messages are more subtle in modern age. In addition, people may not have substantiated and rigid opinions on every issue, which leaves them more vulnerable to media influence.

According to the information-processing perspective, a person first evaluates any media message for salience. If not salient, the message is discarded, but if the message is salient, the information is further processed through the person's cognitive system in accordance with the rules established in his schema system. This may lead the person either to invalidate the information or store it. Entman argues that "when the implications are not obvious — for example when the information is contained in the form of a subtle slant to the news — the probability increases that even activist will store conflicting data without experiencing any immediate dissonance" (p.350). If the information is stored it has a potential to either shape new beliefs or change the old ones.

To summarise, even when "the model of autonomy" — the audience's "inattention" and "selectivity," as dubbed by Entman — is accounted for, the media can influence through agenda setting[34]. It can go far beyond merely telling people what to think about; it can shape the audience's opinions. It tells the audience "what to think" by telling them "what to think about." A salient media message is processed by the established cognitive routines of the schema system. To be accepted and further stored, the message should either a) resonate the values in the person's schema system; b) be subtle so that it is difficult to recognise whether it contradicts

---

[34] On agenda-setting, see Shanto Iyengar, Mark Peters and Donald Kinder, "Experimental Demonstrations of the "Not-So-Minimal" Consequences of Television News Programs," *American Political Science Review* 76, no. 4 (1982): 848-858.

any of the already established values in the schema; or c) be novel or unfamiliar, i.e., information related to some topic on which a person does not have a rigidly formulated opinion, as less familiar topics are more susceptible to media influence. Once the message is processed and stored, it can change an old sets of values, beliefs, attitudes, and preferences or stimulate new ones.

Framing

There is no universal definition of a media frame. Entman (2007: 164) defines framing "as the process of culling a few elements of perceived reality and assembling a narrative that highlights connections among them to promote a particular interpretation. Fully developed frames typically perform four functions: problem definition, causal analysis, moral judgment, and remedy promotion." James Tankard et al. (1991: 3; qqt. in Weaver 2007: 143) suggests that a media frame is "the central organising idea for news content that supplies a context and suggests what the issue is through the use of selection, emphasis, exclusion and elaboration." McCombs et al. (1998) calls framing "second-level agenda setting" and argues that if agenda setting is defined as selecting the news, topics, messages and generally objects for attention, then framing or second-level agenda setting is "the selection of a small number of attributes for inclusion on the media agenda when a particular object is discussed." In his view "the first level of agenda setting is [...] transmission of object salience. The second level agenda is the transmission of attribute salience" (p.704). Continuing Cohen's tradition, McCombs et al. suggests that in addition to telling the audience what to think about, by framing the issues in certain ways, the media also tells them how to think about some objects[35].

---

[35] For more detailed discussion of the literature on framing, see Dietram Scheufele, "Framing as a theory of media effects," *Journal of Communication* 49, no. 1 (1999): 103-122.

Gross and D'Ambrosio (2004) argue that when asked for an opinion, people sample from the accessible information, and it is usually the opinion that circulates most often in the media. According to their research, accessibility[36] of certain information (agenda setting) together with the way that information is contextualised (framed) raises an emotional response. Depending on the way any event is framed or contextualised, the same event can trigger contrasting emotions. Abortion can be framed as a murder or a woman's right to control her own body. Ordinary citizens' understanding of political realities — if not completely, at least partially — depends on the way the issue has been framed.

Entman very well summarises the main functions of agenda setting, framing, and priming. He advances the perspective that elites do care about the opinions of people, primarily because they want to gain the support of the people, citizens' votes, or at least tolerance of the elite's activities. In a world where limitations of time, attention, and rationality are in place, carefully selecting messages and showing the audience the ways in which the elements of these messages fit their own schema system is key to encouraging people to think in certain ways. In other words, agenda setting — which defines problems worthy of attention — "tells people what to think about," framing — which highlights the problems, encourages moral judgments, and promotes favourable solutions — "tells people how to think about objects," and the ultimate effect intended by the actor's framing activities is called priming.

---

[36] On accessibility, see Allan Collins and Elizabeth Loftus, "A Spreading-Activation Theory of Semantic Processing," *Psychological Review* 82, no. 6 (1975): 407-428. They present a spreading activation theory, according to which the information related to any concept is retrieved from the memory. The theory helps to explain the effects of agenda-setting on the audiences' ability to recall a memory of some objects and information associated with some concepts.

Priming

According to Iyengar and Kinder (1987: 63) "[p]riming refers to changes in the standards that people use to make political evaluations." Domke et al. (1998: 52) defines "priming effects" as "the process by which activated mental constructs can influence how individuals evaluate other concepts and ideas." Priming occurs when some issues are highlighted in the news content as more important, suggesting that the audience use the outlined issues as benchmarks for evaluating the performance of the government. For example, when the main emphasis in the news content is given to economic policies, the audience is more likely to evaluate the incumbent government's performance based on his economic policies. The model also suggests that the issues that are not problematised in the media become of secondary importance to the audience. For example, Russian television often problematises social issues, emphasising the incumbent's accomplishments in the corresponding policy sphere. As Scheufele and Tewksbury (2007: 11) argue "[b]y making some issues more salient in people's mind (agenda setting), mass media can also shape the considerations that people take into account when making judgments about political candidates or issues (priming)."

3.4. Media bias

Various types of media bias

In regard to bias in media reporting, many different types of bias exist. Every day, news organisations have to make editorial choices as to which events to broadcast, which message to deliver, and how to present the news. The news and underlying messages are greatly affected during the transmission process and are subject to various interpretations. As Voltmer (2013: 65) argues, "news is a cultural product that provides an interpretation of social reality through the "grammar" of journalism." That is, any material related to any event covered by the media before publication/broadcast as a news piece is first processed by the journalists' schema system (the norms, routines and aesthetic judgements). Bias is widespread and even news agencies claiming to present the most neutral information can be accused of bias. However, bias can come in different forms: some are deliberate, aimed at producing a certain effect on the audience, while others are unwitting and related to daily routines and choices. Denis McQuail (1992) identifies four types of media bias: partisan bias, propaganda bias, unwitting bias, and ideological bias.

- *Partisan bias* is a deliberate and explicit promotion of a political party/candidate or agenda.

- *Propaganda bias* is intended to promote certain causes but does so implicitly. For example, a media report might have a deliberate intention to promote a certain party or a candidate but in a hidden way. For example, a Russian TV news report on the activities of the prime minister may be neutral in tone. However, the impression one gets from watching the report is that Mr. Medvedev is a person who "cares" about his people and is there "to help" and "fix" problems that ordinary Russians face. The problem of this definition of propaganda bias is that it is difficult to identify.

- Another type of bias is *unwitting bias*, which refers to bias that occurs without any intention or prior agenda. This may happen when giving an event primary or secondary importance, placing an event report on the first or second page, and deciding what to include or exclude from the report. These are daily, routine activities. However, they involve judgment about the importance of a news piece/issue.

- The last type of bias identified by McQuail is *ideological bias*. In this case, the bias is hidden and unintentional. This happens when a journalist decides what is important, interesting and worthy to report on, which is an outcome of his value judgments and his knowledge of what is ordinary for the audience and what is 'newsworthy'.

This typology helps draw a distinction between intended and unintended biases. However, in regard to practice, it is quite difficult to clearly differentiate and identify these biases (Street 2001). The same piece of information can be interpreted differently by two readers. For example, in the Russian newspaper "Kommersant," some journalists use irony and implicit critique of the government in reporting, and sometimes interpretations of these reports vary from reader to reader. It is important to bear this in mind also when interpreting the results of content analysis.

More recent typology of media bias was proposed by Robert Entman (2007). He distinguishes between three types of media bias: distortion bias, content bias, and decision-making bias.

- *Distortion bias* is "applied to news that purportedly distorts or falsifies reality" (p.163).

- *Decision-making bias* is used to address "motivations and mindsets of journalists who allegedly produce the biased content" (p.163). To an extent, decision-making bias resonates with McQuail's ideological bias, which is also a product of a journalist's decision based on his value judgments. The only distinction is intention. McQuail claims that ideological bias is unintentional, while for Entman, the decision-making bias is intentional.

- *Content bias* is defined as "consistent patterns in the framing of mediated communication that promote the influence of one side in conflicts over the use of government power" (Entman 2007: 166). In other words, unwittingly employing one-sided framing might be common. However, when the media's preference of one side over the other is noticeable "across time, message dimensions, and media outlets, it means the media may be systematically assisting certain entities to induce their preferred behavior in others" (p.166). Some also refer to content bias as "editorial slant," defined as "the quantity and tone of a newspaper's candidate coverage as influenced by its editorial position" (Druckman and Parkin 2005: 1030). Research by Druckman and Parkin (2005) demonstrates the positive effects of editorial slant or content bias on voters' decisions, although it has also been argued that the significance of the effect is dependent on the level of trust the audience has toward the particular media source (Baron 2006).

As Entman (2007) rightly argues, any extraordinary event is controversial and yields at least a few different perspectives in its interpretation and presentation. To avoid the confusion, he suggests to "study how the news slants in particular instances and whether slant falls into recurrent patterns that [...] "mobilise bias" in the political system by helping some actors regularly prevail over others" (p.166). Thus, an important characteristic of content bias is the recurrence of news reports tilted in favour of a particular actor over time and across media outlets and is "consistent and one sided."

Media bias across regimes

Media bias is also present in democratic regimes[37]. Most of the research on political communication and media effects has been conducted by drawing on data from democracies. Different types of bias (in framing and agenda setting) are also present in democracies. However, although the coverage is biased, media pluralism — the diversity of the "biased" coverage of events — gives the audience an opportunity to receive balanced (i.e., different sources presenting different viewpoints), albeit biased information and interpret it through their cognitive processes. As the audience is exposed to a great variety of opinions, the effects of bias partly neutralise each other.

---

[37] For example, based on the example of the media in the USA, Baron (2006) argues that bias is persistent in the media. If not the result of government pressure or commercial interests, it can be the result of the journalist's own ambition. In other words, journalists may have incentives to insert bias in stories for the sake of career advancement. From a commercial point of view, his study shows that a new organisation is often willing to tolerate journalistic bias as it allows for the payment of lower wages.

Another difference between the media in democracies and non-democracies is the existence of alternative sources to the media. According to Voltmer (2013), in democracies, citizens obtain political knowledge over longer periods of time from different sources (e.g., political parties, trade unions, NGOs, etc.) and do not only rely on the media. In contrast, in countries where political parties, trade unions and other institutions are either weak or have lost credibility, the media becomes the main source of information. The same view has been proposed by Enikolopov, Petrova, and Zhuravskaya in one of their studies on the effects of the media on voting behaviour in Russia (2011: 3255). That said, in new democracies, media manipulation may have even more significant effects on the audience's opinions. They argue that in countries where party systems are unstable, democratic institutions are weak, and voters have limited prior knowledge of parties, candidates and their platforms, many base their decisions on new information obtained mostly from the media during the election campaigns.

To reiterate, bias *per se* is not limited to authoritarian regimes — it is present across all regimes. However, its effect and the extent may vary depending of the context. In countries enjoying media freedom and pluralism, the ramifications of bias are blurred as the audience is exposed to different, although biased, viewpoints.

Functions of the media in democracies

In democracies, the media's main task is to inform citizens, provide balanced coverage of political events, keep political authorities accountable by monitoring their activities, and serve as a "marketplace" of ideas (Voltmer 2013; Dahl 1975). McNair (2007: 21-22) notes that in democratic societies, the media serve five principal functions. First, it informs citizens of events in the world around them. Second, it serves to educate. Its third function, McNair argues, is to provide a platform for expressing opinions, creating a political discourse, and hence reinforcing the formation of a "public opinion." Further, he outlines a "watchdog" role of the media. Lastly, he notes the importance of the media as "a channel for the advocacy of political viewpoints." Voltmer's (2013: 26) list of the main functions that the media fulfil in democracies is similar to that of McNair. She argues that the media serves:

- to hold government officials accountable by acting as a "watchdog" that brings the misuse of power or policy failures to the attention of the public;
- to provide citizens with the information they need to participate in the democratic process in a meaningful and effective manner;
- to serve as a forum for different voices, both official and alternative, to mobilise public support for their cause.

Although the lists are similar, in contrast to McNair, Voltmer does not consider "educating the audience" as the principal function of the media.

A free press is an essential pillar of democracies. However, in states with weak democratic institutions, the picture is somewhat different. As Voltmer (p.23) also notes, "the media are not democratic by nature." They serve dictatorship just as much as they prosper in democracies. They inform, educate, and create public discourse, and to a much lesser extent on rare occasions, depending on the type of non-democratic regimes, political, and economic structures within which the media function, they can serve as a "watchdog" and/or a forum for different voices.

The following section presents a model which illustrates how the media functions in electoral autocracies. The model covers factors and actors shaping the content of news messages; interaction between the media, the ruling elite, and the audience; the influence exerted by the ruling elite on media organisations and its employees; and the possible effects of such influences on news content.

3.5. Model: elections and the media in electoral autocracies

The interaction between the media and its audience is not one-sided. Recent research in political communication takes into consideration the information flow between the political actors, the media and the audience, as well as the context. According to Brian McNair (2007), political communication refers to interaction between political actors, the media and the audience. As Figure 3.1 demonstrates, the role of the media is crucial in communicating between the audience and political actors. For political actors, it is crucial to be able to communicate with voters to legitimise their hold on power. Although until the mid-20th century all forms of political communication were restricted to interpersonal communication between political actors and a small elite group constituting the electorate, the introduction of universal suffrage changed the situation and forced the political actors to use mass media outlets to reach out to the broadened electorate (McNair 2007; Voltmer 2013; Seymour-Ure 1974). Currently, the easiest and arguably the only way of delivering a political message, such as political programs, policy statements, and electoral advertisement to voters, is via the media. According to McNair (2007: 11), the effectiveness of the message depends on the extent to which it has been reported by the media and is received by its audience.

Factors and actors affecting media content

While studying the factors influencing the content of the news media, the political and economic structures within which the media must operate should be taken into consideration. Journalists must be paid, newspapers should be printed and circulated, and all this requires some financial resources. To maintain independence when covering political events, the media organisation should at least be financially independent. This can be achieved in several ways: 1) to have reliable and sufficient advertising revenue; 2) to raise sufficient funds from subscriptions; 3) public financing; 4) or combination of different sources of revenues. Each of the finance sources has its limitations. As to first option of funding, businesses prefer to advertise their products and services on the most popular media, but to top the ratings, all media need a strong financial position. Thus, the media that have stable income, such as the state media or media owned by oligarchs, has the best chances of increasing its popularity ratings and, hence, attract more advertisement revenues. Second, newspapers can raise funds through individual subscriptions; however, a) as newspapers are mostly read in highly urbanised cities, even if the content remains independent, they do not reach the rural population; and b) the price of newspapers relying solely on subscriptions are much higher than those combining revenues from advertising and subscription. Third, in electoral authoritarian regimes with weak democratic institutions, public financing or state subsidies are leveraged to influence the media. Thus, apart from laws and regulations, ownership and sources of finance affect the content produced by media outlets.

Figure 3.1. Elements of political communication

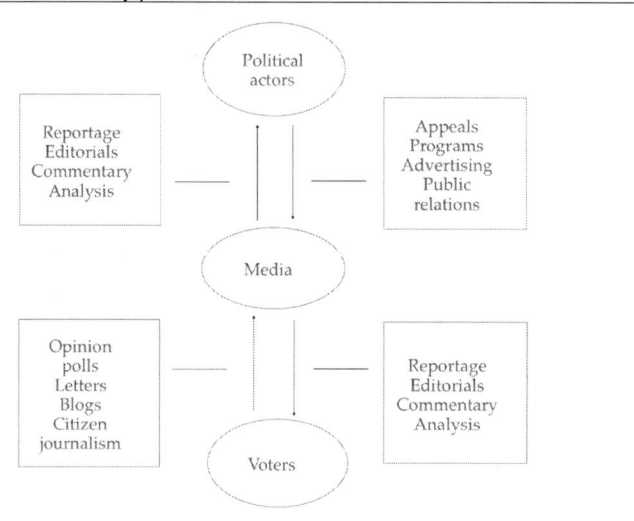

Source: McNair (2007: 7) with slight modifications by the author

Herman and Chomsky (1988) argue that journalists' decisions regarding the newsworthiness of events can often be explained by the "incentives, pressures, and constraints" put in place by structural factors, such as "ownership and control, dependence on other major funding sources (notably, advertisers), and mutual interests and relationships between the media and those who make the news and have the power to define it and explain what it means (1988: X)[38]." In their study, Herman and Chomsky construct a "Propaganda Model" according to which they claim the media in the United States — a country where the media are private and formal censorship is absent — works. They argue that "money and power are able to filter out the news fit to print, marginalise dissent, and allow the government and dominant private interests to get their messages across to the public" (p.2). Although their argument can be criticised for being overly deterministic, leaving only a little room for the role of agency, the structural factors remain relevant. Some of the factors they outline in their work are also applicable for cases well beyond the United States.

Similar ideas about media content being dependent on external factors such as finances, ownership, and personal contacts have been advanced by Herbert Altschull (1995). He argues that "the content of the news media inevitably reflects the interests of those who pay the bills" (1995: 52). Following his argument, those who finance the media will never let their media publish any information that goes against their interests. He differentiated four different patterns of relationships between the media and the "paymasters [39]," designating these relationships as official,

---

[38] They outline the following factors as the most crucial structural constraints: '1) the size, concentrated ownership, owner wealth, and profit orientation of the dominant mass-media firms; 2) advertising as the primary income source of the mass media; 3) the reliance of the media on information provided by government, business, and 'experts' funded and approved by these primary sources and agents of power; 4) 'flak' as a means of disciplining the media; and 5) 'anticommunism' as a national religion and control mechanism' (1988: 2).

[39] A term used by Altschull (1995) when referring to an individual or group who finances media activities. He also refers to them as "financiers."

commercial, interest, and informal. The official pattern is one where the content of the media is determined by the legal framework, i.e., rules, regulations, and decrees. The ownership of some media enterprises by the state, the state's control over licensing arrangements, and management under government regulations are also counted by Altschull as a part of an official pattern. He also notes that no nation is exempt from official control, and the difference between democracies and dictatorships is in "the degree of autonomy" (1995: 52) allowed. The commercial patterns denote cases where the content resembles the views of advertisers and their commercial partners, who often are either media owners or publishers. In the interest pattern, the medium reflects the interests and concerns of the financing organisation; it can be a political party, trade union, religious organisation or any other group following specific goals. The informal pattern refers to cases when the media echoes the perspectives of friends, relatives, acquaintances, or groups supplying money. It is seldom when the relationship is exclusively official or commercial, etc. More often than not, the patterns overlap.

Market concentration is another major issue influencing the media content. The production of news, reports, and other media content is a costly enterprise. As Herman and Chomsky (1988) also note, the costs associated with the start-up of a larger businesses in the sphere of the media with any substantial outreach are so high that they limit the number of competitors, leaving only a few privately owned large media organisations and organisations financed and regulated by the state afloat.

A further noteworthy point that Herman and Chomsky make (1988) is the degree of concentration in news production itself. They argue that the media are tiered. The top tier is defined by media organisations' "prestige, resources, and outreach" (1998: 4). The top tier "… defines the news agenda and supplies much of the national and international news to the lower tiers of the media and thus for the general public." Not all media outlets can afford to pay reporters, photographers and journalists to cover both international and national events. Thus, some outlets borrow the images and news stories from top tier media outlets. Consequently, the power to set the agenda, frame, and prime certain news and issues is concentrated in the hands of a few.

It certainly should be noted that political and economic considerations are not the only factors shaping media content. Extensive studies have been carried out to identify the determinants of media messages. Shoemaker and Reese (1996) detail dozens of possible variables on various levels, including the individual level, media routines, organisation, extramedia, and ideological levels. Every level of influence captures a string of variables affecting media content.

On the *individual level*, factors that are intrinsic to communication employees are discussed. It is argued that the message may differ in accordance with employees' gender, ethnicity, sexual orientation, education, background, professional experience, personal values, beliefs, attitudes, political views, religious orientations, and professional and ethical roles. Journalists may also be influenced by a system of beliefs on a societal level. Journalists' vision of their profession, perception of their rights as journalists, the role in society to which they assign themselves, and their values can be heavily shaped by the ideology of the society in which they live. This set of schemas can vary according to region, across time, and depending on the historical developments in the country. For example, a study of the codes of journalism ethics across the Middle East, North Africa, Europe, and the Muslim countries of Asia showed that although the issue is complex, some differences are obvious. In case of the Islamic world, Hafez (2010) argues that only handful of ethics codes place the freedom of expression above other fundamental rights such as privacy. Norms protecting the private sphere are more widespread in the Middle East and some other Islamic countries than they are in Europe. At the same time, the degree of freedom is more restrictive in the Middle East when interests of the state, nation, or religion are concerned. There are also studies comparing journalists' perceptions of professionalism in Russia and the United States, arguing that the interpretation of the concept by journalists is often determined by historical and cultural traditions as well as more specific socio-economic and political conditions (Wu, Weaver and Johnson 1996). Hallin and Mancini (2004) argue that journalistic professionalisation and levels of media institutionalisation also vary across media systems[40]. Their work provides some interesting insights as to which factors contribute to the development of journalistic professionalism.

Media *routine levels* include another group of factors forming the environment in which media employees work. Routines are 'patterned, routinised, repeated practices and forms that media workers use to do their jobs (105).' They constrain and at the same time provide certain rules that ease the work process of media employees. Three key factors are audience orientation, reliance on sources, and media organisation. Audience orientation: the media are concerned with their target audiences' preferences and interests. Thus, the audience is one of the factors that a medium takes into account when producing news stories. In considering mainstream audience interests and what they deem as important, it is argued that the news should be a) prominent — the story is important if it affects a large group of people; b) touch upon human interest — people are also interested in the lives of celebrities, the dramas revolving around others, and political gossip; c) conflictual — controversial issues attract more attention than non-controversial ones; d) unusual — events should be unusual to be considered newsworthy; e) timely — people want to know

---

[40] They categorise media systems into three groups: 1) the Mediterranean or polarised pluralist model present in France, Greece, Italy, Portugal, and Spain have weaker professionalisation levels among journalists and higher levels of instrumentalisation, either commercial of political instrumentalisation; 2) the Northern European or Democratic Corporatist Model, the example of which can be the media system in Austria, Belgium, Denmark, Finland, Germany, Netherlands, Norway, Sweden, and Switzerland, which have strongly professionalised, institutionalised, and self-regulating media; 3) the North Atlantic or Liberal Model, which features strong professionalisation and non-institutionalised and self-regulated media. They define journalistic professionalism as a type of journalism which "serves a public interest that transcends particular social interests." Two other principal features of journalistic professionalism are "the development of a distinct common culture of journalism," and "relative autonomy in relation to other social actors" (2004: 192).

what is going on in the world now; f) proximity — events occurring nearby are considered more newsworthy than those in distant areas. Organisational routines: every organisation develops its internal routines. In the case of the media, they have established and patterned practices of gathering, evaluating, and processing information. Among other organisational routines, there is a routine reliance on other media, which is also discussed later when presenting the argument by Herman and Chomsky (1988) on news media concentration. It is argued that journalists rely on each other for ideas, which is what makes news so similar across media. External sources: in producing news media, organisations heavily rely on suppliers of information, interviews with politicians, reports, government hearings, and other raw materials, opinions of experts, official sources, etc. These sources also impact the final reporting and content of news messages.

Based on an extensive literature review, Shoemaker and Reese (1996) argue that *organisation level* factors encompass questions related to the organisational structure of the media, the roles performed, the policies according to which organisations function and the methods of enforcing those policies. The authors conclude that most media organisations see profit maximisation as their primary goal. It is important to remember that journalists have to coordinate their media messages with larger corporate enterprises of which they might be part or that may be financing some of this media organisation's activities. However, the principal decisions are left to the owners, and it is up to them to set the policies and implement them. Ownership plays an influential role in shaping news media, as the content of the news can be indirectly controlled by owners through hiring and firing, promotion practices, and self-censorship. To summarise, organisational structure, ownership, and the goals set by the media organisation have influence over media content.

Another principal set of variables potentially influencing media content is located at the *extramedia level*. These are factors beyond the media organisation, such as laws, regulations, domestic markets, global markets, competitors, new technologies, advertisers, audiences and so on. The authors argue that there is anecdotal evidence supporting the claim that media content is influenced by its *audience*. However, it can also be influenced by the advertisers. Although media organisations have a clear idea of their audience, the principal usage of this information is to offer it to advertisers who pay to place their commercials on media channels watched by the desired target group. As advertisement comprises a principal portion of media revenues, the content can often be dictated by the advertisers. Content can also be shaped by a *marketplace* – for example, the size of the market, opportunities for profit, and general economic conditions within which the organisation operates. *Government* influences media content all over the world, albeit to different extent. Sometimes the influence is exerted through laws, regulations, licensing, and taxes. Other times, influence can be generated by producing public information aimed at creating an impression that the government is competent and efficient. It has also been argued that relationships between journalists and state agents impact media messages. Even the words used by officials in presenting certain news can be of some influence.

On *ideological levels*, the principal question is whether media content is influenced by the ideology – defined as a belief system on a societal level – in addition to the role of media in propagating this ideology, and whether media itself is constrained and limited by it.

Although one can name numerous potential factors influencing media reporting in this study concerned with the ruling elite's media manipulation practices, I only look at external factors to use Shoemaker and Reese terminology, factors on the extramedia level, i.e., government control, legal influence, general economic conditions. Ownership and principal source of finance are also seen, as in the case with Russia, as one of the ways in which the elite can control the media, i.e., through ties to owners of large media organisations.

The media in non-democracies

In full and hegemonic authoritarian regimes, democratic institutions either do not exist or exist as a façade. In contrast, in competitive authoritarian regimes, channels through which opposition can compete in executive elections do exist. In competitive authoritarian regimes, "democratic procedures are sufficiently meaningful for opposition groups to take them seriously as arenas through which to contest for power" (Levitsky and Way 2010: 7). "Civil liberties are nominally guaranteed and at least partially respected. Independent media exist and civic and opposition groups operate above the ground" (2010: 8). Opposition is allowed to compete in elections. There is an element of uncertainty in election outcomes; elections are mostly free but unfair. However, creating an uneven playing field by denying the opposition access to media enables the incumbent to win elections without resorting to repression or obvious electoral fraud. In this way, the incumbent's chances of winning elections as well as gaining legitimacy increase. Therefore, rather than fully repressing the broadcast media, competitive authoritarian regime governments prefer using different strategies to manipulate different media outlets. The implementation of these strategies significantly reduces opposition forces' chances to voice their views and opinions, let alone win elections. Mass media manipulation serves as an important instrument for regime stability. In other words, the incumbent manipulates broadcasting media channels to win elections and legitimise electoral success. In such regimes, as the evidence presented in the previous chapter showed, the manipulation of media broadcasting is widespread.

According to Schedler, in electoral authoritarian regime, the only way into office lies in the elections (Figure 3.2 provides an illustration of the process). Many different strategies are employed to manipulate the desired election outcomes. Essentially, the leaders are appointed through the elections, and thus the elections are the "central arena of manipulation." As he further argues, "[u]nder authoritarian conditions, votes are the joint result of voter choices and state decisions." In this way, the manipulation strategies discussed previously can be roughly grouped into: 1) electoral manipulation through state agents (collection of civil bureaucracies, military bureaucracy, legislatures, and judicial institutions); and 2) electoral persuasion.

Figure 3.2. Electoral process

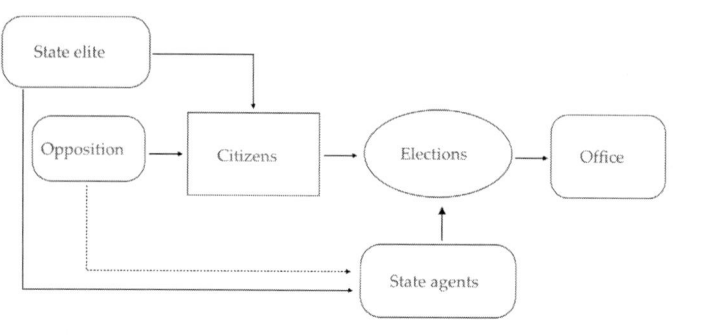

Source: Schedler (2013: 118) with slight modifications

In general, authoritarian governments buy the loyalty of state agents in various ways, thus creating a tie between public officials and the government (Schedler 2013: 123), whereas opposition actors seek to break these loyalties. However, their most significant chance to influence election outcomes is through influencing voters. The real battle in competitive authoritarian regimes occurs here.

Media manipulation is one of the frequently used tactics in competitive regimes. A number of scholars have emphasised the importance of the media in electoral change in these governments. For example, the majority of students of colour revolutions consider relatively free media as one of the crucial pillars of success for electoral protests (McFaul 2005; Bunce and Wolchik 2006). McFaul (2005) argued that one of the critical elements of electoral success in Ukraine (2004), Georgia (2003) and Serbia (2000) was the presence of independent media. According to McFaul (2005: 12), independent media outlets contributed to the decline of Milosevic's popularity. Similarly, in Georgia, the independent media have not only been transmitting corruption exposure shows during Shevardnadze's presidential term, but they also have been broadcasting exit-poll and parallel count results simultaneously with official results released by the Central Electoral Commission. Although the opposition in Ukraine did not have open access to the majority of independent media, the presence of higher levels of Internet connectivity in the country played a crucial role. McFaul argues that "the Orange Revolution (so called after the party colour of "Our Ukraine") may have been the first in history to be organised largely online" (2005: 12).

As was mentioned in the previous chapter, Sarah Birch proposes a typology of electoral fraud. She distinguishes three types of electoral malpractice: 1) manipulation of electoral design; 2) manipulation of vote choice; and 3) manipulation of the voting act (see Table 3.1). The *manipulation of institutions* is understood as a manipulation of the institutional design governing elections for the advantage of certain electoral contestants in violation of the principles of democratic elections. As Birch argues, this includes gerrymandering[41], malapportionment[42], over-restrictive franchise or candidacy regulations, campaign regulations that lead to inequalities among contestants, lack of observer access to electoral processes, etc." (2011: 26). The second type of electoral malpractice is the *manipulation of voters* and the choices they make. This form of manipulation includes undue influence such as creating positive incentives for voters to misrepresent or alter their preferences, including vote-buying and clientelistic transactions; negative sanctions such as intimidation and coercion also fall under this category. Media bias as well as violation of campaign finance regulations can also be counted as manipulation of vote

---

[41] Manipulation of district boundaries to create partisan-advantaged districts, with the aim of gaining additional support for a particular party.

[42] Poor organisation of districts that prevent large portions of the population from being equitably represented in the legislative body.

choice. And the last type is the *manipulation of the voting act*. This type of electoral malpractice includes "the uneven implementation of the regulatory framework, the biasing of administrative decisions in favour of one or more electoral competitors, and, outright fraud" (2011: 27).

Influence: media manipulations

In this study, I aim to concentrate on the forms of electoral malpractice/strategies used in competitive authoritarian regimes that affect voters and their choices through the manipulation of media. These forms of electoral malpractice include distorted and skewed coverage of current political affairs; a biased pre-election news environment; extensive and often positively biased news coverage of the party in power during the parliamentary elections and coverage of the incumbent president during the presidential campaigns; loopholes, laws, and legislations limiting the opportunity for opposition voices to be heard via media; self-censorship of broadcasting media; using state administrative resources to access media; strategies put in place by the state to ensure control over mass media; restrictions on media operations and media content; highly restrictive campaign laws that prevent opposition parties from media coverage. To illustrate different strategies employed by the incumbent to create an uneven field, I use Birch's typology of electoral malpractice (see Table 3.1). Although Birch mentions some practices that "indirectly facilitate electoral abuse", she does not include them in the original typology of electoral malpractice. However, as this type of practices also includes control over the media by the state or president's cronies, I have added an additional cell in the typology: "Corruption and administrative malpractice that indirectly facilitates electoral abuse."

Rather than fully repressing the broadcasting media, competitive authoritarian governments prefer using different strategies to manipulate different media outlets. Implementation of these strategies significantly reduces the opposition forces' chances to voice their views and opinions, let alone win elections. Mass media manipulation serves as an important instrument for regime stability – in other words, the incumbent manipulates the media to win elections and legitimise his/her electoral success (illustration is provided in Figure 3.3).

Table 3.1. Typology of electoral malpractice

Corruption and administrative malpractices indirectly facilitating electoral abuse	Manipulation of institutional design	Manipulation of vote choice	Manipulation of the voting act
- Control over media that indirectly facilitates electoral abuse; - Media ownership.	- Media regulations; - Campaign finance rules; - Rules governing the publication of opinion polls, and contract with workers; - Altering the legal underpinnings of the vote-casting and counting process; - Manipulating the criteria that determine eligibility to take part in the electoral process; - Gerrymandering; Malapportionment.	- Media bias; - The misuse of state resources during the campaign; - Violation of campaign finance regulations; - The "black art" of manipulative campaign tactics. Defined as an act of "seducing or bullying public opinion by media manipulation Hansen 2000: 63; - Candidate intimidation; - Vote-buying; Voter coercion/intimidation.	- The obstruction of ballot access by potential candidates; - The manipulation of voter registration and/or the electoral register; - Failure to provide adequate polling arrangements; - The manipulation of voting; - The manipulation of the process of counting and tabulation of votes; - Misreporting of the results of voting and/or seat allocation; - The obstruction of observer access; Maladministration of election-related legal disputes.

Source: Based on work by Birch, 2011

Table 3.2. Ways of influencing the media

Constraints on a macro-level		Constraints on a micro-level
Incumbent's misuse of state resources to directly or indirectly facilitate abuse of media freedom	*Legal constraints*	*Other ways of ensuring compliance*

- Control over television and most of radio channels via direct state ownership
- Alliance between the ruling elite and media moguls
- Direct or indirect control over facilities rented by media outlets and thus an opportunity to manipulate terms and conditions of lease
- Cooptation
- Control over the media distributive infrastructure (state control over publishing houses and print media distribution infrastructure in the case of print media; and control over the issuance of broadcast licenses in case of broadcast media.) to warrant low circulation of independent newspapers and magazines, ensuring that information is accessible only to certain segments of a population
- Exerting influence via distribution of state financial subsidies
- Distribution of key positions in the media industry to loyalists
- Control over the registration of new media outlets
	- Issuing legislations restricting media freedom
	- Putting restrictions on opposition parties and creating disparities in access to the media
	- Regulations governing broadcast media and obtaining broadcast licenses
	- Lawsuits and criminal cases filed against journalists and media outlets
		- Evicting media outlets from their premises
		- Launching newspapers carrying an existing name
		- Hiring and firing practices
		- Denying access to information
		- Coercive strategies used to force *journalists* into self-censorship: :
		  • attacks on journalists
		  • damaging photos, audio and video equipment, computers
		  • threats against journalists
		  • murder of journalists
		  • detentions by police

Based on the previous studies that have been discussed earlier in this chapter, commonly used manipulation strategies are provided in Table 3.2. They are divided into two more general groups based on the level of influence, which is exerted on macro and micro level. On a macro level, the ruling elite poses serious limitations to the media's activities and curbs media freedom via its control over the legal environment in which the media operates; and through access to state resources they (the incumbent and his supporters) have. Constraints on a micro-level can be viewed on two separate levels: 1) individual journalist level and 2) media organization level. On an individual level, journalists are silenced, pressured into self-censorship in different ways, including violent measures. Additionally, hiring and firing practices employed by the media organizations help to keep the employees in line with media organisation's general views. On the level of a media organization, cases such as the launch of parallel media outlets carrying the same name with an aim of confusing the audience are also employed.

Effects of manipulations on news content

The ruling elite also can affect the content of the news using the same manipulation strategies listed in Table 3.2. The outcomes of these measures are mirrored in the content of media reports. The possible effects of these manipulations on news content are summarised on Table 3.3. Each category in this table has been presented in detail in the previous sections. When constraints on both the macro and micro levels are in place, the news content becomes increasingly one-sided. Content bias is easily observed "across the time, message dimensions and media outlets" (Entman 2007); the agenda is focused mostly on coverage of the incumbent candidate or a successor endorsed by the incumbent; reports related to the candidate from the ruling elite are mostly framed in a positive way. Likewise, when under pressure, news organisations, journalists, reporters, and editors practice self-censorship. The extent of the effects may vary just as the extent of the pressure. Likewise, larger categories of constraints, both on macro and micro level, can be further divided and sub-divided depending on the creativity, skill, and imagination of the ruling elite. However, Table 3.2 and

Table 3.3 present a list of the known and most common media manipulation strategies and their effects on media content.

Table 3.3. The effects of media manipulations on news content

Effects	Definition
Self censorship	The act of censoring or classifying one's own work.
Content bias or Editorial slant	"Consistent patterns in the framing of mediated communication that promote the influence of one side in conflicts over the use of government power...if the patterns of slant persist across time, message dimensions, and media outlets, it means the media may be systematically assisting certain entities to induce their preferred behavior in others" (Entman 2007: 166).
	"The quantity and tone of a newspaper's candidate coverage as influenced by its editorial position" (Druckman and Parkin 2005: 1030).
Framing	"The process of culling a few elements of perceived reality and assembling a narrative that highlights connections among them to promote a particular interpretation. Fully developed frames typically perform four functions: problem definition, causal analysis, moral judgment, and remedy promotion" (Entman 2007: 164).
	"The central organising idea for news content that supplies a context and suggests what the issue is through the use of selection, emphasis, exclusion and elaboration" (James Tankard et al. 1991: 3; qqt. in Weaver 2007: 143).
Agenda setting	"The selection of a small number of attributes for inclusion on the media agenda when a particular object is discussed" (McCombs et al. 1998: 704).
	"Through their day-to-day selection and display of the news, journalists focus our attention and influence our perceptions of the most important issues facing the country...[t]his ability to influence the salience of topics on the public agenda has come to be called the agenda setting role of the media" (McCombs and Reynolds 2009: 1).
	"The mass media force attention to certain issues. They build up public images of political figures. They are constantly presenting objects suggesting what individuals in the mass should think about, know about, have feelings about" (Lang and Lang 1966: 468).
Priming	"Priming refers to changes in the standards that people use to make political evaluations" (Iyengar and Kinder 1987: 63).
	"The process by which activated mental constructs can influence how individuals evaluate other concepts and ideas" (Domke et al. 1998: 52).

The role of the media in the electoral process

Figure 3.3 presents a mechanism according to which the media operates in competitive authoritarian regimes. The model is derived from the theories of competitive authoritarianism, electoral malpractice, and political communication. As is seen in Figure 3.3, in competitive authoritarian regimes, both the opposition and the ruling elite have access to media; however, access is skewed in favour of the incumbent. As Schedler (2013) also notes, the incumbent has access to legal and state resources through which he can manipulate/control/influence the media. As voters in countries with less developed and less institutionalised sources of information mostly depend on the media, their effect on the voters' choice is relatively higher.

The media is an organisation composed of owners, shareholders, editors, journalists, reporters, photographers and other employees. Within the organisation, journalists produce media content, and this content is shaped by many factors, including the journalist's schema system, integrity, etc. Media outlets are divided into three general groups: broadcast, print, and online media. Key features that make these media outlets vulnerable to manipulation from the outside are detailed in further sections of this chapter.

Influence can be exerted on several analytically distinguishable levels. As has been shown earlier (see Table 3.2), constraints on the micro-level can be further divided into those imposed on any given media outlet, or on any individual journalist working in this media outlet. For example, an editor might be more cautious in choosing topics, which might cause potential problems to the outlet, these problems can be either of political or financial nature, or both. On an individual level a journalist might be more careful in selection of frames and topics because of potential risks he/she can face. As this is an important distinction, when looking at constraints I make a separate assessment of potential constraints on the level of an individual journalist, and an individual media outlet.

Media organization: any print or online media outlet is managed by editors and chief-editors on every day basis, in case of television the organisational structure can be more complex and there is a closer control over the content of news produced and aired.

Journalists: The content of the news does not solely depend on the structural constraints present in the country or created by the ruling elite; it is also largely shaped by the producers of the news. The content of news is the product of an interaction between journalists, editors, owners and shareholders of a given media outlet, the choices they make while navigating a complex environment, and calculating both financial, and political risks they face. Any media organisation includes individual journalists whose actions, apart from being constrained by external pressure, are also conditioned by their own schema system and overall journalistic ethics and the level of journalistic professionalism in the country. These are, to an extent, interrelated but can be analytically differentiated. Journalistic ethics and journalistic professionalism − or as Hallin and Mancini (2004) define it, journalism that "serves a public interest that transcends particular social interests" (p.192) and has a well-developed "distinctive common culture of journalism" − are conditions and codes of conduct on a country level and on the level of the journalistic community[43], whereas the journalist's schema system is on an individual level. A journalist might have and maintain his professional integrity (serving a public good with no regard to particular social interests) despite low levels of professionalism in the country, and in spite of some country-specific codes of journalistic ethics (see Table 3.4). For the sake of differentiation, this type of professional integrity is further referred to as personal integrity. A Russian journalist, Anna Politkovskaya, is an example of a journalist with a professional integrity. During the Chechen war, between 1999 and 2000, she was one of very few journalists who dared to write about the events and conditions in Chechnia, being critical of the government's actions during the Second Chechen War and in general. She was murdered in 2006. Politkovskaya maintained professional integrity despite low levels of

---

[43] As has been already mentioned, the level of professionalisation differs depending on various factors. Historical events, social context, and political and economic factors shape professionalisation. This topic is further discussed with examples in the next chapter.

autonomy given to journalists, weaker institutionalisation, and a political environment limiting open criticism and freedom of speech. To summarise, even in the most severe conditions, journalists can and sometimes do maintain their voice, but they do so at their own expense.

Table 3.4. Journalistic ethics and professionalism

Country level	Community level	Individual level
Journalistic professionalism	*Code of journalistic ethics*	*Professional integrity*
Developed through longer periods of time and shaped by historical events and the political, economic, and social context		Developed based on an individual set of values, a schema system, and is a personal choice
Consists of three main pillars: - autonomy — self-regulation; - development of a common culture of journalism — institutionalisation; - a public service transcending particularistic social interests — professionalism or professional integrity (Hallin and Mancini 2004).	The code of journalistic ethics is a declaration by media professional organisations of their professional norms, values, and their social role as journalists (Himelboim and Limor 2008: 240).	Maintaining objectivity and serving the public good with no regard to particularistic social interests.

Arrows: dashed arrow lines — represent interaction, indirect and not clearly defined causal links between the elements. Solid arrows stand for direct relationships between the objects, e.g., the action and consequences, or influence and effect. The arrows linking the state elite to journalists and media organisations stand for the constraining conditions created by the ruling elite to curb media freedom. The arrows that point in both directions linking the "content of news" to "opposition," "ruling elite," "voters," "shareholders" represent an interaction between media content and actors and how media content shapes the debates and influences actors' calculations.

News content — the content of broadcast, print, and online media sources;

Voters — citizens with voting rights;

State agents — the Central Election Commission and other state actors involved in the electoral process who are able to influence the process.

Elite: the business elite (shareholders) — owners of large non-state businesses; and the ruling elite — the ruler and his close circle. The ruler is the head of the state. One of the features of electoral authoritarian regimes is the blurred boundaries between the government, state, and business. The following chapter details examples of how these personal links are used to manipulate the media.

Opposition — both tame and real opposition parties. Although the opposition is present in the model and can be seen as a potential factor with influence on the media, it is not the focus of this study and is presented for the sake of constructing a broader picture.

Sources of information used by journalists also influence the media message. Through this channel (events, reports, press conferences, new policies, interviews, etc.) both the opposition and ruling elite can influence the issues covered in the news.

Mechanisms of influence on media content

The model proposed in this study aims to demonstrate the mechanisms of influence on media content through pressure on news organisations and journalists and interaction between the actors. As seen in Figure 3.3, there is a constant information flow between the audience, the media, and political actors. The ruling elite attempts to influence the content of the media through the manipulation of the legal framework; abuse of state resources; direct ownership of media outlets; buying loyalty of the media owners; or in extreme cases, direct pressure on journalists, reporters, or the news organisations in general. Journalists, in turn, calculate the risks associated with reporting on issues disapproved of by the state and act according to their best knowledge, driven by their professional integrity and their own schema system. Some choose to report issues threatening the state's legitimacy or criticising the government or its policies, while others adjust to demands of the ruling elite. There are plenty of examples for both cases. However, critical voices are rare on television channels and are marginalised in the print media. These are presented in more detail in the case study following this chapter.

As the majority of the population uses television news as the main source of information on political events, and in absence of alternative views and alternatives for the media, voter's opinions to an extent are shaped by the information they receive. The media cannot tell people what to do or what to think. However, implicitly through agenda setting, it can direct the debates in certain directions; using different frames, the media can present reality in a way that gives an advantage to one actor over the other; by priming certain issues, it can nudge the citizens to evaluate the performance of the government using the benchmarks most often discussed in the media. In countries where people have a degree of trust in the media, people are more vulnerable to the media's influence. The ruling elites manipulate the media environment, pressure journalists, and restrict media freedom in a way that best suits their interests. The details on how exactly this is done, which manipulations are used, and how the effects of these manipulations are mirrored in the content of the media is explicated in the case study presented in Chapters 4 and 5.

Figure 3.3. The model of media effects in electoral process

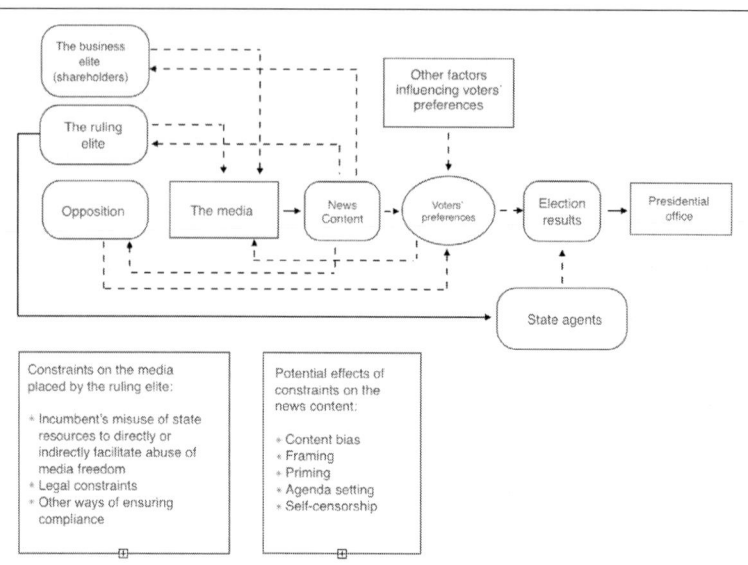

The media are usually divided into three broad categories: print media, broadcast media, and online media. Each medium of communication has its own specific characteristics, methods of presenting information, target audiences, ways of delivering a message, and distribution channels. These characteristics determine the ways in which a certain media outlet can be manipulated, constrained, and its freedom limited. In this section, I present the characteristics peculiar to the media studied in this work. Target audiences, distribution channels, a brief history of creation, actors participating in news production, and the production processes are mainly explicated in this section to lay a foundation for further development of the "model of media effects in the electoral process." In this section, the agency of the media is also discussed. Instead of taking the media as an object subjected to various influences and manipulations from the side of the ruling elite, the media are disassembled into news producers and shareholders with their own interests and calculations who are forced to navigate within the structural constraints they face. As has been summarised in Table 3.2, there are a multitude of ways in which the ruling elite attempts to exert control over the media. They can be roughly grouped into five categories:

1) *Direct pressure on journalists and media organisations* — violent and non-violent ways of pushing a journalist and/or a media organisation into self-censorship. Intimidation, threats, murders of journalists, shutting down newspapers, and attacks on media outlet offices are just a few of them. This practice can be used on any media organisation, whether it is broadcast, print, or online media.

2) *Production and distribution* — control over distributive channels by the state, ruling elite or any other groups who have personal contact with the members of the ruling elite.

Print media: Production and distribution of print media largely depends on printing houses, the country's mail services, and newspaper shops. This in turn makes print media organisations largely dependent either on the state infrastructure or services provided by a third party, leaving print media outlets vulnerable to external influence from the state with regard to distribution. As most distribution channels are under state control, some marginal newspapers may be prevented from distributing papers containing content that is not wanted by the ruling elite. Likewise, there are cases when printing houses refuse to print some newspapers.

In case of *broadcast media*, the state controls broadcast bands and usually has discretion over the issuance of broadcast licensing.

Online media: The medium that is least vulnerable to external manipulation is online media. The World Wide Web enables the distribution of all types of information to international audiences at any time of the day, and compared to traditional media, is the least subjected to censorship. However, the state can easily block some web sites.

3) *Media's sources of finance* — as a profit-making organisation, the media is dependent on actors and groups financing their work. The media's

source of finance can be large business owners, state grants and subsidies, advertisers, and to a much lesser extent, subscribers; or media can be sponsored by donations and grants from foreign NGO's, businesses, foundations, etc. Using financial leverage, the media can be manipulated to produce the desired content. The expansion of the advertisement market allowed the media to sell their product at lower prices. However, attracting advertisers requires broader outreach — higher ratings in case of television, and wider readership in case of print media. The production of news and entertainment programs requires high financial costs, which, again, contributes to the concentration of the main media outlets in the hands of a few[44]. In turn, the outlets that fail to attract advertisement revenues are unable to reduce subscription prices for their customers, and in majority of cases, they face financial problems and lose subscribers. These outlets have a choice between facing bankruptcy or finding alternative sources of finance in the form of financial support from large business owners or state subsidies.

4) *Ownership* — the ruling elite can also influence media content through direct ownership of a media organisation, regardless of the type of media, or alternatively through pressuring or buying the loyalty of media owners.

Private ownership: As has been noted, the content of news, the weight journalists and editors give to some events, or the way the agenda is set are conditioned by the owner's preferences, his vision of the news that should be given preference, and what the general tone of reporting should be.

State ownership: Partial or full state ownership of major media outlets may not be as harmful in institutionalised democracies as they can be in electoral authoritarian governments. In a majority of countries in the post-Soviet region, where the media are owned or subsidised by the

---

[44] This phenomenon was observed by Herman and Chomsky (1988) in their study of media history in the United States.

state, media freedom is rare, and the media are mostly manipulated. Apart from Russia, examples of manipulated media can be observed in hegemonic authoritarian Azerbaijan (Kazimova 2011; Pearce and Kendzior 2012; Pearce 2014), and Kazakhstan[45] (Schatz[46] 2009; Junisbai 2011; Akhrarkhodjaeva 2012). Countries with closed authoritarian regimes, such as Uzbekistan [47] and Turkmenistan [48], use different strategies in dealing with the media; rather than employing covert manipulation strategies, they exert full control over the media and openly assault journalists.

Schatz (2009) states that when addressing manipulative strategies used to ensure regime stability, factors such as actors and institutions should be taken into consideration. Nevertheless, the possession of financial and administrative resources increases the elite's agenda setting power. For example, in Russia, it is often argued that the boom in oil prices after 1998 coincided with the Kremlin's takeover of major television channels and the extension of indirect ownership or control over some major news agencies. As Treisman (2010: 85) notes "Kremlin-controlled gas

---

[45] For general review of media manipulation strategies in the post-Soviet region see, Andrei Richter, "Post-Soviet Perspective on Censorship and Freedom of the Media," *The International Communication Gazette* 70 no. 5 (2008): 307-324.

[46] Edward Schatz (2009) looks at different ways of maintaining power in "soft authoritarian governments," among these tools he also notes the agenda-setting power of media. His comparative case study of Kazakhstan and Kyrgyzstan presents some insights into functioning of media manipulations and other mechanisms of authoritarian rule in these two countries and beyond. On Central Asia, see Olivia Allison, "Selective Enforcement and Irresponsibility: Central Asia's Shrinking Space for Independent Media," *Central Asia Survey* 25 no. 1-2 (2006): 93-114.

[47] For a general comparative case study of media development in early 1990s in Central Asia, see Jeff Brown, "Mass Media in Transition in Central Asia," *Gazette* 54 (1995): 249-265.

[48] In countries like Uzbekistan and Turkmenistan the term "controlled media" is more appropriate. In case of Uzbekistan violence against journalists is widespread, see for example, Sarah Kenzior, "A Reporter Without Borders. Interner Politics and State Violence in Uzbekistan, Problems of Post-Communism," 57, no. 1 (2010): 40-50. On self-censorship in Uzbekistan, see Richard Shafer and Eric Freedman, "Obstacles to the Professionalization of Mass Media in Post-Soviet Central Asia: A Case Study of Uzbekistan," *Journalism Studies* 4, no. 1 (2003): 91-103.

monopoly Gazprom[49], using a mixture of business manoeuvres and administrative muscle, took over previously critical media outlets. State-owned oil company Rosneft swallowed assets owned by the oligarch Mikhail Khodorokovsky, who had been funding political opposition and civil society groups."

5) *Legal constraints* — governments around the world use this strategy to regulate the media. Drafting and approving laws and regulations controlling media's activities is the safest way to influencing media messages. As has been discussed in previous chapters, the ruler often uses and abuses state assets, benefiting from his incumbency advantage. Using incumbency advantage is not unique to non-democratic regimes, as it also takes place in democratic countries. However, as it has also been demonstrated in Chapter 2, the extent of the manipulations of the legal framework is significantly higher in electoral authoritarian regimes, particularly in competitive regimes. Within the legal constraints, the following is discussed: criminal cases against journalists, charges against journalists and lawsuits, the legal environment, libel and defamation charges, criminal charges against journalists, etc.

Print media: Defamation[50], libel, and extremism charges are pressed against journalists of print media either by state authorities, politicians, or other groups; it is used as a way of forcing journalists and media outlets into self-censorship, or as a punishment for disobedience and lack of loyalty.

Broadcast media: Any television and radio broadcasting corporation working in Russia must first register as a media organisation with the Russian Press and Information Committee, and then has to obtain a license as a broadcaster, which is issued by the Federal Commission for

---

[49] State owned gas conglomerate

[50] According to the law of defamation, individuals, groups of individuals, companies or firms have the right to sue anyone who publishes anything that damages their reputation via print, broadcast, or online media.

Television and Radio Broadcasting. This practice is commonly used outside of Russia.

Online media: Until recently, online media and especially the blogosphere, was not heavily regulated by the law. However, in recent years, some states have been changing their regulations regarding online media. For example, Russia introduced a law according to which a blog is considered a media outlet if the number of readers per day exceeds 3000, and the blog must accordingly be registered with a mass media regulator and comply with the same rules as the larger media outlets. Recently, internet companies were required to allow Russian authorities access to users' information (BBC August 1, 2014)

3.6. Conclusions

The potential role of the media in shaping the voter's vision and interpretation of political events, as well as its contribution to the outcomes of elections through the effects it has on the audience — whether the media tell people what to think about or how to think about issues — should not be underestimated. Despite the fact that it is difficult to establish a direct causal link between a media message and the audience's behaviour, we see plenty of examples of indirect effects. For example, a recent publication by the director of the Levada-Centre, Lev Gudkov (2015) showed that the Russian public strongly reacts to the media discourse. Any topic broadly discussed in the media seems to catch up with the public in two or three months, triggering corresponding emotions — hate, aggression, patriotism, antagonism toward the nation's enemies — which are easily forgotten once the topic is dropped from the media.

Much has been written on the mechanisms according to which the media functions in democracies, media effects, and its role as a mediator between the political actors and voters. Scholars have proposed and discredited old media effects models, such as the "hypodermic needle model," "two-way flow model," or the "audience autonomy model," and have presented more refined new models that better explain the interaction between a media message and human cognitive processes. Political communication research demonstrated that agenda setting, framing, and priming are some of the most essential tools used to convey messages to the audience and shape public opinion.

It has also been argued that although media is one of the core pillars of democracy, it is not by nature democratic. Hence, it can be easily used to manipulate public opinion in non-democracies. In electoral authoritarian regimes, where the outcome of elections depends not only on vote buying, repression, or tossing the election results, governments are keen to use the media to construct positive views of the favoured candidate. To do so, various tools are used. With regard to the content of media messages, in addition to agenda setting and framing, which is widely used in the media around the world, in electoral authoritarian regimes, content bias is also often employed.

Apart from the ability to influence media decisions regarding agenda setting and framing of the events, the incumbent can force the state-run media to introduce certain content bias in the reporting, force journalists and media organisations into self-censorship. The incumbent also uses other ways of controlling the media: some of the widely used control mechanisms are intimidation of journalists, rewarding or punishing media outlets either by cutting or increasing financial assistance, as well as introducing laws regulating media outlets' activities. The fact that so many different strategies are used by dictators to tame the media shows the importance that governments attribute to it.

The media operates in a complex environment and depends strongly on socio-economic and political conditions. The media content is produced by journalists who have certain schema systems, values, beliefs, and who work under certain constraints imposed on them by the political, social, and economic environment. To better understand the functioning of the media and the factors influencing its content, one should first outline the environment within which the media, political, and business actors have to operate; and the specific characteristics of media that leaves it vulnerable to external pressure. These factors can be roughly divided into structural constraints, including the media's source of finances, ownership, the structure of country's economy, and presence of independent large businesses; coercive practices; and legal constraints. Journalists, opposition parties, ruling elite, and the owners of large businesses are the actors who navigate their ways through a complex environment.

4. Strategies of media manipulation: The case of Russia

4.1. Introduction

This chapter's primary goal is to present a comparative case study illustrating how media-manipulation strategies function in competitive and hegemonic regimes. By tracing the development of the media landscape, this chapter highlights some of the most influential factors contributing to increased media instrumentalisation, lists various manipulation strategies, and demonstrates how media instrumentalisation is executed.

The chapter is divided into several sections. The section following this introduction outlines the research design. It addresses issues related to the main research question, the research design, the selection of cases, the time frame, and the methods and sources used. In the third section, a short overview of current state of the art is given. In the fourth section, I present arguably the full spectrum of media-manipulation strategies based on the case studies. The strategies or mechanisms of influence are divided into three main groups as outlined in Chapter 3, and are discussed in the following order:

1. *Constraints on a macro level:*

a) Incumbent's misuse of state resources to directly or indirectly facilitate the abuse of media freedom; and

b) Legal constraints.

2. *Constraints on a micro-level*

3. *Other ways of ensuring compliance:*

a) Organisational level; and

b) Individual level.

Some additional manipulation strategies are derived from the case study. Furthermore, some of the most significant factors and actors involved in shaping the media landscape are discussed and the dynamics of actors' interaction within particular economic and institutional constraints are presented. The fifth section presents the results of interviews with journalists and their perspectives on how the system functions. In the section that follows, trust in media is assessed. The last section maps the incumbent government's media-manipulation strategies, their effects on the media professionals (i.e., journalists, editors) and their calculations. It also highlights the differences in competitive and hegemonic regimes' batteries of manipulations.

4.2. Research design

As has already been outlined in the Introduction, my principal research question is divided into two parts and in this chapter the first part is addressed: What are the media-manipulation strategies employed by the ruling elite in competitive authoritarian regimes? The question consists of three principal components: 1) types and extent of media-manipulation strategies; 2) mechanisms of influence; and 3) the media's reaction to that influence.

To explore the mechanisms of the media manipulations employed by the ruling elite in electoral authoritarian regimes and the effects of those manipulations on news content, I use a longitudinal comparative in-depth case study design. A case-study approach assists in the acquisition of valuable insight into the inner workings of the regime and the mechanisms that it uses to influence information flow in a given country. As Denscombe (2007: 36) notes, this research design "[...] offers the opportunity to explain why certain outcomes might happen — more than just find out what those outcomes are." That is exactly the aim of this chapter: to explain variations in coverage of presidential candidates during their election campaigns. The variation in coverage between two different elections and regimes is analysed in the fifth chapter. I take a single country and study it during two different periods, the first of which presents a typical case of a competitive authoritarian regime and the second of which features hegemonic authoritarianism. Furthermore, I study various actors and the dynamics of their interactions in a changing political and economic environment.

I look at both the causes and effects of media-manipulation strategies. The dependent variable consists of news content and the independent variable consists of media-manipulation strategies that affect the content of media coverage. To explore the causes of media-manipulation strategies, I compare those strategies and the extent to which they are used by the ruling elite at two different points in time. On the effects side, which is discussed in the next chapter, I look at news content.

Case selection

The selection of a case is grounded on the fact that it is typical, i.e., similar in many respects to other cases; to an extent, the results of this study can be applicable elsewhere. Certainly, one should be careful when attempting generalisations based on research into a single case. Although each case might have some unique features, a typical case would share many characteristics and serve as an example for a broader sample. The extent of one case's generalisability depends on its similarity to other cases in the sample (Denscomb 2007).

For this research, I choose a typical case of a competitive authoritarian regime that later slides into hegemonic authoritarianism. Choosing one country at two different points in time and two different political regimes helps control for variables such as culture, religion, historical background, geographical location, etc., while helping identify the differences between the inner workings of competitive versus hegemonic regimes. The case is chosen from a broader universe of countries with competitive authoritarian regimes. The concept of competitive authoritarianism has been thoroughly detailed in Chapter 1: instances of competitive authoritarian regimes are neither rare nor in any way unique to any particular region. Levitsky and Way have classified nineteen countries from various regions as being competitive authoritarian between 1995 and 2008. Of those I select Russia for the case study, as it satisfies the principal conditions for my case selection. According to the academic literature (Goode 2010; Levitsky and Way 2010; Hale 2010; etc.[51]), it is a typical and at the same time a prominent case of competitive authoritarian regime transforming from competitive to hegemonic authoritarian regime. In addition, reliable data such as opinion polls, electronically accessible and fully transcribed news reports of various media outlets operating in the country are available.

Table 4.1. presents Russia's election years between 1995 and 2012. This time frame has been selected for several reasons. The first reason is data availability: electronic versions of most of Russia's newspapers and TV programs have only recently become available. The second reason is institutional stability. Since the collapse of the Soviet Union, the post-Soviet states have adapted new regime institutions, i.e., a set of rules and procedures governing political participation (Gasiorowski, 1996: 470). The logic underlying this reasoning is that it takes time for newly established

---

[51] J. Paul Goode. 2010. "Redefining Russia: Hybrid Regimes, Fieldwork, and Russian Politics," *Perspectives on Politics* 8 (4): 1055-1075; M. Steven Fish. 2005. *Democracy Derailed in Russia: The Failure of Open Politics*. Cambridge: Cambridge University Press; Gordon Hahn. 2004. "Managed Democracy? Building Stealth Authoritarianism in St. Petersburg." *Demokratizatsiya* 12 (2): 195-231; Lilia Shevtsova. 2009. "The Return of Personalized Power," *Journal of Democracy* 20 (2): 61-5; Cameron Ross. 2005. "Federalism and Electoral Authoritarianism under Putin." Demokratizatsiya: The Journal of Post-Soviet Democratization 13 (3): 347-72; Grigorii Golosov. 2010. "Contemporary Regional Politics in Russia: A Chronicle of Degradation," *Russian Analytical Digest* 77, Institutions in Russia: 10-13, April 26; Nikolai Petrov, Masha Lipman and Henry E. Hale. 2010. "Overmanaged Democracy in Russia: Governance Implications of Hybrid Regimes." Carnegie Papers Russia and Eurasia Program No. 106, February; Henry E. Hale. 2010. "Eurasian Polities as Hybrid Regimes: The Case of Putin's Russia," *Journal of Eurasian Studies* 1: 33-41; Robert W. Orttung. 2010. "Understanding Recent Developments in Russia's Political System," *Russian Analytical Digest* 77, Institutions in Russia, 6-9, April 26.

institutions to become attuned to the existing system, to function in a more systematic way, and to follow a particular logic.

Table 4.1. List of parliamentary and presidential elections in Russia, 1995-2012

1996	1999	2000	2003	2004	2007	2008	2011	2012
Pres.		Pres.		Pres.		Pres.		Pres.
	Parl.		Parl.		Parl.		Parl.	

To select the units of analysis, a "purposeful sampling" approach is used. Purposive sampling is a form of sampling in which the selection of cases is based on the researcher's judgment as to which subjects best fit the study criteria. It gives an opportunity to select "information-rich" cases and investigate the insights of the phenomenon (Patton, 2001: 230). I select the most informative cases, i.e., Russia's 2000 and 2008 presidential elections, which served as a point of change in regime dynamics. Russia's political system is presidential; and as the presidential elections play a crucial role in regime dynamics they are selected for this study.

Freedom House's annual survey of global press freedom, Freedom of the Press, helps draw a rough sketch of the media landscape in the post-Soviet region. According to Freedom House's survey, none of the post-Soviet states except for the Baltic States are classified as free. Most of the countries in the region are ranked as "Not Free." Figure 4.1 shows press-freedom scores for Russia and average scores for the region in general from 1994 to 2011. The graph shows a downward slope in many post-Soviet countries since 1994. Although Russia was ranked as "Partly Free" in the mid-1990s, its scores began to dwindle in the early 2000s. By 2008, Russia's scores were on par with the regional average. By 2011, Russia scored twice as poorly as it did in 1994.

Figure 4.1. Freedom of the Press, 1994-2011

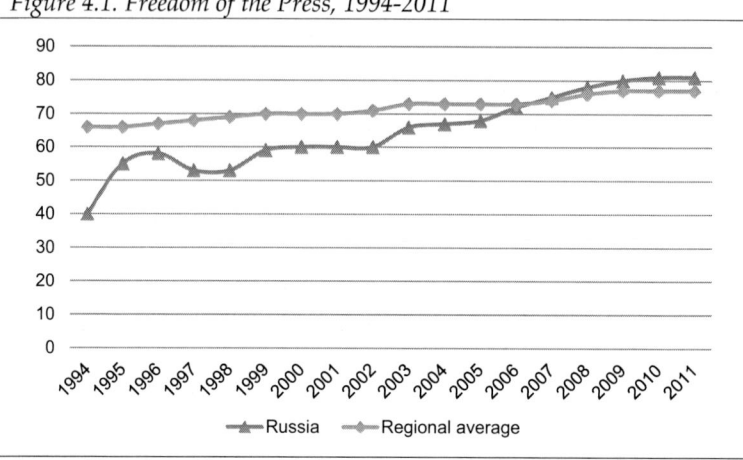

Source: Freedom House, 2012

Another index that assesses press freedom worldwide has been created by Reporters Without Borders. Their index reflects the level of freedom enjoyed by news organisations and journalists. Figure 4.2 shows that the media's working conditions in Russia have steadily worsened and that although Russia's scores were slightly better than average, starting in the early 2000s freedom of the press has been declining. Although press-freedom indices compiled by organisations such as Freedom House and Reporters Without Borders might vary slightly, the general pattern is consistent: i.e., the media enjoyed relative freedom in Russia in the 1990s, and that freedom began to deteriorate starting in 2000. As the state began to regain power, the media landscape began to change. Under President Vladimir Putin, Russia took an authoritarian turn. The country's flawed or electoral democracy of the early 1990s gradually transformed into an authoritarian regime; more specifically, the regime changed from competitive to hegemonic.

Figure 4.2. World Press Freedom, 2002-2011

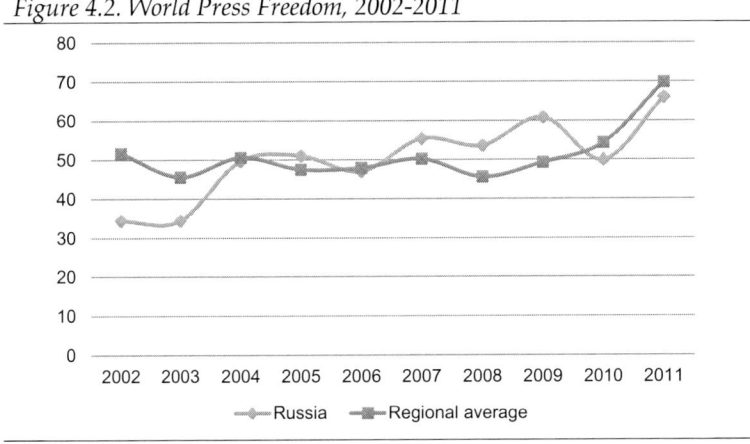

Source: Reporters Without Borders, 2012

For this research, the evolution of Russia's media was divided into two periods. The first period is the period of relatively free media under the competitive authoritarian regime, which began with the collapse of the Soviet Union and experienced considerable changes. The second period is the period between 2000 and 2008, which was marked by the regime's backslide into authoritarianism, declining press freedom, and a higher degree of media instrumentalisation. Tracing the changes in the media environment helps outline some of the main factors contributing to this phenomenon, most notably, expansion of the extent of the government's manipulation of the media. The comparison between 1991-2000 and 2000-2008 helps shed light on the mechanisms and strategies used in competitive authoritarian regimes and how they differ from those in a less competitive environment.

A content analysis of Russia's news media is presented in the next chapter. That analysis illustrates the link between differences in media content and increased pressure exerted on the media. The 2000 presidential election is used to illustrate media content in competitive authoritarian regimes, whereas the 2008 presidential election serves to illustrate media content in a more tightly controlled environment. Multiple sources and multiple methods are used in this work. Interviews, opinion polls, statistical data, secondary literature, and country reports are consulted. The following two sections provide brief information about the methods and sources used in the study of media manipulation. The description of the content analysis of media reporting will given in the next chapter.

Methods

Document analysis: The information on which the case studies are based is collected from various sources using both qualitative and quantitative data. I look at media statistics to assess the level of the country's press freedom and the significance of its record of violating that freedom. To evaluate press freedom, I employ various reports and data provided by Freedom House, Reporters Without Borders, and Internet access is obtained from OSCE (Organization for Security and Co-operation in Europe) reports, secondary sources, and the websites of television channels and newspapers. I also look at legislation concerning the media to give a full spectrum of governmental strategies to curb press freedom. According to Freedom House reports, laws that hinder press freedom have been passed throughout the post-Soviet region. I use country reports from Freedom House, OSCE, official government sources and newspaper reports to describe the legal framework in which the media must operate. The media's ownership structure is also examined to determine whether media outlets are independent, owned by the state or owned by cronies. Based on the reports of the Glasnost Defence Foundation, Freedom of the Press, and the Media Sustainability Index, I document various strategies used to manipulate the media. Likewise, secondary sources—i.e., the rich research literature on Russia's media—are consulted. Most of the quantitative data and interview findings are cross-checked using other sources.

Opinion polls: Additionally, to obtain at least a rough understanding of the weight given to the media in constructing or shaping public views, public opinion polls are considered. Trust in media helps determine whether people believe information presented in the media. For this purpose, I use opinion polls gathered by the Levada Analytical Centre, independent and professional research institution.

Interviews: To enrich the case study, I conducted eleven interviews with journalists, reporters, and editors working in some of the most popular newspapers and online media, whose target audiences are intellectuals, academics, entrepreneurs, and politically active members of society. The interviewees were journalists and editors working at "Kommersant," "Vedomosti," "Novaia Gazeta," "Nezavisimaia Gazeta," "gazeta.ru," "lenta.ru," "Russia Today," "NTV," and "Radio Mayak." Interestingly, most of those professionals have changed employment at least once, thus demonstrating the fluidity of the media market. Each interview lasted approximately one hour. Most of the interviewees chose to maintain their anonymity. The interviews were partially transcribed; all of the interviews were recorded and saved in data files. Two approaches were used for sampling: purposeful sampling and snowball sampling. Respondents were chosen from the pool of journalists working in particular media outlets studied in more detail in this work. During the interviews, they were also asked to recommend colleagues who would be relevant to the research.

The primary purpose of these interviews was to establish a link between the formal and informal pressure (i.e., media-manipulation strategies) exerted by the ruling elite on the media (i.e., media organisations and journalists) and the effect of that pressure both on the media and on news content. The interviews were semi-structured and the questions were designed not only to determine which factors shape and frame the agenda but also to shed some light on questions of self-censorship. Open-ended semi-structured interviews were chosen because they provide a sufficient structure while maintaining a "natural" method of communication (Patton 2010: 342f). Other sources include interviews from 2015 published on "colta.ru," interviews conducted in the early 2010s by Schimpfossl and Yablokov (2014), and a study by Koltsova (2006).

The discussion and presentation of responses is approached in two ways. Some of the information provided by journalists is presented in the section detailing constraints on the macro and micro levels, i.e., section 4.4, Mechanisms of influence. This information primarily involves cases in which a respondent provides an example of constraints experienced by a media organisation. Questions of self-censorship, agenda setting, framing, and overall freedom as perceived by the interviewed are presented and discussed in section 4.5, Journalists' reporting practices.

Sources

OSCE country reports: The ODIRH (Office for Democratic Institutions and Human Rights) provides a detailed assessment of election quality in all of the countries of the OSCE. Respect for fundamental freedoms — i.e., equality, universality, political pluralism, confidence, transparency, and accountability — is taken as a benchmark for assessing the elections.

IREX Media Sustainability Index (MSI): The MSI provides in-depth analyses of the conditions affecting independent media in 80 countries. Since 2000, it has assessed changes in media systems across countries and over time.

Freedom House (FH): Freedom House provides both qualitative and quantitative assessment of freedom of the press for each country. Each year, it produces a detailed analysis of press freedom worldwide. Their quantitative data are used to rate overall press freedom. Countries score from 0 (best) to 100 (worst). The total score determines a country's status as Free, Partly Free, or Not Free. Assessment is based on 23 methodological questions and 132 subquestions divided into three subcategories: the legal environment, the political environment, and the economic environment. A country's final score represents the total of the scores assigned for each question. A score from 0 to 30 receives a status of Free; a score from 31 to 60 receives a status of Partly Free; and a score from 61 to 100 receives a status of Not Free. FH's qualitative assessment of press freedom includes detailed reports on media freedom across countries and over time.

According to FH, more than 60 analysts (including both the principal research team and outside consultants) are involved in the rating process. Their ratings and reports involve some subjectivity; because they are compiled based on questionnaires completed by country experts, they might be biased. To decrease the risk of presenting misleading information, I combine FH's press-freedom data with the data provided by Reporters Without Borders.

Both data sets are used for illustration purposes only, to show changes in press freedom both in Russia and in the post-Soviet space in general. Moreover, although just like any other data source, FH and Reporters Without Borders' reports should be used with caution. With respect to press freedom in Russia and in the region, the trends reported do not show substantial differences. Both reports paint a similar picture and similar changes in freedom levels.

Reporters Without Borders (RWB): Another quantitative assessment of press freedom is provided by RWB. That organisation's report is based on a questionnaire sent to freedom-of-expression-related NGOs in various parts of the world and to 150 correspondents, journalists, researchers, jurists and human-rights activists. RWB's quantitative data include the number of various types of violations, the number of journalists killed and jailed because of their professional activities, the number of media professionals abducted, exiled, and attacked, and the number of incidents of media censorship. These data are collected and counted by RWB employees. Information about the degree of self-censorship, government interference in editorial content, the transparency of government decision-making, the effectiveness of legislation, the concentration of media ownership, favouritism in allocating state subsidies, and discrimination related to access to journalistic training is gathered from questionnaires sent to both media professionals and outside partners. RWB notes that its data set should be used to assess press freedom of press, not media quality.

Glasnost Defence Foundation (GDF): Founded in 1991, GDF's main priorities include monitoring violations of journalists and media in the Russian Federation, providing legal assistance and advice to journalists and representatives of media organisations in disputes related to their professional activities, generating analytical digest of Internet news feeds, and so on. The group produces detailed reports on all types of press-freedom violations involving media organisations and media professionals, including the number of those violations. Although GDF's numbers might not be absolute, given that it is logistically difficult to account for every violation in an area as large as Russia, its data are useful for two purposes. First, they provide examples of various types of violations that are primarily referred to in this work as "manipulation strategies." Second, their quantification of violations help better illustrate the difference between the situations in 2000 and 2008; because the data are gathered from the same or similar sources and regions, they are comparable, although some data might be missing for 2000.

TNS Russia: TNS provides information about media audience measurements, media intelligence and custom market research. Data on television audiences are gathered using peoplemeters, which are devices connected to TV sets in participating households. Using a remote control, the participants register when they start and finish watching TV. In this way, the device automatically records channels watched, the time at which they are watched, and the length of time that they are watched.

To collect data on newspapers' readership, telephone interviews are used. More than 500 professional interviewers ask the participants questions about what newspapers they read within the previous six months. The method of collecting data about the reading audience is the same for all Russian cities.

Information about the Web index is compiled by identifying the participants using a counter installed on monitored sites. Data about the sites on which such counters are not installed are gathered with the help of special software installed on the participants' computers.

Data provided by TNS are also cross-checked with information from secondary sources. Scholars and media experts studying Russian media provide similar information. TNS findings on the popularity of particular media outlets are not inconsistent with the data gathered by Stephan White and Ian McAllister (2006), Colton and McFaul (2003), and IREX (MSI data compilation).

Levada Analytical Centre (LAC): This is a non-governmental research organisation based in Russia. It has an extended network of 67 regional offices across the county and numerous partnerships with public opinion research centres in other post-Soviet states, including the Baltic States. Among other research projects, LAC has gathered data on "Media: behaviour and attitudes towards different Media in Russia, 2008-2010" and "President's approval ratings," the results of which are presented in this work with the goal of revealing the Russian public's trust in the media. LAC's research remains relatively independent of the state. However, it should be noted that when interpreting the results of opinion polls, one must consider that respondents' answers depend on how the question is worded. To minimise this risk, LAC asks the same question using different wording. When presenting opinion-poll data, answers to multiple questions pointing in similar directions are provided.

4.3. Literature review

Much has been written about the media landscape in Russia and its role in Russian politics. The literature on Russia's media can be roughly divided into six general categories: 1) the effects of the Russian media on election results (Colton and McFaul 2003; White, Oates and McAllister 2005; Oates 2006; Enikolopov, Petrova and Zhuravskaya 2011); 2) the Russian media and the dynamics of its evolution (Koltsova 2001; Koltsova 2006; Zasurskii 2004; Roudakova 2009); 3) the type of media system in Russia (Becker 2004; Vartanova 2011); 4) Russian journalists and journalistic professionalism (Voltmer 2000; Pasti 2005); 5) television viewers in Russia

(Mickiewicz 2005); and a theme closely related to the topic of this work, 6) instrumentalisation of the Russian media by the political elite (Lazitski 2013; Orttung and Walkier 2014; Silitski 2009), tightening control over Russian television since Putin's rise to power, and television content intended to support the regime (Lipman 2009; Lipman 2014; Gehlbach 2010; Burrett 2014; on television content, Laruelle 2014; Rollberg 2014).

1) The media's effects on voters: The first stream of literature aims at measuring the effects of media on voters' behaviour using the example of the Russian media. For instance, Enikolopov, Petrova and Zhuravskaya (2011) compare the 1999 parliamentary election outcomes among different regions and show that watching independent TV channels both decreases the aggregate vote for the government party and increases the vote for opposition parties. Their research indicates that voters who watch independent TV are more likely to vote for the opposition. A similar study has been conducted by White, Oates and McAllister (2005). Their analysis of the media's effects on the 1999 parliamentary and 2000 presidential elections based on a national survey show that ORT (a state television channel that favoured the Kremlin) had an impact on election outcomes. According to their findings, although everybody watched television, its effects were more prominent on those who supported the Kremlin-backed party because they considered state television both objective and trustworthy (206). Although there are various measurements of the media's effect on audience attitudes, every approach has flaws. One way to measure that effect is through public opinion polls. However, while interpreting the results of such polls, one must bear in mind that the manner in which a question is formulated has an effect on the answers. Therefore, the question must be very carefully formulated to avoid distortions, misunderstandings, etc. Furthermore, the respondents are not always completely honest. The second way to measure the effects of the media is through experimental research carried out in laboratories. The problem with this method is that under experimental conditions, the effect of context is undermined. In other words, even if the experiment shows that the effect of the media is significant, when put in their political context, those effects might be different (McNair 2003). The third way to measure the effects of the media is to observe voting behaviour. In this case, one would measure public opinion before the elections and then count the actual votes after the elections. However, attributing changed opinions (when those changes occur during a campaign) to the media is just one way to interpret the facts: there could be many other explanations (McNair 2003).

2) *Russian media and the dynamics of its evolution:* Scholars have also addressed questions about the Russian media and the dynamics of its evolution. Much has been written on Soviet and post-Soviet journalism in Russia (Voltmer 2000; Koltsova 2001; De Smaele 2007), the information climate during the Glasnost period (McNair 1991), changes in the media environment and media ownership (Mickiewicz 1997; Koltsova 2006; Arutunyan 2009; Beumers, Hutchings and Rulyava 2009; Lipman 2014). Other works have focused on the history of the transformation of media and politics in Russia (Roudakova 2009). Moreover, there has been extensive coverage of topics related to the Russian media and society (Mickiewicz 2006; 2008; White 2008) along with interactions between politics and the media (Lipman and McFaul 2003; Belin 2004; Fossato 2006).

3) *Attempts to categorise the Russian media using media systems typology* have also been made. For instance, Becker (2004) uses typology by Siebert, Peterson and Schramm (1956), whereas Vartanova (2011) refers to typology proposed by Hallin and Mancini (2004). These studies provide insightful case study of Russian media system from different perspectives during different periods. Nevertheless, all of these studies are single case studies that neither consider regime type nor include a comparative dimension. Another article by Koltsova (2001) studies power relations in Russian politics and its effect on mass media production.

Anyone even remotely acquainted with Russia's media landscape would agree that the Russian media is not completely controlled by the state: despite the state's tight control over broadcast media, some islands of relatively independent reporting exist. Dunn (2014) draws parallels between this phenomena in Russian media and lottizzazione—an Italian term used to describe a "two-tier system" in which different media outlets enjoy different levels of freedom. First-tier media outlets are mostly controlled, and those in the second tier (some print media outlets and mostly online media) are permitted some degree of freedom. According to Dunn, this system contributed to political stability and predictability while avoiding "the absence of a safety-valve, inefficiencies caused by the lack of access to accurate and up-to-date information and excessive damage to the country's image in the outside world" (1449).

In recent year, much has been written on Russia's changing media; one of the main topics of those writings is the government's increasing control over media and media content. With respect to media content, some study the messages and ideas promoted by the political authorities on television. For example, Rollberg (2014) argues that some popular miniseries in contemporary Russia have a statist agenda and carry certain either implicit or explicit political messages. Conveying these messages to the public helps maintain the current regime. Tina Burrett (2014) studies the Kremlin's influence on television coverage. She examines the coverage of Russian-Japanese relations and the territorial dispute over the Southern Kuril Islands on state-controlled television channels. Like Rollberg (2014), Lauruelle (2014) looks at how political authorities use television to promote certain ideas in the case of Russia's national-identity debates. Tightening control over the media is not only studied by academics but also widely discussed in the media. Some scholarly works (Gehlbach 2010) compare the Soviet and post-Soviet systems and analyse the extent to which the Kremlin established control over the Russian media during Putin's presidency. Likewise, Lipman (2014) examines new state-imposed constraints imposed on nongovernmental media and Internet communications after Putin's 2012 return to office.

4) *Journalists and journalistic professionalism:* Other works have concerned journalists and journalistic professionalism (Voltmer 2000; Pasti 2005). Based on thirty interviews with Russian journalists working at the

end of the 1990s, such works argue that there are two groups of journalists in Russia: "the old generation" (i.e., those who had been journalists since the Soviet era) and "the new generation" (i.e., those whose journalism careers began after 1990). Pasti's main argument is that the old generation views journalists' main task as collaborating with authority, whereas the new generation views journalism as a PR tool that can serve the benefit of business, politicians, and other influential groups. Although that finding is interesting, it could be that "the new generation's" perception is conditioned by the socioeconomic and political circumstances of the 1990s, which have changed in more recent years. Additionally, a journalist's views might vary depending on his or her media outlet. Most of the journalists whom I interviewed said that a journalist's task is to provide the audience with balanced information about current events. Similarly, Katrin Voltmer (2000) studies levels of journalistic professionalism and whether they have changed since the Soviet era. Based on a comparison of news content on "Izvestiya" in 1988 and 1996, she argues that in the Russian journalism community, old and new journalistic norms co-exist.

5) *Television viewers in Russia:* Most of the works on Russian media focus on media laws, regulations, media systems, and the media's effects on election results. Very few, however, concern themselves with the direct study of Russian television viewers. Ellen Mickiewisz's (2008) work attempts to fill this gap by conducting sixteen focus group interviews involving 158 participants in four cities. Her work attempts to analyse people's perception of television and news content. Similarly, Mickiewicz (2005) analyses Russian television viewers' cognitive processes while watching the news.

6) *Instrumentalisation of the media by the state* is the subject of more recent studies by Walker and Orttung (2014). Like Silitski (2009), Walker and Orttung (2014) argue that leaders of modern autocracies use the media to maintain their power. Walker and Orttung look at the media as an instrument for preventing the defection of regime elites. Although Silitski does not focus solely on the media (or as he calls it, "political technology")

he argues that "information and propaganda campaigns" are "aimed at discrediting and destroying opponents before they even enter the political contest (2009: 43)" and are one of the three main tools used by autocrats to extend their terms in power. Lazitski (2013) looks more closely at various strategies employed by the ruling elite to influence viewers. Comparing the American and Russian media, she argues that in both cases "media endearment techniques," such as misinformation, censorship, omission, spinning and twisting, the construction of false reality, intimidation, entertainment, simplification, and lowering/marginalising the quality of content are used. The extent to which the two countries' media landscapes can be compared is arguable. One could claim that despite the dominance of certain frames, media pluralism continues to exist in the United States and the state elite does not exert either direct or indirect control over main TV channels. Nevertheless, the study outlines some interesting techniques used by the elite. Although the literature on the Russian media covers a broad range of themes, a detailed, systematic comparative analysis of media instrumentalisation in Russia across two regime types is missing.

As has been noted above, scholars such as Walker and Orttung (2014), Silitski (2009), and Lazitsky (2013) have opened up the topic of media instrumentalisation. However, their work lacks a systematic approach to studying the strategies used by the ruling elite to influence the media. Nonetheless, the literature on the Russian media is quite insightful, reveals details of the internal functioning of the media system, can be used to build a typology of media manipulations strategies and is generally useful for this case study.

In the following section, I present a case study of the Russian media and the manipulation strategies employed to tame it. By placing relevant actors in their context, I look at how their actions are constrained by structural and institutional factors such as media ownership, the availability of financial resources, the legal framework, etc. The case study reveals some insightful details that have not yet been studied. The principal goal of the following two subsections is to identify and map media-manipulation strategies and to determine whether and how they affect journalists, editors, and other media professionals' calculations in regard to media reporting.

4.4. Mechanisms of influence

The ruling elite's [52] strategies to influence media content and the mechanisms through which that influence is exercised are the core of this

---

[52] *The ruling elite* is the chief executive (the ruler) and the government (his ministers). Composition of Russian political elite has been widely discussed in the literature. The research can be divided into two groups, those studying the elites during the period of Eltsin's presidency, and focusing on questions related to old Soviet nomenklatura, whether the elite composition went through any substantial changes (Hanley et al. 1995; Kryshtanovskaya and White 1996; Lane and Ross 1998; Rigby 1999; Rivera 2000); and the second group of scholars concerned with the elite composition in Putin's era (Bremmer and Charap 2007; Kryshtanovskaya and White 2005; Renz 2006; Treisman 2007; Rivera and Rivera 2006). This work is concerned both with key actors of media industry during Eltsin's presidency and Putin's term. The owners of major media outlets in the country during both time periods and their relations with the governments are explicated. In case of Russia, the ruling elite is the president, ministers, and a close circle of loyal supporters. In this model the ruling elite uses state resources to exercise control over the media. However, it is done in many different ways, which are explicated later in the chapter.

The business elite is composed of the owners of large non-state businesses. However, it is difficult to draw a solid line between business and political elites in Russia. The composition of business elite has changed since Putin came to power, oligarchs* who owned major businesses in Russia during Eltsin's presidency were replaced by silovarchs**. Later in the chapter, owners of major media outlets and the links they have to the ruling elite are presented. In Russia they are mostly referred to as oligarchs. These are a group of people who was able to get a grab of the most lucrative business sectors during the privatisation of 1990s. Some of them also controlled large media companies. Oligarchs had and some still retain the control of some popular broadcast and print media outlets, as well as some widely used online social media. The issues of full and partial ownership and instrumentalization of the media by the oligarchs is discussed further in this chapter.

book. Those strategies are detailed in this section. The subsections are arranged by the type of constraints involved, as discussed in Chapter 3. These constraints are categorised into three main groups:

1. *Constraints on a macro level:*

a) The incumbent's misuse of state resources to directly or indirectly facilitate the abuse of media freedom; and

b) Legal constraints.

2. *Constraints on a micro-level:*

c) Other ways of ensuring compliance

Every subsection gives a chronological overview of events. The concluding part of every subsection provides a table that attempts to summarise strategies used in two different points of time, i.e., 2000 and

---

Oligarchs — Under Boris Eltsin Russian economy can be characterised as the one in which a group of owners of big businesses occupied massive oil and metal enterprises (Treisman, 1999). The wealth was mainly concentrated in the hands of so called oligarchs (see Guriev, 2005). According to Mancur Olson (1971), the oligarchs, as a small group with many common interests and substantial common resources, can heavily influence the politics and in Russia this was the case. In 2000, the oligarchs took control over the Russian Union of Industrialists and Entrepreneurs (RUIE). Since then, they had been actively involved in economic policy, and other strategic issues, partly influencing political decisions via RUIE (Guriev, 2005).

**Silovarchs* — Treisman (2007) coined the term "silovarchs" combining the words "silovik" — a group of people comprised of those who previously worked at security services, and "oligarchy." During Putin's term, according to Treisman oligarchs or "Yeltsin's accidental billionaires" were replaced by silovarchs, fusing secret police network with financial capital (142). Silovarchies are the "states in which veterans of the security services or armed forces dominate both politics and big business [...]. They differ from ordinary oligarchies in that silovarchs can deploy intelligence networks, state prosecutors, and armed force to intimidate or expropriate business rivals (142)."

Opposition includes any kind of opposition parties, be that tame opposition, or real opposition. Opposition's influence on media content is beyond the scope of this work, in addition, during Putin's and Medvedev's presidency opposition's role diminished significantly.

The media — in general, the term used to refer to journalists, reporters, editors, and media organizations as a unit. But when discussing mechanisms of influence, the effects and coping mechanisms of the media are discussed on two different levels: individual level, i.e., journalists, reporters; and on a level of organization, i.e., the media outlet itself directed by editor-in-chief.

2008. However, because the boundaries between these time periods are sometimes murky, the distinction between these two time frames is slightly blurrier than desired.

Misuse of state resources

Media ownership: As discussed in the previous chapter, journalists' decisions about the newsworthiness of events can often be explained by the "incentives, pressures, and constraints" imposed by structural factors such as "ownership and control, dependence on other major funding sources (notably, advertisers), and mutual interests and relationships between the media and those who make the news and have the power to define it and explain what it means" (Herman and Chomsky 1988: X). Likewise, Shoemaker and Reese (1996) argue that ownership plays an influential role in shaping news media because news content can be indirectly controlled by owners through hiring and firing, promotion practices, and consequently, self-censorship. This subsection is devoted to a discussion of media ownership and the media's principal sources of finance. By employing certain hiring and firing practices, some media outlets in Russia attempt to influence news content. Interviews with journalists reveal how this practice functions. The consequences of state (or government-crony) media ownership on media organisations and journalists are presented in subsection "Hiring and firing practices".

The dissolution of the Soviet Union has also marked the abolition of censorship. The Constitution of the Russian Federation [53] not only abandoned censorship but also guarantees freedom of expression. Caught between privatisation and the state's fiscal deficit caused by the collapse of the old system and falling oil prices, the state was deprived of the capacity either to control or to subsidise media outlets. As the state released its grip on the media, it also cut subsidies, leaving media outlets responsible for financing their own activities. A decline in real wages also reflected on a decline in newspaper circulation. Furthermore, because product markets were underdeveloped, advertising revenues were insufficient to finance media outlets. In the absence of any alternative source of funds, media directors (who could neither self-finance nor expect state subsidies) could only survive by finding sponsors who were interested in using the media to advance their political agendas[54].

Nevertheless, in the early 1990s, despite potential challenges such as a limited market for commercial advertisements and an absence of state subsidies, hundreds of new media outlets including local to national newspapers, radio stations, and television channels were launched. In 1993, "NTV," a new television channel founded by Vladimir Gusinsky, received

---

[53] The Constitution of the Russian Federation, Chapter Two: Rights and Freedoms of Man and Citizen, Article 29 states: 1) Everyone shall be guaranteed the freedom of ideas and speech; 2) The propaganda or agitation instigating social, racial, national or religious hatred and strife shall not be allowed. The propaganda of social, racial, national, religious or linguistic supremacy shall be banned; 3) No one may be forced to express his views and convictions or to reject them; 4) Everyone shall have the right to freely look for, receive, transmit, produce and distribute information by any legal way. The list of data comprising state secrets shall be determined by a federal law; 5) The freedom of mass communication shall be guaranteed. Censorship shall be banned.

[54] More on this subject can be found in Brian McNair, "Media in Post-Soviet Russia: An Overview," European Journal of Communication 9 (1994): 115-135; Katrin Voltmer, "Constructing Political Reality in Russia," European Journal of Communication 15, no. 4 (2000): 469-500; see also Olessia Koltsova, News Media and Power in Russia, Routledge: New York, (2006). On changes of Russian media landscape since Glasnost, see Ivan Zasurskii, "Media and Power in Post-Soviet Russia," New York: M.E. Sharpe, Inc., (2004).

a broadcast license. In 1994, "Channel One" (also known as "ORT"), one of two major state television channels, was partly privatised; "Channel Two" (also known as "RTR" and later as "Rossiia") remained under state control. These three channels were and still are the biggest television channels with the largest territorial coverage and largest viewership numbers in Russia.

Throughout the 1990s, most media owners used media as an instrument to advance their interests, either during the period of privatisation — to buy out state owned enterprises at low costs[55] — or (later) to back up politicians who would promote their business and political interests[56] (i.e., the interests of oligarchical media owners). Russian-media expert Olessia Koltsova states that ownership of three major television channels represented three different ownership models present in Russia at that time; those models are set forth below.

1. *Internal ownership.* NTV can be regarded as an example of internal ownership because NTV owner and media tycoon Vladimir Gusinsky (who also owned the Media Most holding company) received direct revenue from the media outlet itself. According to Koltsova's research, which was based on expert interviews, NTV adopted the following strategies to avoid dependence on the Russian government: 1) attracting external finance by selling shares on the New York Stock Exchange; 2) launching a satellite to avoid the need to depend on the state's signal; and 3) attracting Western

---

[55] Centrally planned economy did not allow emergence of business elite, thus when the Soviet Union collapsed and the rapid economic reforms, the core of which was privatisation of state enterprises were launched, there was no business class capable of buying out national property. Therefore, allocation of state property had to be based on other that highest bidder principle, but often times it was quite arbitrary. Some shrewd entrepreneurs or opportunists found media to be an excellent channel of influence this decision making process either through publicly bashing competitors or by threatening to expose "kompromat" material.

[56] Many oligarchs opted to backing up Eltsin's candidacy for the presidential office when his approval ratings fell and the threat of the communists winning the elections, which could lead to re-nationalisation of the state enterprises at the expense of newly born oligarch's class became real.

support by presenting itself as an independent media outlet fighting for freedom of press.

NTV was only one subsidiary of Gusinsky's Media-Most holding company. Other subsidiaries included "Segodnia," a daily newspaper, and "Itogi," a weekly magazine. Gusinsky also owned a stake in "Ekho Moskvy," a popular radio station. In addition to the media outlets listed above, Gusinsnky's Media-Most company had either full or partial ownership of several television channels ("NTV Plus," "TNT," and "RTVi") and journals ("Sem' dnej," "Karavan istorii," "Delovaia hronika," "Yezhenedelniy zhurnal," "Taburet," and "Put' i Vodidetel"). The national broadcast channel NTV, the newspaper Segodnia, and the radio station Ekho Moslky were considered to provide relatively balanced coverage. Many media experts and scholars referred to NTV as an independent, private channel offering relatively balanced news coverage (Lipman and McFaul; Koltsova 2006; Oates and Roselle 2000); its coverage of the Kursk submarine disaster[57], the war in Chechnia, and the Beslan school hostage crisis[58] showed indicia of "serious and independent reporting" (Oates and Roselle 2000: 32).

2. *Mixed state-private*. Channel One (previously ORT) is a television channel that was half privatised and half state-owned, thus providing an example of mixed state-private ownership. According to various sources, Boris Berezovsky — an entrepreneur and oligarch who, together with Roman Abramovich, controlled the richest oil company at the time, "Sibneft" — also owned up to 49% of the channel's shares, with the rest belonging to the state. Interestingly, Koltsova's interviews show close links between Boris Yeltsin (Russia's president from 1991-1999) and Berezovsky. Because the state could not subsidise two state channels (Rossiia and

---

[57] Kursk submarine disaster — on August 12, 2000, 118 people died when the Kursk submarine sand during a naval exercise in the Baltic Sea.

[58] The Beslan school hostage crisis — took place on September 2004, when terrorists took hostage more than 1200 children at school in Russian town of Beslan.

Channel One), it allowed Berezovsky to fund Channel One in exchange for his loyalty to the government. According to studies by the European Institute for the Media (1996) and other experts (Oates and Roselle 2000; Mickiewicz 1997), Channel One promoted Yeltsin's candidacy during the 1996 presidential election campaign (EIM 1996; Zasurskii 2004; Koltsova 2006; Dunn 2014); during the 1995 parliamentary elections, it gave preferential coverage to pro-government parties.

3. *External state ownership.* Rossiia (previously known as RTR) is fully owned and subsidised by the state, thus providing examples of external state ownership.

Following Russia's severe economic crisis of 1998, significant changes occurred. The collapse of the Southeast Asian commodity market led to devalued commodity prices. Although the economy had already begun to recover in May 1999, Yeltsin's popularity reached its lowest level (6%) that year (Treisman 2011). In August, Yeltsin appointed Putin as his Prime Minister. During Putin's term, Russia experienced a dramatic economic recovery. Introduction of new economic reforms such a flat tax and most importantly, increased international oil prices led not only to economic recovery but also to rapid GDP growth.

Oil prices doubled from 12.72 USD per barrel in 1998, to 28.5 in 2000, and 111.62 in 2012. As commodity prices increased, both Russian and world economies began to recover. Whereas World Bank data on country GDP shows negative growth of -5.3% in 1998, growth had rebounded to 10% by 2000. Inflation was reduced from 72.4% in 1999 to 37.7% by the end of 2000 (World Bank inflation data).

In addition to introducing economic reforms, Putin launched a fight against the oligarchs in an effort to establish control over them. During Putin's first term, Gazprom's leadership team was changed, oligarchs and media tycoons such as Boris Berezovsky and Vladimir Gusinsky were forced into exile under corruption charges, "Yukos" oil company head Mikhail Khodorkovsky was arrested, and central control over regional governors was tightened. Putin promised to fight corruption and crime and to restore "order." In 1999, when Putin had just come to power, his approval ratings were approximately 31%; within a year his popularity increased, allowing him to win 2000 presidential elections with 53.4% of the vote (see Figure 4.3).

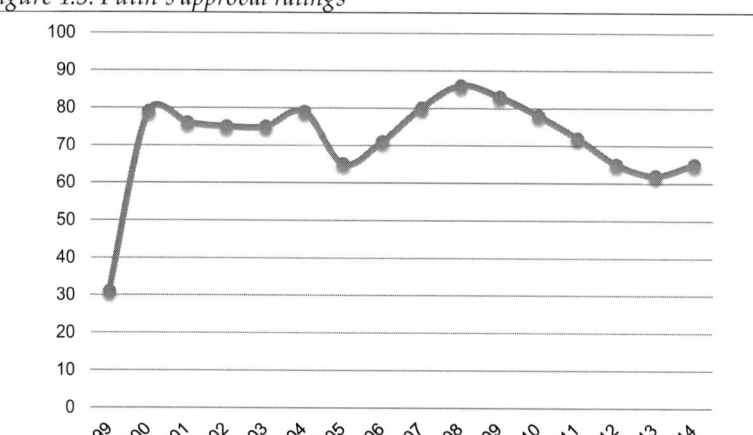

Figure 4.3. Putin's approval ratings

Source: Levada Center, 2014

After winning the 2000 presidential election, Putin not only established control over the oligarchs but also set out to crack down on the media. Nationwide TV channels were his first and primary target. Boris Berezovsky was forced to sell his shares of Channel One to Roman Abromovich, who claimed his loyalty to Vladimir Putin, while Vladimir Gusinsky's media company Media-Most was bought by the Gazprom-Media. However, while exercising full control over television, the Kremlin allowed some diversity of information in the print media and on the Internet. Most print-media outlets were still privately owned. Nevertheless, the most popular of those media outlets supported the Kremlin's policies; several influential dailies had been purchased by companies that had close connections to the government (BBC: Russia country profile, 2012). For example, the weekly newspaper "Kommersant," founded in 1989 by a group of journalists, was bought in 1996 by Alisher Usmanov, a co-owner of a large steel company, "Metalloinvest"; that company had connections to Gazprom. Indeed, Usmanov was a founder of "Gazprom-Invest," a company that managed Gazprom's investment projects. As of 2008, most Russian TV stations were either directly state-run or owned by companies that had close connections to the government. The state controlled the three most popular TV channels with the highest coverage rates. That same year, Gazprom acquired the radio station Ekho Moskvy, shut down the newspaper Segodnia, and fired the staff of the weekly journal Itogi. Journalists who had previously worked at NTV moved to independent television channel TV-6, which was later shut down. Gazprom has also acquired the majority of shares in the newspaper Izvestia.

To sum up, ownership is one of the levers that the ruling elite can use to influence the media. There are several types of ownership through which the ruling elite can shape media-reporting practices: *1) direct ownership* of media outlets, for example, Rossiia; *2) partial ownership,* for example, Channel One; *3) ownership via state companies,* for example, "Gazprom-Media"; and *4) crony ownership* or ownership of media organisations by those close to the ruling elite. The ways in which ownership can shape reporting is presented in subsection 4.6.4. Reporting; how reporting changed over time and the result of my news-content analysis are discussed in Chapter 5.

As seen in the summary in Table 4.2, in 2000, two of three most-viewed federal channels (Channel One, Russiya, and NTV) were either owned or sponsored by business groups that were not dominated by the state or the ruling elite. This changed by 2008, when the majority of popular media outlets (both print and broadcast) were under state's influence via either direct or indirect ownership. Since 2008, the popularity of online media has increased. In 2008, the most viewed online sources were "gazeta.ru" and "lenta.ru." gazeta.ru belonged to Alexander Mamut, its ownership structure has not changed since; however, lenta.ru was recently acquired by Mamut and Vladimir Potanin's company "Rambler-Afisha."

Table 4.2. Owners and financiers of large media organizations, 2000 and 2008

Owner	Key industry and company	Shares in media various outlets	
2000			
Boris Beryuzovskii	Sibneft	Berezovskiy was a partial owner and financier of ORT/Channel One	
Vladimir Gusinskii		Media-Most: *Print media:* Segodnia, Itogi, Sem' dnej, Karavan istorij, Delovaya hronika, Yezhenedelnij zhurnal, Taburet, and Put' i Vodidetel.	*Radio station:* Ekho Moskvy *TV Channels (either full or partial ownership):* NTV (both national and international broadcasting), NTV Plus, TNT, and RTVi
State	VGTRK	RTR/ Rossiia Kultura	
2008			
Alisher Usmanov	Metalloinvest— steel industry, Megafon Gazprom-Invest	*Print media:* Kommersant *Social media (shareholder):* LifeJournal—Kommersant owns shares of Sup, owner of popular blog service in Russia LiveJournal Odnoklassniki mail.ru Group VKontakte	*Online media:* gazeta.ru—Kommersant has shares of Sup, which in turn has bought gazeta.ru
Alexander Mamut and Vladimir Potanin	Rambler-Afisha Interros group— metallurgy, mining, leisure, construction and real estate pharmaceuticals industry, and media	In 2012 Usmanov sold his interests in Sup Media to Alexander Mamut *Television:* - REN TV *Social media:* - LifeJournal	*Online media:* - Gazeta.ru - Lenta.ru - Rambler-finance - Rambler-search - and other less relevant to this study media services

Alexey Miller - Chairman of the board of directors	Gazprom — 38.37% of company's shares are owned by the Russian Federation, 12% belongs to Rosneftigaz and Rosgazifikatsiya, the rest 49.84% are owned either by other legal entities and individuals or traded on international stock markets as ADR (American Depositary Receipt)	Gazprom-Media — was founded in January, 1998 and owns a wide range of television, radio, printing press, cinema production, advertizing, movie theatres, and internet assets. *Gazprom-Media Holding includes:* - *TV companies:* NTV; TNT; NTV-PLUS. - *Radio stations:* Echo of Moscow; CITY-FM; Relax-FM; Detskoe radio; Comedy Radio. - Publishing house Seven Days: 7 Days TV-Program; Caravan of Stories' Collection; Caravan of Stories. - *Newspapers:* Tribuna; TV guide Panorama TV. - Film- production company NTV-KINO - Cinema-theater Oktyabr - Internet video hosting Rutube - Gazprom-Media Technology - Gazprom-Media (TV and Radio advertising) - Gazprom-Media Digital (Internet advertising) - Telebasis, Komstek engineering company and Advertising company SMS (real estate management and ownership).	*Gazprom-Media subsidiaries:* - Seven Days Publishing House - Publishing House Tribuna - Radio 'Echo of Moscow' - NTV-Plus - NTV — Kino and Central Partnership Production - Media Press - Comedy Club Production - GPM-Digital - Comedy-TV - Friday! TV-channel - Broadcasting Corporation Prof-Media - NTV Broadcasting Company - TV-channel '2x2' - TNT-Broadcasting Network - Alaskar-Media - Central Partnership - Red Media - RUTUBE - TV-channel TV-3
Partial state-ownership	51% of assets owned by the state, the rest is owned by private shareholders	Channel One	
State		VGTRK *National TV channels:* Rossiia 1, Rossiia K, and Rossiia 2, Russia 24, RTR-Planet, Euronew-TV channel *Radio channels:* Radio Rossii; Mayak (Lighthouse), Kultura (Culture), Vesti FM, and Yunost (Youth), and Rossiia	A state *Internet channel* "Rossiia" combining dozens of online resources *Non-air television channels:* Digital television — consists of nine channels: Russian romance, Russian bestseller, Science 2.0, My planet, Rossiia HD, Sport, Sport 1, Fight club, Sarafan

Changing ownership is not the only way the ruling elite can ensure the media's compliance with its views. Some other strategies to influence media are as follows: the ownership of production and distribution facilities; state subsidies and selective funding; barter deals; blackmail; selective recovery of debts; control over office facilities; cooptation; and control of access to information. To illustrate how each of this strategies work in reality, I give a short overview of each of these strategies and provide some examples.

Production and distribution: According to Freedom House reports from 2005, although a few independent and critical media outlets existed, most of them depended on state distribution services and printing facilities. The state owns the national postal service and many printing houses. Most of the TV and radio signal transmitting networks also belong to the state. Koltsova's (2006: 51) investigation shows that some regional elites used this privilege to prevent certain newspapers from being printed and to limit certain television companies' transmitter access.

State subsidies and selective funding: Every media organisation needs financial resources that it can use to conduct its activities. A media organisation can be financed via subscriptions, advertisement revenues, foreign funding, state subsidies, and/or third-party sponsorship. To attract more customers business firms aim to advertise their products and services on the television channels with the widest coverage and the newspapers with the highest circulation rates and widest readership. Thus, small media outlets receive minimum revenues from subscriptions and advertisement. As a result, they either run the risk of bankruptcy or must find alternative sources of funds.

Although state-subsidised media outlets have an obvious advantage, state actors have leverage over such outlets and can withdraw subsidies as a punishment for overly independent editorial judgment. In regard to state subsidies, state actors might selectively fund the mass media. As Koltsova (2006: 52) argues, "individual decisions concerning subsidisation are often made by officials with executive power, as well as deputies who have their own funds. This opens up wide possibilities for state agents to service their external partners (e.g., media organisations whose backers have brought a particular state agent to power)."

Selling large numbers of newspapers to big companies might also limit newspapers' freedom to choose their tone and topic. For example, during the interviews[59], one of the respondents mentioned that on occasion, large numbers of printed newspapers are bought by big companies. "If 20% of any given newspaper's circulation is bought by, let's say, "Aeroflot" or "RZhD"[60], then to an extent your business becomes dependent on them. However, it is clear that if RZhD buys your newspapers you should not be criticising RZhD. If one day one of them refuses to buy then what can you do? So, in the end you have to decide what is more important to you, your business or something else. And as you know, in Russia, the business is quite state controlled. If you want a guaranteed distribution, and who would not want it…? You have to be careful about what say." To avoid disruptions in demand, newspapers experiencing such conditions must be careful about their content.

In summary, state subsidies allocated to compliant media, along with limited access to printing facilities and distribution services, make independent media outlets not only much less profitable but also dependent on the state.

Barter deals: In addition to the above-mentioned strategies, Koltsova argues that in late 1990, barter deals were made. Examples include providing access to confidential information (not for publication but for the personal use of media professionals). Another example is the granting of certain privileges in the form of social-welfare benefits.

Blackmail: In the mid-1990s, cases of extortion and blackmail against journalists and media organisations were quite frequent (Koltsova 2006). It

---

[59] Reporter from "Nezavisimaia Gazeta"
[60] Russian Railways

is worth noting that blackmail worked both ways. State agents and business owners used extortion against journalists, and journalists used extortion when they were in possession of compromising materials. With time, blackmail has been gradually disappearing, and fewer cases were noticed in the later 2000s (GDF 2008). For example, in January 2008, Alexander Semenov, a journalist at the newspaper "Ulyanovsk today," was accused of extortion and sentenced to one year and ten months of imprisonment. In September, Alexander Zizhigin, a former journalist at the newspaper "Russian North," was sentenced to two years of probation and a fine of 14,000 rubles. Boris Zemtsov, the deputy editor of "Nezavisimaia Gazeta," was charged with violating Article 163 ("Extortion") of the Criminal Code.

Selective recovery of debts: Not only selective funding but also selective debt recovery has been used as a strategy of influence. The early 1990s left many organisations and firms in debt. One example of the selective-recovery strategy is how "Vneshekonombank" handled the matter of credit that it extended to NTV and Channel One. In 1999, after talks with the head of the president's administration, "Vneshekonombank" refused to extend NTV's credit; however, in the case of Channel One, "Vneshekonombank" did not insist on immediate return of the credit, even though the amounts of the two companies' credit were comparable and in the case of the NTV extension, had even been earlier agreed upon (Koltsova 2006: 52).

Control over office facilities: Olessia Koltsova's work on Russia's news media (2006) provides a detailed account of the media's environment and power struggles in the early 2000s. Among other forms of ensuring compliance, Koltsova argues that state actors' direct or indirect control over facilities rented by media outlets provided them with an opportunity to manipulate terms and conditions of their leases. She provides a few examples of the following practices:

- Manipulating the terms and conditions of the lease
- Refusing to extend rent contracts
- Requiring annual rent contracts
- Increasing rent payments

- Offering unsuitable offices

Cooptation: Koltsova (2006: 53) also mentions that state actors use cooptation strategies. For instance, journalists might be involved in different commissions and committees in which they are given positions that can be used to advance their private interests.

Control of access to information: Another way to influence media content is to control access to information. This method has been used throughout the studied period. For example, on August 22, 2000, the media was not allowed to attend the meeting between Vladimir Putin and the relatives of the crew on the board of the "Kursks," a nuclear-powered cruise missile submarine of the Russian Navy that sank in the Barents Sea on August 12, 2000 (GDF 2000). Similarly, in the Pskovsk region and in Yekaterenburg, media representatives were denied access to a meeting between the workers of an agricultural farm and the governor of Pskovsk. In Yekaterinburg, special police forces (OMON) have proposed forbidding journalists to enter hotspots. According to them, "journalists chase" a beautiful picture, "go to Chechnia to get their dose of adrenaline, while the employees of special police forces risk their lives to safeguard these journalists." The police claimed that only well-trained reporters/journalists from the central TV channels should be given access (GDF 2000). Likewise, in February 2008 in Nizhniy Novgorod, television journalists from "Volga" were chased away from a military base at which a fire had broken out. The military interrupted the reporters' work, claiming that they had been ordered to "get rid of journalists and destroy their equipment" (GDF 2008).

Some quantitative data on types of practices used against media professionals and media organisations are described provided by the Glasnost Defence Foundation, see Table 4.3. Interestingly, the number of cases against journalists increased around the 2004 elections, with a particularly large number occurring in 2003, 2004, and 2005. These practices might result from "disciplining" the media to engage in reporting that is acceptable to the ruling elite.

Each of the strategies discussed above has its own specificities. Some, such as production and distribution, state subsidies and selective recovery of debts, require state involvement. Barter deals and blackmail can be used equally by state and non-state agents. However, these two strategies were more widespread in Russia during the early 1990s, when both power centralisation and the level of institutionalisation were lower. Other forms of manipulation—i.e., cooptation, control over access to information, and control over office facilities—can be used not only by state agents but also by the owners of office facilities rented to the media. State agents and property owners not only exercise control over information about their activities but also can choose to allow or deny the media access to that information; cooptation can also be used by various actors willing to pay for compliance on the part of media outlets.

Table 4.3. Strategies of media control and manipulation, 2000-2008

Year	2000	2001	2002	2003	2004	2005	2006	2007	2008
Unfair dismissal of editors or journalists	11	15	6	14	5	11	16	12	8
Denying access to information	215	180	161	109	213	233	240	238	237
Evicting a media organization from the leased office facilities		5	5	7	16	10	7	7	4
Refusal to print (spread) newspapers	31	21	26	65	33	38	50	34	28
Disconnecting from radio broadcasts	28	44	40	24	19	23	18	27	22
Withdrawal (purchase or arrest) of circulation	17	15	8	32	30	28	28	92	27
Closing down newspapers	-	-	11	7	16	23	26	15	31
Launching a newspaper carrying already existing name	-	-	-	-	17	7	8	5	9
Refusing new media outlets registration	-	-	-	-	0	0	0	0	0

Source: Glasnost Defense Foundation

Media ownership is the strategy that can have the most durable, systematic effect. Most importantly, it enables control over the media from the top, unlike in case of cooptation, pursuant to which only a few media professionals can be asked to comply. If the ruling elite wants to establish full control and introduce content bias in a systematic way, throughout a longer time period and across different media sources, it must adopt one of the following strategies. First, it can address the situation involving media moguls as it did in the 1990s, both during the 1996 presidential elections (when Channel One and Rossiia fully supported Yeltsin's candidacy (EIM 1996) and in 2000 (when those same television channels supported Putin (EIM 2000). In this case, however, the media moguls are free to change their minds, and they usually place their own interests above those of the ruling elite. Second, the ruling elite might nationalise the most popular media outlets and exert direct control over them, which is what happened to Channel One. Third, the ruling elite can place their cronies or those dependent on the incumbent elite in charge of the most important media outlets. The first strategy was used during the 2000 presidential election, and the second and third strategies were used in the 2008 elections. As shown in Chapter 5, the content of news has changed significantly in accordance with these strategies.

Legal constraints

In addition to exerting control over the main television channels via direct or indirect[61] ownership, the ruling elite can employ other methods to influence media and its content. One of these methods is to use the legal

---

[61] Here indirect ownership refers to ownership of media outlets by third parties with close links to the ruling elite, or in other words by cronies.

framework[62] in which the media operates. As with any other business, the media is subject to state regulations. A report by Sada Aksartova et al. on "Television in the Russian Federation" provides a detailed analysis of state laws and regulations that directly or indirectly affect the media. The report provides a general overview and analysis of legal aspects; in addition, it outlines problematic issues. Overall, regulations can be separated into three groups: legislation, which incorporates the Law on Mass Media, the Law on Advertising, the Law on Licensing, etc; licensing of electronic media, which provides that any electronic media with an audience of more than 200,000 people must obtain permission to broadcast, which is issued by the Federal Competition Commission; and pricing for signal transmission (Aksartova 1995: 5). According to that report, state authorities can influence the media on a legal basis using several levers: "ownership rights, state subsidies, distribution of transmitters and signal" (1). The state can support loyal media outlets by providing them with some tax exemptions, offering better prices for distribution.

Superfluity of rules: In terms of laws and regulations, in the early 1990s "superfluity of rules" was observed and documented by Koltsova. The chaotic political situation of the early 1990s led to the disordered creation of rules, leading to a situation in which "all the relevant rules taken together turn out to be entirely or almost unobservable" (2006: 54). One example of this phenomenon is the creation of a new regulation by a local sanitary inspectorate. As Koltsova argues, the primary rationale for the regulation could be a new opportunity to collect bribes in situations of non-compliance. This later became a widespread strategy (alongside with the use of tax police and fire-control authorities) to influence media organisations. For instance, "a man with a warrant for sanitary inspection

---

[62] This section provides some examples of how regulations have been used to influence the media, but for more detailed description and analysis of regulatory system in Russia, see Sada Aksartova et al. "Television in Russian Federation." For analysis of earlier periods, see Monroe Price (1995). Low, Force, and the Russia Media, Cardozo Arts and Entertainment Law Journal 13: 795-846.

came with twelve gunmen to close a TV company in Rostov because the temperature in its office was two or three degrees lower than the norm" (55).

Another example of superfluity of rules which took place in the year 2000 is a special deal that the newspapers "Volgogradskaya Pravda," "Moskovsky Komsomolets," Volgograd," "Komsomolskaya Pravda," and "Volgograd" had to make with the federal security service for the Volgograd region. According to GDF, some parts of this "agreement" openly violated the norms of the Law on Mass Media. For instance, editors were forbidden to comment on the FSB[63]'s official reports.

Other examples of how state authorities use the regulatory framework to influence the media include an incident in 2004, when the parliament considered adopting "media law amendments banning any television or video information on terror acts, exception information allowed for publication by law enforcement agencies" (Freedom House, 2005). This proposal has been seen as a limitation on the right to information. Although the parliament initially voted against the changes, after the September 2004 terrorist takeover of a school in Beslan, antiterrorist legislation was passed to permit the suspension of media activities for up to 60 days in the event of a terrorist threat. The Law against Extremist Activities, which prohibits the dissemination of information supporting "extremist activities," has been used by authorities to shut down media outlets (after three warnings have been given). These types of laws have been used to restrict coverage of topics such as the conflict in Chechnia. In 2006, the parliament passed amendments to the Law against Extremist Activities; those amendments were signed into law by the president. According to the amendments, media criticism of public officials can be punished by up to three years in prison.

---

[63] Russia's Federal Security Services

Libel and defamation: On August 11, 2000, in the Rostov region, the prosecutor's office held a briefing in which prosecutors accused journalists from Moscow newspapers "Version" and Novaia Gazeta of defamation. The reason for the accusation was those newspapers' reports on cases of corruption in the prosecutor's office (GDF 2000).

Table 4.4. Legal constraints on micro-level: number of legal charges, 2000-2008

Year	2000	2001	2002	2003	2004	2005	2006	2007	2008
Charges against journalists and media lawsuits	377	447	427	378	373	382	299	220	201
Lawsuits filed against journalists and media claims	-	-	-	-	144	203	131	118	106
Number of lawsuits, which were satisfied	-	-	-	-	94	134	80	58	46
collected as compensation for moral damage	-	-	-	-	22	0	0	30	0
Criminal cases against journalists and the media	28	44	40	34	35	42	48	46	43

Source: Glasnost Defense Foundation

The government also uses libel suits to control the media. For instance, in January 2002, after energy company "LUKoil" brought a lawsuit against "TV-6," judicial authorities ordered the independent television broadcaster to shut down. In June 2003, another independent nationwide television station, "TV Spektrum" (TVS), was replaced by a state-owned sports channel. That same year, the parliament passed legislation allowing government authorities to close print or broadcast media outlets that disseminate "biased" political commentary. Independent reporting is further hindered by criminal defamation charges. In 2005, several journalists were charged with defamation for writing about government officials' sexual orientations and for accusing officials of organising the murder of the former owner of "Radio Vesna."

Table 4.4 provides data gathered by the Glasnost Defence Foundation on press freedom, focusing on legal charges filed against journalists. Interestingly, since 2000, the number of charges dropped significantly. This might be the sign that by 2008, a majority of the most critical voices had been silenced or that the regime switched to more coercive measures (see Table 4.6).

More recently, since 2010, Russia introduced a battery of legal constraints on both traditional and online media. A few of those constraints were mentioned during the interviews with employees of different media outlets. For example, the editor of the "Politics" section at Novaia Gazeta, Kirill Martynov, mentioned the law on foreign financial grants. According to that law, any organisation that receives a foreign subsidy must fully disclose its finances and no foreign grant can exceed 20% of an organisation's funds. As Martynov also notes, when access to foreign finances is limited, media outlets must turn to state subsidies, rendering them dependent on the state.

Furthermore, as is mentioned in the report by Aksartova et al. (2003) "…all laws, especially those with few precedents, mass media laws are open for broad interpretation." Martynov notes that the new Law on Extremism has similar qualities, i.e., it is open to interpretation. For example, criticising bureaucrats might potentially be interpreted as sowing hatred of the social group of bureaucrats. Another example is that because of the wide interpretation of this law, when preparing a report on neo-Nazi organisations the newspaper was not allowed to publish pictures of the groups' participants because they had Nazi symbols tattooed on their bodies.

According to Martynov, the Law on Privacy also causes problems. He claims that when reporting on terrible conditions at orphanages, he was forbidden to report the names of children who had been bitten because underage children's names and faces cannot be reported in the print media without the consent of the guardian. In the case of the orphans, it was the guardians who were the very people treating the children badly. Thus, the names of the children, the names of the guardians, and the name of the orphanage could not be provided because to do so would violate the Law on Privacy. In principle, if one wishes to stretch this law even further, even stories about state officials spending a significant excess of their official incomes cannot be reported because information about private affairs and living expenses is legally protected.

Many respondents have mentioned the increasing role of "RosKomNadzor" (the Federal Service for Supervision in the Sphere of Telecom, Information Technologies and Mass Communications), which was established in 2008. Its primary task is to regulate the compliance of the media (both traditional and online) with the law.

Just as in the case of the battery of manipulation strategies described under the subsection "Incumbent's misuse of state resources to directly or indirectly facilitate the abuse of media freedom," in the case of the legal framework, some manipulation was in place, primarily because of the lower levels of institutionalisation in the 1990s. Strategies such as the selective use of rules or their superfluity became less commonly used. However, the ruling elite identified more institutionalised and centralised ways to constrain the media, including legal amendments banning any television or video information about acts of terrorism, the Law against Extremist Activities, and the establishment of an institution (RosKomNadzor) that checks media content (see Table 4.5).

There are also other ways (both violent and non-violent) to pressure the media into self-censorship, including intimidation, threats, murders, shutting down newspapers, and attacking media offices. These practices can be used on any media organisation, whether broadcast, print, or online. Destruction of print editions by state agents is another method of pressuring the media, sometimes by destroying already-printed editions. For example, according to the GDF, on August 17, 2000, in the Republic of Mari-El, a printed edition of the newspaper "Sovershenno sekretno" was destroyed because of an article titled "Dictatorship of kulak," which described the characteristics of a criminal. Other editors were warned that if any of those reports were reprinted, they would be charged with defamation.

Table 4.5. Legal constraints placed on the media

As of year 2000			As of year 2008		
Television	Newspapers	Online media	Television	Newspapers	Online media
- Selective use of rules - Superfluity of rules - Libel and defamation			- Media law amendments banning any television or video information on terror acts, except information allowed for publication by law enforcement agencies		
			- Law against extremist activities prohibiting the dissemination of information supporting "extremist activities" - Legislation allowing government authorities to close print or broadcast media outlets which spread "biased" political commentary - Establishment of *RosKomNadzor* - Libel and defamation		

Direct pressure on journalists and individual media outlets

A GDF-compiled list of the practices used to pressure media professionals is given in Table 4.6. As seen in that table, there are many ways in which the media are harassed. The most commonly used methods are legal in nature, including the following: 1) filing charges against journalists and lawsuits against media outlets; 2) filing lawsuits against journalists and media outlets; and 3) denying access to information. There were more than one hundred such incidents reported each year. The second most commonly used methods involve directly pressuring journalists by engaging in the following: 1) terminating circulation, either through purchases or arrests; 2) refusing access to printing facilities; 3) attacking journalists; 4) filing criminal cases against journalists and media outlets; 5) closing down newspapers; 6) disconnecting radio broadcasts. There are at least 25 cases each year of each of these types of intimidation. Interestingly, police detention increased from 15 cases during 2000 to 140 during 2007, which was a pre-election year. Closer observation of Table 4.7 reveals that cases of direct pressure on the media have increased, at least with respect to situations such as police detentions, threats against journalists and media outlets, and seizure and damage of photos and other equipment. This increase can be explained by the tightening control over the media and the regime's decision to use measures that are more repressive than subtle, this could also partially explain the decreasing number of legal charges against journalists by 2008 (as was presented in Table 4.4)

Table 4.6. Strategies of media control and manipulation on micro-level, 2000-2008

Year	2000	2001	2002	2003	2004	2005	2006	2007	2008
Number of journalists' murdered	16	17	19	20	14	7	9	8	5
Number of deaths of other media employees	-	-	-	-	0	0	1	0	0
Number of missing journalists	-	-	-	-	4	1	1	0	2
Attacks on journalists	-	-	-	96	58	63	69	78	64
Attacks on media outlet offices	-	-	-	24	13	12	12	12	6
Detention by police (FSB, etc.)	15	23	18	22	37	47	75	140	103
Threats against journalists and the media	14	21	29	24	28	25	43	27	29
Withdrawal of photos, audio and video	-	-	-	-	4	2	4	11	17
Damage photos, audio and video equipment, computers	-	-	-	-	6	5	0	4	11
Interference with Internet publications	-	-	-	-	9	9	8	27	38
Other forms of pressure on journalists	-	-	-	-	226	311	300	315	356

Source: Glasnost Defense Foundation

4.5. Journalists' reporting practices

Although some of the most influential strategies used to control the media can be delineated based on data and materials gathered from secondary sources, it is interviews that help us see journalists' perceptions of the media environment, whether they feel constrained, and which constraints they consider to have the greatest effects on their reporting.

Several topics were covered during the interviews conducted for this study in autumn 2015. The first topic focuses on technical questions involving both everyday routines and respondents' perceptions of journalistic professionalism. This category includes questions about agenda setting, decision-making mechanisms related to publishing reports, and hiring and firing practices. The second topic focuses on questions about press freedom in Russia and how it has changed in recent years. The third topic focuses on risks, limitations, and any other difficulties experienced by either a journalist on the individual level or the media outlet on the organisational level. The fourth topic focuses on media coverage of candidates and elections.

In addition to data gathered for this work, additional secondary sources were used, including three published works based on interviews with journalists working in Russia, mostly on TV stations. The questions posed in those works relate to topics that are very similar to those discussed here; accordingly, they can be used as additional source material.

First, I consider Olessya Koltsova's (2006) "News media and power in Russia." In that book, Koltsova presents interviews with journalists, reporters, columnists, anchors, editors, and administrators working for regional television in Russia; in addition to media professionals, she interviewed a group of actors to whom she refers as "agents of external influence and experts (20)." She conducts approximately 80 interviews. Based on her research, I attempt to draw a picture of journalists' reporting practices in the early 2000s.

Second, I look at an article published by Schimpfossl and Yablokov (2014) that contains 13 interviews with reporters and media personalities working on the main federal channels, Channel One, Rossiia, NTV, and REN TV. Some of the questions are more technical, "related to everyday journalistic practices and procedures: how agendas are set, how decision-making mechanisms operate, and how hiring practices work." This and the following source are used as data in addition to the interviews conducted for this work, aiming to present a fuller picture of journalists' reporting practices in 2008 and beyond.

Third, I use Colta.ru (2015), an online media article based on interviews conducted by three former employees of VGTRK and REN TV, and a producer from "TVC" channel. There are four interviews, three of which are anonymous. These interviews provide a very rough outline of the censorship of Russian Federal Television channels in 2014-15.

Agenda-setting and priming

During the interviews, the journalists were asked about everyday routines to identify the criteria used to choose which events will receive media coverage. Most of the respondents referred to common journalistic practices, choosing topics based on either their core audience's interests or the events' importance. Both the television and print media topics to be covered are first proposed and discussed during daily meetings. Topics are proposed either by editors or by the reporters themselves. Typically, primary importance is given to events that claim human lives, followed by natural disasters, catastrophes, political news, and other issues; alternatively, stories are chosen and prioritised depending on an outlet's focus. Coverage might also vary slightly based on the type of media involved. If the media outlet is television, then the reporter searches for images, if it is print, then less-visual events also can be covered.

This approach might be different in the context of the main federal television channels. Interviewees gathered by Colta.ru (2015) argue that control is more direct and that news reports and political programming are discussed and written down prior to airing. However, none of the interviewees who worked at print media outlets confirmed this to be the case at their workplaces. One interviewee noted that it is mostly in the state-owned media that topics are chosen by authorities instead of by reporters.

Another interesting point was made by one of the editors at "Kommersant," who said that when choosing topics, they cannot ignore audience demand and to an extent—willingly or not—they have to follow the agenda set by television. Taking into account both that the main television channels are state controlled and that topics and theses are determined by state authorities, one can assume the state significantly contributes to priming the audience.

Self-censorship

Multiple sources indicate that compared to print media, television is closely monitored by the state. It has been argued that the content of Russian federal channels is prominently pro-Kremlin. The evidence supporting this argument is also presented in Chapter 5.

Various views have been advanced in an attempt to explain reporters' rationale for producing pro-Kremlin news reports. Self-censorship was one of the most prominent explanations. However, in a recent publication based on thirteen interviews with media personalities on major television channels (Channel One, Rossiia , NTV, and REN TV), Schimpfossl and Yablokov (2014) argue that pro-Kremlin reporting is primarily attributable to "conformism" among journalists, not self-censorship. Those authors' respondents claimed that they do not employ any self-censorship but instead attempt to report on things in a way that is both adequate and appropriate given the current political situation. Olesya Koltsova's interviews with journalists working in various regions showed similar findings.

I conducted interviews with print media journalists working in Moscow. Interestingly, none of the eleven admitted self-censorship, however, five of them said that they think about the possible consequences of their reports before they publish. However, my respondents also claimed that there are cases in which even awareness about possible consequences does not stop them. Most argued that it is possible to print reports on controversial but worthwhile topics. Respondents from the Kommersant and Vedomosti newspapers claimed that as soon as clear facts can be provided, editors accept articles for publication. However, as was also noted in one of the interviews published in Colta.ru (2015), the rules leave room for interpretation. One example given by a respondent from Nezavisimaia Gazeta was as follows: "Of course, if we write something like "Putin is a killer," this might not be approved for publication, but we do not have any evidence or material supporting this type of claim. Other than that, in my department I do not feel constrained in choosing topics." A respondent working at Kommersant made a similar observation: "Assume you have a good material on a controversial topic and evidence that supports it. Editors might ask for additional materials, for example, getting an interview from the head of the state. On the one hand, that seems impossible and like an excuse not to publish, but on the other hand, if you are a good journalist, then nothing should be impossible."

Only two interviewees admitted self-censorship. A reporter from Nezavisimaia Gazeta said that self-censorship actually operates on both an individual level and on an editorial level. On the one hand, a journalist attempts to be careful about what he says, whereas on the other hand, an editor must consider both the newspaper's business interests and the quality of the report. With respect to censorship at the individual level, the respondent said that there was a case in which one of the newspaper's employees published something on his personal blog during the weekend; "RosNeft" (a large Russian petroleum company, with which the outlet had a contract) found the post to be controversial. As a result, "RosNeft" terminated the contract. The interviewee said that he himself does not write anything "silly" on social media. Another respondent, who preferred to maintain her anonymity, cautiously noted that while working on television, she received death threats from state officials for investigating a case. She was very discreet and did not reveal any details. However, according to her, since then she has attempted to avoid political journalism. Another reporter working at Kommersant mentioned being more careful in choosing his words and topics; however, he argues that this is not because of censorship from above or pressure, but rather, is consistent with the following approach: "no need to anger a bear."

It is interesting that despite the worsening media environment and decreasing number of critical voices, few actually admit self-censorship. This phenomenon can be considered from different perspectives. Although one could say that the respondents do not feel safe openly discussing self-censorship, various scholars have conducted anonymous interviews (Koltsova 2006; Schimpfossl and Yablokov 2014; interviews conducted for this work), and diverse groups of reporters have been questioned, all with similar results. There might be multiple explanations for this phenomenon, two of which I highlight: a) uncertainty, and b) hiring and firing practices. Both explanations are based on observations from the interviews.

Principle of uncertainty

When asked to compare levels of media freedom in the early 2000s and the 2010s, the majority of the interviewees noted that the media environment has worsened. However, when asked about changes at their own workplaces, such as daily routines, editor-imposed censorship, self-imposed censorship, how the agenda is set, or choices about how to frame news events, most of the respondents claimed that they have the freedom both to choose their topics and to frame those topics as they see fit. Simultaneously, the majority of respondents noted that if any news excerpt is unpopular, there might be "payback," but only after the fact. Although material is not censored before publication, if a report is found inappropriate by external actors (i.e., state officials, the business elite, or the ruling elite), the media outlet might receive a warning or, as one of the interviewees[64] said, it is "not that the media is under direct pressure, but if a critical article appears in a newspaper, the next day, the building of that media outlet might be shut down under the pretence that the building is in a state of disrepair or undergoing reconstruction, and other things of that sort." This shows that on the one hand, there is no direct censorship, whereas on the other hand, there is some uncertainty about potential responses to controversial publications.

This principle of uncertainty and how it works can be observed both in interviews that I have conducted and in interviews from secondary sources. It seems that stability and compliance can also be ensured through an informational vacuum about the rules of the game, so that nobody really knows how to act, what is allowed, and what is not allowed. This way, even if there is no direct pressure, a journalist "double checks" before taking any action, and based on the decreasing number of critical voices in Russian media, it can be assumed that most of the time, reporters prefer to be cautious. Because any reaction to a publication occurs after the fact, it is difficult to predict whether one will "get away with it" or receive a warning from RosKomNadzor. Even very formal regulations are blurry. For example, another interviewee[65] mentioned that the regulations state that swear words cannot be used in publications, however, there is no list of which words are forbidden. Thus, a journalist must consider whether or not the commission could consider a particular word to be a swear word.

Another example of uncertainty was given by a Kommersant reporter, who said that he does not feel any pressure when writing or publishing his materials and that there are no prior rules about or prohibitions of any topics. However, there is a shared understanding, common-sense knowledge among journalists that some topics are better left uncovered.

---

[64] Reporter from Nezavisimaia Gazeta

[65] Reporter from Russia Today

Unless a reporter openly violates unspoken rules, there is no way to determine whether negative consequences will follow. Thus, to be on the safe side, some might take precautions in choosing topics, whereas others might decide to speak openly about controversial issues. Again, based on the principle of uncertainty, the critical voice is either punished or not. Perhaps that is one of the reasons that there remain some islands of a relatively free press in Russia. Additional examples of such uncertainty can be seen in an interview conducted by Schimpfossl and Yablokov (2014: 309):

> One interviewee told us a story about when they had invited a writer who fell out with Putin on the very day when the interview was scheduled to take place: "We asked ourselves: maybe we should not have him [the writer] here anymore? And without any instruction from above our team decided to cancel the interview. Our producer gave him [the writer] some lame excuse that some technical equipment broke down here in the studio or something. The program is pre-recorded, so we could have actually just cut out some bits if necessary, but we wanted to cover our backs… He [the writer] instantly wrote about it on Twitter, and in the end we had a scandal."

An interview with a former VGTRK employee published on Colta.ru (2015) may serve as another example of uncertainty:

> For example, there was a parade in Serbia. Not really in honour of Putin, in honour of the victory, but Putin was there… The parade was really amazing, beautiful. "Rossiia -24" was feeding a signal from Serbian TV and broadcasting the parade in Moscow. Serbs organised everything, we organised a translator who translated the words of the parade presenter. There was only a small complaint that the interpreter was a girl. The editor-in-chief was absent: his deputy was replacing him. Prior to leaving, the editor-in-chief told his deputy, "We will show only a part of a parade, and the rest can be transmitted through a small window." Apparently, this issue had not been agreed upon with the officials. What happened next was that after broadcasting part of the parade, as told by the editor-in-chief, the deputy chief moved the parade into a small window. At that moment, the phone starts ringing, Dobrodeev[66] calls three or four times, screaming to put

---

[66] Oleg Dobrodeev is a general manager of VGTRK

the parade back on and broadcast it till the end. Yelling at the same time about a woman translator—why could you not find a male translator? There's a dance that was because of this parade ... Of course, we returned the parade to the air, however, even after that there were phone calls: "How could you, what are you doing?" In principle, it was supposed to be editor-in-chief's decision, but this is how it turned out in the end. The editor guessed wrong.

As Schimpfossl and Yablokov (2014: 309) also note, "[t]he need for a reporter to sense what is appropriate at a particular moment in time might lead to insecurity and overly cautious approaches." It is not about knowing, it is more about sensing, which creates the uncertainty that forces a person to think twice before taking any step: there is no need to resort to direct censorship or coercive practices.

Hiring and firing practices

Hiring: Schimpfossl and Yablokov (2014: 3010) argue that many of their respondents "hold the view that, if a media personality and reporter does not agree with the editorial policy of one media organisation, he or she is free to change to another organisation." They conclude that their interviewees "seem to freely promote their masters' view." Koltsova's interviews with reporters have revealed similar findings. Apart from uncertainty, another way to ensure compliance without resorting to open censorship is through the use of hiring and firing practices. During my interviews, some of the respondents argued that when hiring, the editor makes sure that the new employee fits well into the existing team and that his views do not either deviate from those of the team or contradict the outlet's editorial policies. As a respondent working for Russia Today said,

> "Why would an employer hire someone who would go against the employer's views? Most often people gather around themselves those who share their ideas. We do have some variations in opinions in out media outlet, but in general we share principle ideas. We invite people who are more like us."

Another interviewee gave an example from his own experience. He reported that a few years ago, while applying for a job at state-owned media, he was informed by the editor-in-chief (behind closed doors) that the conditions had changed. Previously they could propose their own topics; now, however, the topics and theses were provided by the authorities or third parties. The assumption is that if one does not agree with the new conditions, one cannot join the team.

Firing: Journalists from the main federal channels who gave interviews to Colta.ru (2015) also noted that anyone whose views contradicted those promoted by management were free to go. Those who left did not make a big fuss: they just left. Others stayed for various reasons. In the end, however, this policy ensured a team that was both homogeneous and compliant with spoken and unspoken rules. As was the case with NTV. This independent TV station provided a critical reporting during the first Chechen war as well as balanced coverage of the parliamentary elections of 1995. The channel was considered as having "a strong news and analytical component" (Belin 2002: 19). However, in 2001, the company was acquired by Gazprom-Media, and the management of NTV was replaced, while dozens of its regular employees have resigned (Belin 2002).

Hiring and firing practices and/or the internalisation of externally imposed unspoken rules could be responsible for journalists' behaviour. However, such controls may vary not only based on the type of media but also from person to person.

4.6. Trust in the media

Only when the media is trusted and taken seriously by the audience can we speculate that the media matters. In the case of the population of Russia, the number of people who trust the media is greater than that of those who do not. Public opinion polls (Levada, 2009 – data gathered for the period between March 2008 and March 2009) and studies (Oates & Roselle 2000; White and McAllister 2006; White, Oates, McAllister 2005) show that a majority of the population not only receives its information from broadcast media but also does not distrust that information. Based on a survey conducted in Russia by the Levada Center in 2008, 46% of the population considered mass media absolutely free or mostly free from government control. Moreover, the questionnaire showed that only approximately 12% of the respondents did not trust the media at all and that approximately 35% believed that it was mostly controlled (Table 4.7). A plurality, approximately 50%, considered the media coverage of the candidates for the presidency during the 2008 presidential elections to be objective (Table 4.8). According to the same polls, 52% believed that central television and radio provided all the candidates with equal opportunities to express their views before elections. Only 27% thought that Medvedev received greater preference (Table 4.9). General trust in the media has slightly increased (Table 4.10).

Table 4.7. Government control over the mass media

Question: Do you think the mass media are free from government control now or are they controlled by the state?		2006 (July)	2008 (July)
	Absolutely free	12	12
	Mosly free	31	34
	Mostly controlled	36	35
	Fully controlled	12	10
	Difficult to answer	9	9

Source: Levada Analytical Center, 2009
Note: N=1600

Table 4.8. Objectivity of Russian mass media

Question: Do you think that Russian Mass Media furnish objective coverage of contestants for Russian presidency during elections?	Definitely yes	11
	Yes, rather than no	38
	No, rather than yes	29
	Definetely no	11
	Difficult to answer	12

Source: Levada Analytical Center, 2009
Note: N=1600

Table 4.9. Presidential treatment of candidates on central television and radio

Question: Central television and radio provided all the candidates with equal opportunities to express their views before elections, or did they give some candidate greater preference? Who in particular?		
	Andrey Bogdanov	1
	Vladimir Zhirinovsky	3
	Gennady Ziuganov	2
	Dmitri Medvedev	27
	Everyone had equal opportunities	52
	Difficult to answer	17

Source: Levada Analytical Center, 2009

Note: N=1600

Table 4.10. Trust in the media

Question: To what extent can today's press, radio, and television be trusted?		1999	2000	2001	2002	2003	2004	2005	2006	2007	2008
	Quite	25	26	30	23	22	26	24	24	25	28
	Not quite	44	44	47	44	46	45	45	43	39	40
	Not at all	19	18	17	21	22	18	18	21	22	18
	Difficult to answer	12	12	6	12	10	11	13	12	14	14

Source: Levada Analytical Center, 2009

Note: N=2100

4.7. Conclusions

A list of the manipulations discussed in this chapter is provided in the following two tables. The types of practices used to influence the media are given in the first column, and subtypes of these practices are given in the second column. The following columns present the effects of these practices on various types of media (i.e., broadcast, print, and online), and the general box presents outcomes common to all three types of media within each type of media manipulation. The first table (Table 4.11) provides a summary of the practices used before and during the 2000 election campaign, and the second table (Table 4.12) is devoted to the 2008 elections.

As seen in these tables, the range of manipulations widened by 2008. Both the cases and types of manipulations involving misuse of state resources and coercive practices against journalists increased. Interestingly, based on this comparative case study, it can be concluded that in competitive authoritarian Russia, the extent of media manipulations was generally smaller. Although the list might seem to be long, it is worth noting that some of the manipulations (blackmail, barter deals; selective recovery of debts) were related to weak institutionalisation during the period in which Russia was building a new system after the collapse of the Soviet Union. Over time, manipulation strategies became more centralised; legal ways of constraining media freedom have increased and practices such as barter deals and blackmail decreased.

Control via the ownership and financing of media outlets remained as one of the most commonly used methods of influence. This might be because media ownership is the strategy that can have the most durable and systematic effect. It allows control of the media from the top, i.e., control is centralised, which makes it easier to dictate the rules. In addition, this control is not an illegal practice, unlike threats, etc., against journalists. Control through ownership was used both in 2000 and 2008; however, the power balance was different in the two cases. In 2000, if the ruling elite wanted to have the media on its side, it had to ask the media outlets' owners and financiers. At that time, the main television channels belonged to media moguls or oligarchs. In the event that the interests of the oligarchs coincided with those of the ruling elite, media support could be provided. This was the case in both the 1996 and the 2000 elections. In both cases, the main opponent was the candidate from the Communist Party, who was inclined to renationalise certain industries. This plan was not in the interest of the oligarchs, who made their fortunes during the privatisation of the early 1990s. The state was largely dependent on business groups because it could not afford to fully finance the federal channels. On the one hand, this ensured some pluralism, whereas on the other hand, at crucial moments such as elections, the media continued to support the candidate who represented the ruling elite. However, these arrangements changed by the 2008 elections, when oligarchs no longer had as much power. By 2008, the media was controlled in two different ways. The most popular media outlets were either nationalised and the ruling elite was able to exert direct control over them, or the ruling elite installed their cronies (or people dependent on them) to run the principal media outlets.

As has been noted elsewhere, each of the strategies discussed in this section has its own specificities. Some of them are legal (e.g., defamation, libel, broadcast licence), whereas others are not (threats, murder, etc.); some are centralised and allow overall control of either the media or certain media outlets (e.g., ownership, legal framework), whereas others point at a particular media outlet or media professional (e.g., cooptation, control over office facilities). Moreover, some manipulation strategies were the result of destabilised institutional settings present in the early 1990s (e.g., blackmail, barter deals). Another distinctive characteristic of manipulation strategies is whether the strategy is accessible only to state agents or whether other actors can also use it (e.g., manipulations involving selective debt recovery and state subsidies can be used only by state agents, whereas cooptation, access to information, or individual threats against media professionals can be used by other actors, although most of these types of strategies are the most effective when used by the ruling elite).

Considering these specific characteristics of manipulation strategies, it can be concluded that to influence the media on a large scale, the following strategies are the most effective, in descending order: 1) ownership; 2) legal framework; 3) access to information; and 4) cooptation. Threats, control over office facilities, destruction of media outlets' property or videotapes, blackmail, interference with newspapers' printing and distribution processes, access to information, and cooptation are used on a smaller scale, primarily at the local-government level.

The case study also shows that media freedom and pluralism depends, at least to an extent, on the main source of media organisations' revenues. During the early 1990s, thousands of independent new media outlets emerged, most of which were founded by journalists and editors who split off from their old companies. This period was marked by a relatively free press. However, soon these newly established outlets experienced financial difficulties. Many shut down, whereas others were either bought by or offered financial assistance by oligarchs, who requested those media outlets to advance their particularistic interests in exchange for funding. Because there were a relatively large number of oligarchs, although speech was not "free," at least some media pluralism could be observed. In the early 2000s, the Russian state's newfound capability to purchase, finance, and influence the media marked the demise of freedom of speech and media pluralism.

This study also demonstrates that the media is not only a tool in the hands of the ruling elite; it also can show us how the system works. Every regime has characteristics that make it work in a certain way: this is observable also when looking at how the ruling elite and the media interact. Here, two points can be highlighted: *faded boundaries* and *uncertainty*. Faded boundaries involve weak democratic institutions and blurred boundaries among the state, ruling elite, and business. This phenomenon is particularly visible in the context of a) the control exerted by the ruling elite over state-owned television; and b) the control exerted over the media through the loyalty and crony ownership of media outlets. Uncertainty can ensure the regime's stability. No one really knows how to act—what is allowed and what is not. Thus, to be safe, one might think twice before publishing anything controversial. For example, because of vague regulations, journalists might not be completely confident about what they can report, what they are allowed to discuss, and what is forbidden. On television, the agenda is discussed weekly; in newspapers, however, things are different. It is unclear what can be safely reported. The boundaries are unclear, thus leaving a way to confine the media within a frame while avoiding the application of direct pressure. Most of the interviewees said that they do not feel any direct pressure or limits on their creativity in choosing topics and frames. Although self-censorship might exist, it is not the result of direct pressure, control, or limitations on freedom; instead, self-censorship is the result of both carefulness and a wish to avoid possible inconveniences. This argument summarises the interviews that I conducted with various journalists.

Table 4.11. Constraints placed on the media: Year 2000 and prior

Mechanisms of influence	Sub-types	Consequences: Television	Consequences: Newspapers	Consequences: Online media

Misuse of state resources	- Ownership:
	  . direct ownership of state but alternative sources of finance
	  . partial ownership
	- The media's source of financing:
	  - The state subsidies/Selective funding
	  - Financial rewards for compliance and fulfilling agreements/orders of larger businesses and/or state actors
	- Personal ties with
	  - owners of media outlets
	  - media distribution channels
	  - owners of facilities rented by media outlets
	  - businesses on whose financial support a media outlet relies (sponsorships, advertisement)
	- Control over distribution channels; ex. state postal services, broadcast frequencies, etc.
	- Direct or indirect control over facilities rented by media outlets and thus an opportunity to manipulate terms and conditions of lease
	- Cooptation
	- Broadcast license
	- Blackmail
	- Selective recovery of debts
	- Control over office facilities
	- Barter deals
	- Control over access to information
		- Decision over what content is allowed to be aired
		- Disconnecting from radio broadcasts
			- Refusal to print/distribute newspaper
			- Withdrawal, destruction, purchase, or arrest of newspaper circulation
				-

		- Unfair dismissal of editors or journalists - Unfair dismissal of editors or journalists - Denying access to information - Evicting a media organization from the leased office facilities		
Legal constraints	- *Glavlit* (the Chief Board of Literature and Publishing established in 1922) transforms into the Committee on Press (1992) responsible for registration of media and allocation of frequencies and state funds for media. - State controls issue of broadcast license - Selective use of rules - Superfluity of rules	-	- Closure of newspapers	-
		- Criminal cases against journalists and the media - Charges against journalists and media lawsuits - Lawsuits filed against journalists and media claims		-
Other ways of ensuring compliance	- Coercion	-	-	-
		- Detention by police (FSB, etc.) - Threats against journalists and the media outlet - Journalists' murder		-

Table 4.12. Constrains placed on the media: Year 2008 and after

Mechanisms of influence	Sub-types	Consequences		
		Television	Newspapers	Online media

Misuse of state resources	- Ownership:
	  . Higher levels of direct ownership and partial ownership
	  . Ownership via state companies
	  . Crony-ownership
	- Limiting the media's source of financing:
	  . State subsidies
	  . Advertisement
	  . Foreign funds
	- Ensuring loyalty of media professionals by cooptation
	- Control over distribution channels; ex. state postal services, broadcast frequencies, etc.
	- State or crony ownership of printing facilities
	- Control over issue of broadcast license
	- Control over access to information
		- Decision over what content is allowed to be published
		- Disconnecting from radio broadcasts
		- Unfair dismissal of editors or journalists
		- Evicting a media organization from the leased office facilities
		- Withdrawal of photos, audio and video
			- Refusal to print/distribute newspapers
			- Withdrawal (purchase or arrest) of circulation
			- Unfair dismissal of editors or journalists
			- Eviction from its premises editions
			- Closing down newspapers
				- Interference with Internet publications

		- Refusing new media outlets' registration		
Legal constraints	- Media law amendments banning any television or video information on terror acts, except information allowed for publication by law enforcement agencies - Law against extremist activities prohibiting the dissemination of information supporting "extremist activities" - Legislation allowing government authorities to close print or broadcast media outlets which spread "biased" political commentary - Establishment of *RosKomNadzor*	-	- Closing down newspapers	- Interference with Internet publications
		- Criminal cases against journalists and the media - Charges against journalists and media lawsuits - Lawsuits filed against journalists and media claims		
Other ways of ensuring compliance	- Coercion and other practices	-	-	- Interference with Internet publications
		- Detention by police (FSB, etc.) - Threats against journalists and the media outlet - Damaging photos, audio and video equipment, computers - Journalists' missing - Attacks on journalists - Attacks on media outlet offices - Launching a newspaper carrying already existing name - Withdrawal of photos, audio and video		-
	- Hiring and firing practices	- Ensuring that mostly journalists with political views similar to those of the media outlet employing them are hired, whereas those that do not share the views are fired		

5. Analysis of news content: presidential election campaigns 2000 and 2008

5.1. Introduction

Eighty-three per cent of the population in Russia watch TV on a daily basis (White and McAllister 2006; Levada Analytical Center 2009); 49% of Russians believe in objectivity of the media (Levada Analytical Center 2009) However, what messages are transmitted via the most popular media outlets in Russia? What type of information do millions of people receive before the voting day? In many modern autocracies, rulers prefer employing media propaganda to using direct repression and force (Silitski 2009). How exactly this media use is accomplished at the news content level itself is discussed in this chapter. The main questions posed here concern the content of news, framing, and representation of candidates.

To answer these questions, the content analysis method is used. Employing the qualitative[67] and quantitative[68] content analysis method, I examine the media coverage of presidential electoral campaigns for 2000 and 2008. The goals of the study are to ascertain how biased the media coverage was and to examine the effects of the incumbent's media manipulations strategy on news content. The analyses are also aimed at showing how the media distorts and skews coverage of political affairs and how this distortion differs across different media types and outlets.

---

[67] Analysis of framing used in addressing candidates and their policy platforms.
[68] Calculating frequency with which certain topics or candidates are mentioned.

The chapter presents the results of news content analysis during the presidential election campaigns of 2000 and 2008. First, a systematic plan for the research is detailed. The following section proceeds with case selection concerning media outlets and discussion of methods used in this study. Sections four and five present the results. In the sixth section, a discussion of these results from a comparative perspective is provided. Conclusions follow.

5.2. Research design

In chapter 3, it was argued that different factors could affect news content. Those factors include constraints created for media organisations and journalists by the ruling elite to skew the playing field to its own advantage. Some of the most visible effects of media manipulations on news content are mirrored in agenda setting and the framing of stories. Posing a relevant set of questions helps to identify the content bias in framing and in agenda setting using content analysis. Table 5.1 summarises the information provided in Chapter 3, it presents definitions of different types of effects, highlights the indicators, and provides illustrative examples. In this chapter, I examine each in turn, except for "self-censorship," which was already discussed in Chapter 4. Content bias and its extent is measured by examining framing (i.e., tone of the coverage) and agenda setting (i.e., topics most frequently mentioned). To see whether the ruling elite use the priming as an active tool for winning the votes, I look at the issues highlighted by each candidate during the campaign period and see if the media's agenda corresponds the issues outlined. This will show if the issues mentioned most often by the incumbent also reappear frequently in the media. Indicators for each are provided in Table 5.1.

Table 5.1. Effects of media manipulations on news content

	Definition	Indicators	Examples
Content bias or Editorial slant	"Consistent patterns in the framing of mediated communication that promote the influence of one side in conflicts over the use of government power… If the patterns of slant persist across time, message dimensions, and media outlets, the media might be systematically assisting certain entities to induce their preferred behaviour in others" (Entman 2007: 166). "The quantity and tone of a newspaper's candidate coverage as influenced by its editorial position" (Druckman and Parkin 2005: 1030).	To recognise content bias, news content is analysed over six weeks of time. Positive or otherwise coverage of the candidates is quantified and compared. The number of times any candidate was mentioned and the tone used to describe the candidate is coded.	Content analysis of Russian media shows that the state-run media is heavily biased; the incumbent receives either neutral or positive coverage, whereas the opposition is mostly ridiculed and presented as incapable. In addition, the number of news messages mentioning the incumbent in a positive light is significantly greater than the coverage of all the other candidates taken together.
	Framing		
	"The process of culling a few elements of perceived reality and assembling a narrative that highlights connections among them to promote a particular interpretation. Fully developed frames typically perform four functions: problem definition, causal analysis, moral judgment, and remedy promotion" (Entman 2007: 164). "The central organising idea for news content that supplies a context and suggests what the issue is through the use of selection, emphasis, exclusion and elaboration" (James Tankard et al. 1991: 3; qqt. in Weaver 2007: 143). "The selection of a small number of attributes for inclusion on the media agenda when a particular object is discussed" (McCombs et al. 1998: 704)	The tone of the coverage, identification of the problem, causal analysis, moral judgement and a solution proposed for the problem. 1. Tone used in presenting each candidate in the media: - Positive - Negative - Neutral 2. Tone used in presenting the policy programme presented by each candidate: - Positive - Negative - Neutral	An example of a framing would be a presentation of a conflict raised around one of the opposition leaders, Mikhail Kas'ianov — who was nominated as a candidate for the presidential elections of 2008 — and the Central Election Commission, which rejected his candidacy on the grounds that more than 10% of signatures were invalid.

		Agenda setting	
	"Through their day-to-day selection and display of the news, journalists focus our attention and influence our perceptions of the most important issues facing the country…[t]his ability to influence the salience of topics on the public agenda has come to be called the agenda setting role of the media" (McCombs and Reynolds 2009: 1)	Topics covered most often in the news, when the names of the candidates are mentioned. 3. Number of times each candidate was mentioned 4. Number of times each candidate's policy programme was discussed 5. Policy topics most frequently mentioned policy topics by the candidates	For example, some of the most often mentioned problems in news media before the 2008 elections were social issues, and the incumbent government's success in handling them.
	"The mass media force attention to certain issues. They build up public images of political figures. They are constantly presenting objects suggesting what individuals in the mass should think about, know about, have feelings about" (Lang and Lang 1966: 468)		
Priming	"Priming refers to changes in the standards that people use to make political evaluations" (Iyengar and Kinder 1987: 63).	Priming is an effect that agenda setting has on the audiences' evaluation of the government's performance. Priming effects can be identified by interviewing two different audience groups exposed to different media agendas. Similarly, opinion polls indicating the most important issues in the eyes of the audience can be a good indicator. However, this work is not concerned with the effects but rather the manipulations used to produce an effect. Thus, interviews are not conducted but opinion polls and some secondary literature on the topic are consulted.	For example, as was also mentioned earlier in this chapter, according to recent studies of the Levada Center (Gudkov 2015), topics widely discussed in the media catch up with the public in a few months, triggering corresponding emotions such as aggression, hate, and patriotism.
	"The process by which activated mental constructs can influence how individuals evaluate other concepts and ideas" (Domke et al. 1998: 52).		
Self-censorship	The act of censoring or classifying one's own work.	Interviews with journalists and materials gathered from secondary sources presented in Chapter 4.	

To examine how biased the media were in framing stories related to candidates and their platforms, I examine how the candidates were presented in the media and how the events revolving around the candidates were framed. Answering these questions also helps to reveal the frames and themes that are used on the state-run television channels and that are aimed at increasing the chances of the candidate from the ruling elite to win the elections. To identify whether content bias was present in agenda setting, I look for topics that occur most often and the extent of coverage each candidate receives. Examining the principle differences between selected broadcast, print, and online media content illustrates several points: 1) the level of freedom permitted to different types of media; 2) the qualitative difference in agenda and framing across various media outlets, i.e., which events were provided broader coverage on state television channels and which events were deemed more important by the editors of more-critical print outlets; and 3) how candidates were presented on pro-government channels and whether that presentation differed in relatively critical media. Additionally, examination of the differences between media coverage of elections in 2000 and 2008 reveals the dynamics of change from competitive to hegemonic authoritarianism.

5.3. Content analysis

To analyse media content, I use the content analysis method. The content analysis method is usually used to describe systematically the meaning of qualitative data (Schreier, 2012: p. 1). It can be used to analyse a wide variety of material, such as texts generated from conducting interviews or a range of materials from various sources (e.g., newspapers, blogs, magazines, and journals) (pp. 2-3). Content analysis helps to reduce the amount of data because different categories are assigned to segments of the text. The method requires careful analysis of parts of the text related to the research question. Each part of the text is assigned to a relevant category or sub-category, which allows comparing and relating different parts of the text that can later be used to observe patterns among units of analysis. The category frame used for the analysis can be developed in three different ways. The categories can be data-driven, built on prior research, or they can be developed with the help of a deductive-inductive approach. In this study, I use the latter approach, i.e., deductive-inductive. The principal advantage of this approach is that the source of categories can be both theory/prior knowledge and the data under examination.

Boyatzis (1998) argues that developing themes and codes is a three-step process. The first stage involves solving issues on sampling and design; in the second stage, themes and codes are developed; and in the last stage, the codes are validated and used. The following sub-sections present the development and implementation of categories and codes based on this three-step process.

Stage I: Sampling and design

I examine media coverage of presidential election campaigns that occurred in Russia in 2000 and 2008. The official start date for media-based campaign activities was four weeks before the election day. The start day of analysis is February 10 for the 2000 elections and 15 January for the 2008 elections, which is six weeks before election day. See the summary in Table 5.2.

Table 5.2. Elections of 2000 and 2008

Case	Presidential Elections, 2000	Presidential Elections, 2008
Election date	March 26	March 2
The official start date for campaign activities	February 25 (4 weeks before the election day)	February 2 (4 weeks before the election day)
Start day of media analysis	February 10 (six weeks before the election day)	January 15 (six weeks before the election day)
Candidates	Vladimir Putin Gennadii Ziuganov Vladimir Zhirinovskii Grigorii Yavlinskii	Dmitry Medvedev Gennadii Ziuganov Vladimir Zhirinovskii Andrey Bogdanov

Segmentation of the audience: Any type of advertisement, including political advertisements, is targeted at groups of people or the target audience whose support/attention the creators seek to gain. Thus, I divide the audience into several groups based on their preferences of media. According to David Stroemberg (2004: 266), less-educated voters prefer visual and audible information obtained from television to reading newspapers. This is partly because although the introduction of broadcast media made the distribution of information to rural areas easier and less expensive, it has also contributed to a decline in the circulation of print media outside the major cities. In the case of Russia, White and McAllister (2007: 215) argue that a majority of the population receives political information from television because the circulation of print media outside the largest cities is very poor. This poor circulation can easily be a consequence of the vast territory that the country occupies and of financial difficulties that newspapers encounter in distributing the paper issues, which in turn makes newspapers available mostly in urbanised large cities. Therefore, better-educated, urban population have an opportunity to choose between different sources of information such as newspapers, television and the Internet. The more vibrant population, with short attention spans and a willingness to obtain quick information on current events, prefers the Internet. Hence, the audience is divided into three segments: 1) average voter; 2) well-educated — mostly urban population including professionals, office workers, business elite, and intellectuals; and 3) young people. This segmentation helps to identify the most popular media outlets for each segment of the population to have samples of media outlets targeted and read by a majority of voter representatives of different groups.

Sampling of media outlets: The selection is based on an analysis of the media environment, area coverage, readership, and viewership ratings of print and broadcast media outlets. The outlets to be analysed include television, newspapers, and the Internet. The main criterion in selection of media outlets was high level of popularity within different segments of the population (i.e., the general population; well-educated professionals; and the young generation).

All three types of media distribute information on a regular basis. They are similar in terms of regularity of information distribution and of their content reaching a wide audience. However, in contrast to television and print media, the Internet enjoys a higher level of freedom of information flow but also lower rates of accessibility. Taken together, newspapers, television, and the Internet distribute a majority of media content. Thus, in this work, not only traditional media outlets, such as newspapers and television, but also online media are analysed. The number of media outlets analysed is comparatively small. However, a majority of the population receives information from media outlets selected for this study. The following sub-section presents an overall picture of the media market in Russia.

Media outlets

This sub-section provides a brief overview of some of the most popular media outlets within different media categories; broadcast, print, and online media are presented and discussed. The information provided in this section refers to the period under study, i.e., 2000-2008.

Broadcast media: Television was the most popular source of information in Russia in the early 2000s, as it was during the electoral campaigns later in 2008. Stephan White and Ian McAllister (2006) argue that a majority of Russians chose television as a primary medium. Their survey shows that 92% of respondents as of 2001 watched TV, and the most-watched channels were Channel One (84% of the population) and Rossiia (71%). As of 2004, 82% of the general population watched television, and only 22% read newspapers. Another survey conducted by the Levada Center in March 2008 shows that 83% watched television every day and only 19% read newspapers on a daily basis (see Table 5.3).

Table 5.3. Percentage of media audience according to media outlets

	Daily basis	Week or more	Several times a month	Less than once a month	Hardly ever
Television	83	13	1	1	2
Radio	42	22	3	9	24
Newspapers	19	56	9	6	9
Fiction	14	26	17	22	20
Magazines	6	39	22	16	17

Source: Levada Analytical Center, 2009
Note: July 2008; N=1500

In 2000, the top three television stations in Russia were Channel One, Rossiia and NTV (EIM 2000). The channels have not lost their popularity and remained the most watched in 2008 (MSI, 2009). Figure 5.1 shows the ratings of the channels. The two most popular ones, Channel One and Rossiia, have been included in this study.

Channel One provides national coverage and broadcasts to 98.8% of the country's territory. The station started operating in 1995, replacing the old USSR's "Ostankino" state television company. According to a variety of sources, Boris Berezovsky[69], an entrepreneur and oligarch, owned up to 49% of the channel's shares; the rest belonged to the state. Some sources (Koltsova 2006) show the existence of close links between President Boris Yeltsin and Berezovsky in the 1990s. Because the state was incapable of subsidising two state channels (Rossiia and Channel One), it allowed Berezovsky to fund Channel One in exchange for loyalty to the government. Later, in 2001, Channel One was acquired by one of the oligarchs close to the Kremlin.

Figure 5.1. TV Ratings as of 2009

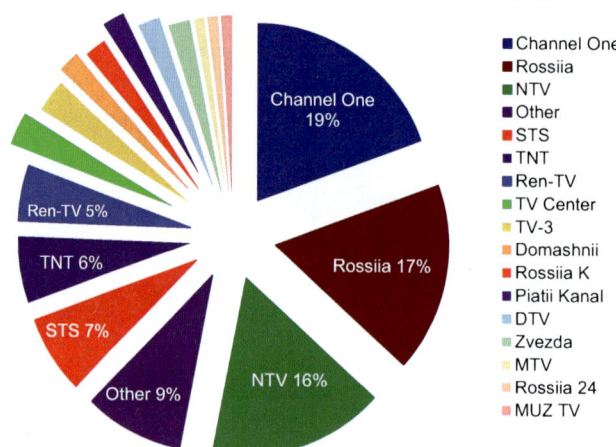

Source: TNS Russia

Rossiia is another state-owned TV channel broadcast nationwide. Its coverage is approximately 98.5% of the country. The station is fully owned and subsidised by the state. In the 1990s, because the state did not have the

---

[69] Details about Boris Berezovsky were provided in Chapter 4.

capacity to finance the channel fully, the media outlet had to seek alternative sources of funding (Koltsova 2006).

Print media: As of 2008, according to MSI (2009), there were approximately 35,500 newspapers, and 23,500 magazines in Russia. Although print media readership has declined in recent decades, some segments of the population still read newspapers regularly. According to a representative survey conducted by Colton and McFaul (2003), three per cent of respondents said that newspapers are their main source of information. Some of the most popular newspapers among the urban population are Kommersant, Novaia Gazeta, Komsomolskaya Pravda, Izvestiya, and Nezavisimaia Gazeta (BBC country profile). The two most important newspapers for the Russian business community and the community of highly qualified professionals are Kommersant and Vedomosti. The most prominent newspaper seen as openly critical of the government is Novaia Gazeta.

Kommersant was founded by a correspondent of "Ogonyok," Vladimir Yakovlev in 1989. The newspaper has published regularly since January 1990. Its daily circulation in 2006 was 120 thousand copies; the newspaper is highly respected for its general quality and is read both in the business community and by a broader public of intellectuals and academics. Between 1999 and 2006, it was under Berezovsky's influence, but later was purchased by Alisher Usmanov (Forbes April 23, 2012) – co-owner of "Metallinvest" and general manager of "Gazprominvestholding". The company was founded on July 28, 1997, to manage Gazprom's investment projects, which points to close business relationships between the state-owned gas company and the media owner, i.e., Usmanov[70].

Vedomosti, which was founded in 1999, is a joint venture of The Financial Times, Dow Jones and Sanoma, a Finnish media group. It is one of Russia's leading business newspapers (BBC, 16 May 2008). Their target audience is business professionals. Vedomosti is one of the most important newspapers in the Russian business community; as of 2006, its circulation had reached 70 thousand copies, and the paper had seven regional editions (Koikkalainen 2007). Both Vedomosti and Kommersant are some of the most-known and most-read newspapers among the business community, although Vedomosti is considered a purely financial market-oriented newspaper (Koikkalainen 2007). Due to the editorial line and the principal market of the newspaper, it might be expected that Vedomosti's coverage of candidates from the Communist party would be either negative or neutral. However, if these newspaper characteristics were the only reason communists do not obtain positive coverage, then one should expect the coverage of an event to be similar in both cases (i.e., both in the case of Russian presidential elections of 2000 and 2008).

Novaia Gazeta is a daily opposition newspaper founded in 1993 due to a split among journalists at Komsamolskaya Pravda. The first edition of the newspaper was published in April 1993. It is known for its critical reporting on political and social issues in Russian and its tradition of investigative

---

[70] Usmanov is also an owner of DST Global (Digital Sky Technologies owns large shares in popular social networks such as "Odnoklassniki" and "VKontakte"), Mail.ru group, and musical TV channel "Muz-TV". Furthermore, "Kommerstant" also concealed a deal with the "Sup" company – the owner of popular Russian blog service LiveJournal – in which "Sup" bought "Gazeta.ru", whereas "Kommersant" bought shares of "Sup" (peoples.ru). The "Kommersant" company includes a weekly newspaper "Kommersant", weekly "Kommersant in regions", analytical weekly "Kommersant Vlast'", economic weekly "Kommersant Dengi", automobile journal "Avtopilot", monthly journal about shopping "Kommersant Katalog", monthly journal "Sekret Firmi", journal "CITIZEN K", and weekly journal "Kommersant WEEKEND" (km.ru). The owner of Kommersant, Usmanov, also has partial or full ownership of gazeta.ru, LiveJournal, mail.ru, Odnoklassniki, VKontakte, and Muz-TV.

journalism. During the war in Chechnia, the newspaper presented the most critical assessment of the government's politics in the region. A controlling share of Novaia Gazeta belongs to its employees.

Online news media: There is an important distinction that must be drawn between online media and information disseminated through social networks, personal weblogs, and other popular social platforms. As has already been mentioned, traditional news media are produced by professional journalists and reporters. With the emergence of the Internet and the increasing popularity of online media, the traditional media landscape went through profound changes. News items are no longer produced solely by professional journalists or news organisations but also by the audience itself. The advent of online platforms for dissemination of information and communication, accessible to the broad public, created another type of reporting – via social networks, e-mails and mailing lists, and personal blogs. However, this work concerns itself only with media content produced by professional journalists because the most efficient means of delivering information biased in favour of the incumbent is through the most popular media outlets because the most effective means of influencing media content is targeting professional journalists and media organisations. On the one hand, news produced by journalists is easily accessible, widely broadcast, and can be considered more trustworthy by the audience; on the other hand, news organisations can be targeted as a group, whereas scattered bloggers, opinion leaders, and others are more difficult to control – but at the same time can be easily removed from the web. Therefore, focusing on the news produced by journalists and media organisations has more relevance for this research.

According to Freedom House reports, 27% of the Russian population used the Internet as of 2008. Although the government did not restrict the Internet, Internet service providers were required to cooperate with security services. The providers were required to allow the police and other security services to monitor traffic, e-mails and web posts. According to TNS Gallup (2008) data for 2008, a majority of Internet users check websites such as gazeta.ru and lenta.ru for news; the two websites were visited by 24.9% and 24.4% of the Internet audience, respectively. Among those aged between 18 and 34, i.e., the younger population of the country, these online sources were also visited the most. Gazeta.ru's audience comprised 24% of those 25-34 years old and 19.3% of those aged from 18 to 24. Lenta.ru's ratings were slightly higher: 25.2% of those who were 25-34 and 24.1% of those whose age was from 18 to 24 (see Table 5.4[71]).

gazeta.ru — launched in 1999 was, according to some sources, a part of Yukos' media assets (Arutunyan 2009). However, after imprisonment of company executives, Gazeta.ru became a part of Sup media, which was partially owned by Alisher Usmanov through his media company Kommersant. In 2012, Usmanov sold his interests in Sup Media to Alexander Mamut[72] – the owner of Rambler-Afisha. In 2014, Mamut and the owner of Prof-Media, Vladimir Potanin[73], signed a merger contract. More importantly for this study, in 2008 both internet news portals belonged to media holdings of business people close to the ruling political elites. Lenta.ru was registered in 2001, and soon after became a part of "Rambler-Afisha." As of 2015, both gazeta.ru and lenta.ru are united under Rambler & Co (Vedomosti, 21 April 2014). Table 5.5 gives an overview of the media outlets selected for content analysis.

---

[71] Other online media outlets such as "dozhd.ru" and "slon.ru" became highly popular after 2010. Dozhd.ru, an online television company quite popular among intellectuals and politically active youth, was launched in the late 2000s and thus does not fall into the timeframe of this work. For more detailed information, please see Lenta.ru.: http://lenta.ru/lib/14198587/

[72] According to some sources Mamut is Putin's close ally (The Telegraph, 4 February 2011), other sources mention his connection to Eltsin and his family, as well as his former partnership with Berezovsky and later Abramovich (lenta.ru, 15 March 2015).

[73] Vladimir Potanin is an owner of a large company, "Interros," which was founded in the 1990s by Vladimir Potanin and Mikhail Prokhorov. The main activities of the company include metallurgy, mining ("Noril'skii Nikel"), leisure ("Roza Hutor"), construction and real estate ("Profesteyt"), pharmaceuticals (Petrovaks Farm), and media (currently Ramble&Co, Prof-Media before its merger). Additional information can be obtained on the company's website http://www.interros.ru/company/.

Table 5.4. Popular online media in Russia, 2008

	Total (12-54)	Men	Women	18-24	25-34	35-44	45-54
gazeta.ru	24.9	25.1	24.7	19.3	24.0	34.5	28.6
lenta.ru	24.4	26.3	22.2	24.1	25.2	25.6	26.3
rian.ru	23.9	22.6	25.3	20.3	22.6	25.4	28.6
vesti.ru	23.3	24.4	22.1	19.2	23.5	28.1	24.5
tden.ru	21.3	21.5	21.1	19.8	23.9	22.2	21.6
rb.ru	15.3	15.8	14.8	10.2	17.5	16.6	21.9
newsru.com	14.2	14.9	13.4	11.9	14.0	16.6	16.4
moskva.ru	13.6	13.5	13.7	14.5	11.9	12.0	12.5
izvestia.ru	12.6	10.2	15.3	9.7	14.6	15.5	14.4
vedomosti.ru	12.1	12.6	11.5	9.7	11.0	15.8	17.2
kommersant.ru	12.9	12.2	13.6	10.3	14.8	13.9	17.1
aif.ru	11.1	10.3	12.2	11.3	9.9	12.1	11.6
ng.ru	9.5	10.9	7.9	7.3	8.6	12.0	12.5

Source: TNS Gallup
Note: Share of visitors among Internet audience in percent

Data collection

Campaign coverage by the news media was obtained from the "Integrum" database, which contains fully transcribed electronic text versions of press, radio and TV broadcasts. The database enables search within the documents. Media reports were downloaded from this database starting from 10 February 2000 for the elections of 2000 and from 15 January 2008 for the 2008 elections. TV news stories were obtained as news transcripts. The media reports from the media outlets given in Table 5.5 were identified as relevant if they contained the name of a presidential candidate. The reports were later filtered to remove excerpts about people with surnames identical to those of any of the candidates. Overall, for 2000, 842 news pieces from four different media outlets were analysed. Of these, 160 were newspaper articles and 682 were television news excerpts. For

2008, 1462 media reports in which names of any of the four candidates were mentioned in seven various media outlets were analysed. Of those 445 were television news, 448 newspaper articles, and 569 online media publications.

Table 5.5. Selected media outlets, Russia

Audience	Educated/Professional/Elite			Younger generation	Average population/rural/less-educated
Media type	Newspapers			Online news media	TV
Media outlets					
Year	2000				
	Kommerstant	Novaia Gazeta	-	-	Channel One Rossiia
Year	2008				
	Kommerstant	Novaia Gazeta	Vedomosti	lenta.ru gazeta.ru	Channel One Rossiia

Depending upon the topic discussed in the text, every paragraph containing the idea related to one of the categories created was coded. The categories were developed based on prior research and an in-vivo coding strategy. Therefore, the codes developed for the 2000 and 2008 elections differ slightly. The codes are created based on the prior research, and the literature forms the core of the coding framework, which is similar for both election years. Later, codes are added.

In order to check how far media reporting reflected the agenda raised by the candidates themselves their campaign materials were also subjected to content analysis. Campaign materials have been accessed in the Collection of Documents Produced by Russian Political Parties and Organisations, which is held by the Research Centre for East European Studies at the University of Bremen [74] and additionally via Integrum database.

---

[74] Accessed at: http://www.forschungsstelle.uni-bremen.de/en/9/20120703150035/20130211111310/.html

Stage II: Themes and codes

The main categories of content analysis were developed prior to coding. These categories were based on general issues that were raised during the campaign by the candidates, such as policy platforms. Other categories were constructed based on the literature, which specifies particularities of the case, such as the war in Chechnia, that appeal to national sentiments. Categories such as character have also been included. Most of the categories have sub-codes that indicate the tone of the report, that is, whether it was positively or negatively framed.

Categories related directly to discussion of candidates are grouped into three; the first group includes policy issues, the second group largely encompasses categories related to personal traits of candidates, and the third is a residual group in which in-vivo codes and categories are located, such as candidates' views on the War in Chechnia and social, political and economic conditions in the region.

Coding framework

Code	Foreign affairs
Definition	Includes topics concerning Russia's interests abroad, relations with other countries, and meetings and negotiations with representatives of foreign countries. Any opinions and views expressed by the candidates concerning foreign affairs.
Example	Speaking about foreign policy, Medvedev assured that Russia is not going to break relations with so-called problematic countries. "Not cutting off diplomatic relations with so-called problematic countries – causing the world community distress – is our duty. The most unproductive would be to terminate the relationship and move on to bombardments. I think that in today's world, everyone understands this", Medvedev said (lenta.ru, 22.01.2008).
Sub-codes	Positive Negative Neutral

Code	**Governance**
Definition	Includes discussions of topics related to "the formal and institutional processes that operate at the level of the nation-state to maintain public order and facilitate collective action" (Stoker 1998: 17). For example, topics such as the government and state's efficiency in making decisions and in implementing them.
Example	Only two assumptions are possible: either they are not quite adequate, or they have their own version of further political developments. There are quite strong objective contradictions between the oligarchs and Putin concerning the FSB (). Putin as an interim president and the defender of the people should think of ways to bring justice. And Putin's intention to do so with the help of "siloviki" is becoming more obvious, which in turn is worrisome because the root of the problem is not in the sphere of security forces or the methods of governance, but rather – as Putin noted himself – in areas of ideology, law, and the economy (Novaia Gazeta, 06.03.2000).
Sub-codes	Positive Negative Neutral

Code	**Other**
Definition	A residual category. Issues that were raised and discussed by the candidates but that did not reoccur later were allocated to this category. It includes topics such as the environment.
Example	The second "i" stands for infrastructure. Dmitry Medvedev spoke not only of the usual energy and transport but also about the development of the Internet, fundamental science, and education. However, "to rid Russia of the well-known problems," creating another state corporation was proposed – a joint-stock corporation, the main function of which will be coordination of building and exploitation of roads (Kommersant, 16.02.2008).
Sub-codes	Positive Negative Neutral

Code	**Corruption**
Definition	Contains discussions about corruption matters in any sphere, be it corruption present in the education system, the health care system, or the state bureaucracy, such as abuse of office and embezzlement. Candidates' proposals for addressing corruption and their opinions and views on corruption are coded under this category. The issue was assigned a separate category because it could be used as a valence issue due to rampant corruption in Russia. According to Transparency International, in 2000, Russia scored 2.1 on the Corruption Perception Index, in which 0 is highly corrupt and 10 is very clean. This score remained relatively stable throughout the 2000s.
Example	"Without a fight against corruption, there can be no economic growth in Russia, and this remains one of the issues of the highest priority," – said by interim president of the Russian Federation Vladimir Putin when answering questions from journalists after the meeting of the Board of Interregional Association "Siberian Agreement".
	Putin has expressed an opinion that "there is only one remedy against corruption – consistent, principled, tough, and perseverant compliance to law." He emphasised that a successful fight against corruption will make "our country economically attractive and politically developed" (Channel One-Vremya, 18.02.2000).
Sub-codes	Positive Negative Neutral
Code	**General rhetoric**
Definition	A category created to identify rhetoric mostly emphasised by the candidates to appeal to national sentiments, such as yearning for stability after the wobbly 1990s, nationalism, religion or creating and blaming an external enemy, as was done in Soviet times.

Example	*External threat*
	At first glance, Russia became more aggressive in dealing with the outside world. Putin states, "the world is becoming more and more "complicated and hard", that under the pretence of freedom, sovereignty is crushed and Russia is being dragged into wasteful confrontation and a new race of weaponry advancement. And in general, do not teach us democracy; better go and teach your wife to cook soup." In the majority of western states, this statement causes uniformly negative sentiment. Soon, we will hear again about "dangerous Russia" and "protofascism". However, in reality, a foreign policy, the principle thesis of which is "The world is multi-polar, Russia is a great power and influential member of all global processes", was formulated in the early 1990s and since then has not changed. Boris Yeltsin allowed himself tougher talk than Putin does. An example would be Yeltsin's hard threats addressed to the United States in 1999 in Beijing. He said, "Clinton allowed himself to put pressure on Russia. He apparently forgot for a few seconds what Russia is. Russia has a full arsenal of nuclear weapons. Let him not forget in what world he lives" (Vedomosti, 20.02.2008).
	Nationalism
	Dmitry Medvedev, the First Deputy Prime Minister of the Russian Federation stated, "We are the most powerful agricultural country in the world. This is because our territory allows for it. Right now, our task is to ensure food independence for years to come. And not only should we be able to feed ourselves but also supply our neighbours" (Channel One-Vremya, 13.02.2008).
Sub-codes	Stability Religion
	Nationalism External threat

Code	**Economy**
Definition	Contains discussion of economic concerns such as the federal budget deficit, inflation, debt, jobs, and unemployment.
Example	Discussion of state support for private Russian businesses abroad intensified after the speech provided by the first deputy prime minister and candidate for the president's office – Dmitry Medvedev – at an economic forum in Krasnodar. "It is the state's duty to ensure that the business has confidence that it can always rely on support from the state in the arena of world markets", Medvedev said. According to his words, this statement applies specifically to those areas in which there is global competition, including energy and engineering (Rossiia-Vesti, 05.02.2008).
Sub-codes	Positive
	Negative
	Neutral

Stage III: Validating the codes

A problematic issue that should be mentioned is that, when interpreting the results of the study, only one coder was involved in the coding process. However, an inter-coder reliability test was performed to check for reliability. Randomly selected texts were reviewed by the second coder to see whether the two rounds of coding coincided. Fifteen randomly selected texts were cross checked. Twenty-three out of twenty-six codes were coded similarly, representing an 88.5% agreement between the coders. The agreement coefficient is zero when absolutely no consensus has been reached between the coders. In such a situation, the data are not reliable. An agreement of 100% refers to the case when the coders reach agreement on every code, which means that the data are reliable. However, neither extreme is statistically plausible unless the coders copy from one another. Scholars suggest 66.7% of agreement as acceptable; when more-certain conclusions should be drawn from the data, the required threshold is 80% (Krippendorff 2004: 241). Although 88.5% agreement between the coders suggests that the results should be reliable, it is important to bear in mind that the number of cross-checked texts is relatively small, suggesting that the points mentioned above concerning the problems that arise when identifying biases due to subjectivity in interpreting texts should also be kept in mind.

5.4. Presidential elections of 2000

Background

In late 1999, due to President Boris Yeltsin's resignation, the Prime Minister, Vladimir Putin, assumed the duties of the President until the election of a new president[75]. Elections were held three months earlier than

---

[75] Under the Constitution, Article 36 (1), Law on the Election of President of the Russian Federation, the Prime Minister assumes the duties of the President until a new President is elected (OSCE 2000).

originally scheduled. A total of 33 candidates were nominated to run for the office. After a three-stage registration process[76], only 11 candidates were registered. Vladimir Zhirinovskii, the leader of the LDPR (Liberal Democratic Party of Russia) was added to the ballot list later due to problems encountered during his registration with the Central Electoral Commission. (For a short description of the candidates' biographies, see Table 5.6.).

Table 5.6. Names and brief description of the candidates

Candidate	Description of the candidate
Vladimir Putin	"A former KGB agent and former head of the FSB – the KGB's domestic successor – Vladimir Putin was named prime minister to replace Sergei Stepashin in the fall of 1999. President Boris Yeltsin resigned on 31 December 1999, making Putin acting President."
Gennadii Ziuganov	"A chairman of the Central Committee of the Communist Party of the Russian Federation (KPRF) and, as a State Duma deputy, leader of the KPRF faction in the State Duma. He ran for president in 1996, when he won sufficient votes in the first round to face Boris Yeltsin in the second round."
Grigorii Yavlinskii	"The head of the centre-right Yabloko movement, a deputy and faction leader. Yabloko, with Mr. Yavlinskii in the lead, won seats in the State Duma in 1993, 1995 and 1999. Yavlinskii also ran for president in 1996, receiving just over seven per cent of the vote."
Aman-Geldy Tuleev	"The second governor in the presidential election is KPRF-affiliated Aman Tuleev of the Kemerovo region. Tuleev was elected governor of Kemerovo in 1997 with almost 95 per cent of the vote."
Ella Pamfilova	"The leader of a civic organisation called "For Civil Dignity." Pamfilova was active in democratic politics in Russia for many years and in the December 1999 State Duma election led "For Civil Dignity" in an unsuccessful quest for seats in the lower house of the Russian Parliament."

---

[76] The first stage is the nomination; under the law, electoral associations (parties or blocs) or citizens forming "initiative voters' groups" can nominate a candidate. At the second stage, a candidate must gather signatures of eligible voters in support of his/her candidacy. Normally, no fewer than 1,000,000 signatures must be gathered; however, in the case of "case of early or repeated election", the law requires only half of the signatures. Thus, each candidate had to present 500,000 signatures (OSCE 19 May 2000, 17-19).

Stanislav Govorukhin	"A famous Russian film director and a State Duma deputy in the Fatherland faction".
Vladimir Zhirinovskii	"The nationalist leader of the Liberal Democratic Party of Russia (LDPR), who also ran for president in 1996 and won 5.8 per cent of the vote. He was at the heart of two CEC registration battles in the last year. First, his LDPR was refused registration by the CEC for the State Duma election on the grounds of inaccurate financial disclosures by several of its candidates, a decision that was later overturned by the courts. Despite these obstacles, LDPR won seats in the Duma for the third time since 1993. Second, Zhirinovskii himself was refused registration as a presidential candidate due to failure to declare an apartment owned by his son, only to be reinstated and allowed on the ballot by the Board of Appeals of the Russian Supreme Court."
Konstantin Titov	"The Samara region, of which Konstantin Titov is the governor, is one of the most prosperous regions in post-Communist Russia. Mr. Titov was able to attract a large amount of foreign investment and, as such, his region is one of the few that makes a net contribution to the budget of the Russian Federation. He is also chairman of the political council of the centre-right party, Union of Right Forces, which cleared the five per cent minimum vote threshold and, surprisingly, came in third in the 1999 State Duma elections."
Yuri Skuratov	"The suspended Prosecutor General of the Russian Federation. Former President Boris Yeltsin suspended Skuratov and tried to fire him but was unable to get the votes necessary in the Federation Council, the Russian Parliament's upper chamber. Skuratov made serious allegations of financial improprieties in the Yeltsin Administration, including the First Family".
Aleksei Podberezkin	"Leader of the civic and political movement, "Spiritual Heritage," Podberyozkin led his organisation to break its alliance with KPRF prior to the 1999 State Duma election. Spiritual Heritage participated on its own in that election but failed to reach the five per cent vote threshold needed to gain seats in the Duma."
Umar Dzhabrailov	"A co-owner of the Radisson-Slavyanskaya Hotel, a prosperous Moscow hotel, shopping and business centre."
Yevgenii Savostyanov	"A chair of the board of an organisation called the Moscow Fund for Presidential Programs and a former Yeltsin aide."

Source: IRI, Russia: Presidential Pre-Election Assessment Report, 20 March 2000, pp. 2-3.

Table 5.7. Election results, 2000

Candidates	Number	Total Vote in Percentage
Vladimir Putin	39,740,434	52.9
Gennadii Ziuganov	21,928,471	29.2
Grigorii Yavlinskii	4,351,452	5.8
Aman-Geldy Tuleev	2,217,361	3.0
Vladimir Zhirinovskii	2,026,513	2.7
Konstantin Titov	1,107,269	1.5
Ella Pamfilova	758,966	1.0
Stanislav Govorukhin	328,723	0.4
Yuri Skuratov	319,263	0.4
Aleksei Podberezkin	98,175	0.1
Umar Dzhabrailov	78,498	0.1
Against all	1,414,648	1.9
Electorate	109,372,046	-
Total Valid Votes	74,369,773	68.0
Invalid Votes	701,003	0.6
Total Votes	75,070,776	68.6

Source: CSPP 1996 - 2004

Within a few months, relatively unknown Putin's approval ratings skyrocketed, increasing from 31% in 1999 to 79% in 2000 (Treisman 2010). On March 26, 2000, the acting president won the presidential election with a majority. Putin had captured 52.9% of the vote, compared with 29.2% for Ziuganov, the leader of the Communist Party (KPRF – Communist Party of Russian Federation). Grigorii Yavlinskii, the head of the liberal party "Yabloko," was in third place, with 5.8% of the votes. Aman Tuleev, Kemerovo governor, received 3%, and Vladimir Zhirinovskii garnered 2.7%. The remaining six candidates, including Samara governor Konstantin Titov and former Prosecutor General Yuri Skuratov, each collected less than 2% of the vote. Overall voter turnout was 68.7%. Out of 11 candidates for the presidential office, only three were considered serious contenders. According to opinion polls and experts' predictions, candidates other than

Vladimir Putin, Gennadii Ziuganov, and Grigoii Yavlinskii were likely to obtain less than 3% of the vote (see Table 5.7).

Candidates' campaign strategies

Candidates' campaign strategies varied, for instance, Vladimir Putin said he would not campaign. Although at the end of December 1999, he published an article, "Russia on the threshold of the new millennium," and a compilation of journalists' interviews with Putin was published as a book [77]; also some newspapers also published "An open letter from Vladimir Putin to Russian voters," in which he announced that he is not planning any special campaign events; however, he considers it important to present the plan he has for the future of the country. Some of the priorities he outlines were property rights, a decent life for everyone, and prioritising national interests in the international arena (Kommersant 25 February 2000). Putin did not otherwise publish a pre-election programme, declaring that he would not campaign, and he refused to participate in television debates, presenting himself as "a man of action, not words." His successor, Dmitry Medvedev, used the same tactic in the 2008 presidential elections. Nevertheless, Putin received extensive coverage in the media as a prime minister and interim president, although a broad overview of his political and economic views could be deduced from some of his speeches and publications. For example, in "Russia on the threshold of the new millennium," emphasis was placed on building a well-functioning, effective and stable economy alongside a need for a strong state. He also advanced the idea that the state should not only enforce the law but also should comply with it, the same rhetoric was used by Medvedev later in 2008. Another important point that Putin made concerned the Russian ideal, claiming that Russia has its own unique path. Some of the topics that were

---

[77] The book was discussed in the news and by the Central Election Committee concerning whether it should be a part of an election campaign.

mentioned most frequently were "state," "government," "economy," "development," "freedom," and "property" (Polit-Gramota 2013).

Ziuganov's electoral programme was largely based on his party's programme for the parliamentary elections of 1999 (KPRF 1999). In terms of economic reforms, although Ziuganov did not propose re-nationalisation of the economy, he proposed state ownership of natural monopolies. He promised lower prices for energy and transport and called for support of a public sector that would increase social benefits, improve education, and contribute to culture and science. With respect to foreign policy, he proposed unification of Russia, Belarus, and Ukraine. He also accused the United States of having "expansionist interests" and opposed improving relations with NATO. Similar to Putin, Ziuganov favoured a stronger state and a spiritual revival of Russia. In the case of Chechnia, Ziuganov supported Putin's policy but proposed a plan of economic recovery in the region.

Grigorii Yavlisky's programme was pro-market economy, lower taxes, and an effective state. He proposed stronger control over the use of budget funds and promised to fight the "shadow economy" (Rossiiskaia Gazeta, 22 March 2000; Yabloko 1999). Not unlike Putin, Ziuganov, and Zhirinovskii, Yavlinskii also promised to raise social benefits and stop the delay of wage payments. He also promised to focus more on civil rights and media freedom and emphasised the importance of an independent judiciary. With respect to the Chechen war, Yavlinskii emphasised the need for open negotiations with legitimate representatives of the region (EIM 2000).

Zhirinovskii's programme included ten key points: 1) vertical power; 2) economic amnesty – those who return money to the Russian economy are not to be prosecuted; 3) the USSR's debt recovery; 4) state monopoly on certain products; 5) increasing budget funds to expand social spending; 6) supporting national agriculture; 7) fighting corruption and crime; 8) reducing taxes to 30%; 9) supporting the army; and 10) a new foreign policy (Rossiiskaia Gazeta, 18 Febryary 2000). Zhirinovskii's foreign policy programme was the most striking. He proposed to incorporate Belarus,

Ukraine, Kazakhstan, and parts of the Baltic States into Russia and to achieve closer relations with countries such as Iraq, Libya, Cuba, and Vietnam (EIM 2000). He also mentioned that the West is interested in Russia's losing its power and therefore all foreign consultants should be removed from the government (Rossiiskaia Gazeta, 18 February 2000). Aman Tuleyev's programme was similar to Ziuganov's; it was even noted that he was actually supporting Putin's candidacy for presidential office but was running to undermine Gennadii Ziuganov (EIM 2000). The reasons for this programme ranged from wanting to challenge Ziuganov for the leadership of the KPRF to simply helping the Putin camp to split the communist vote among several candidates. Titov's programme was similar to Yavlinskii's.

One of the most notable aspects of Vladimir Putin's campaign during the presidential elections in 2000 was his refusal to participate in any of the TV debates or to use the state-owned media free time and space provided to all candidates. At the same time, he extensively used his position as a prime minister and an acting president to criss-cross the country, performing all types of duties in the last few weeks of the electoral campaign. His travels and activities were widely covered in the media. In most cases, he was portrayed as a man of action.

Because Putin refused to participate in debates with other candidates, they had no other choice but to attack one another. As is noted in the EIM report, the candidates focussed on criticising those whose political views were closest to their own. For example, Ziuganov was attacked by member of KPRF Tuleyev, whereas Yavlisnky was criticised by similarly liberal-minded Titov and Govorukhin. The absence of Putin from TV debates made them less interesting because some candidates also decided to send their representatives to participate in the TV-debates on their behalf. In addition, when campaigning for their own candidacy, Podberezkin and Tuleyev expressed their support for Putin. Govorukhin, Pamfilova, Dzhaibrailov and Zhirinovskii united against Yavlinsky, arguing among other things that his party over-spent the permitted budget for the campaign (EIM 2000).

The war in Chechnia also played a role in the campaign. Most of the television channels and newspapers reported about the war. Interestingly, all of the candidates supported the government policy in Chechnia. Only Yavlinskii was critical, but his criticism was directed at the tactics used rather than at the war as such. Among newspapers, Novaia Gazeta was critical about government actions and losses the war caused on both sides. Television channels were rather supportive of government on this issue[78] (EIM 2000; OSCE 2000).

Results of content analysis

Putin received much wider coverage in broadcast media than in print media. Between 15 February and 26 March, among the analysed media outlets he was mentioned 1928 times and in 545 documents on television, and 824 times in 146 documents in newspapers. Ziuganov was mentioned only approximately 50% as often on television (281 times). Yavlinskii and Zhirinovskii received relatively equal numbers of mentions both on TV (Yavlisnkii: 142; Zhirinovskii: 157) and in newspapers (54 and 40, respectively[79]).

Agenda setting – most frequent topics

Television: Putin's promises to address social issues received the highest coverage. Table 5.8. presents the most frequently addressed topics. Among them were raising wages and pensions, improving life in Siberia, taking better care of orphanages, and better medical care. Putin's promises

---

[78] Information is based on reports by EIM and OSCE: EIM (2000). Monitoring the Media Coverage of the March 2000 Presidential Elections in Russia, Final Report, August 2000; OSCE (2000). ODIHR Election Observation. Russian Federation, Presidential Election, Final Report, March 26, 2000.

[79] For details, see Table 5.13.

appealed to various strata of the population including military, veterans, women, and workers.

Print media: Some of the most frequently covered topics in the print media included the economy, governance, and social issues. When reporting on Putin, topics such as economic development, stability, and corruption were also mentioned. As on television, economic and social policies received coverage, albeit on a smaller scale than on television. Candidates other than Putin generally did not receive significant newspaper attention; however, Novaia Gazeta openly supported Yavlinsky's candidacy and his economic policies were mentioned on Kommersant. When discussing Ziuganov's candidacy, the same topics – economic and social policies and issues of governance – were covered most often. The issue of the North Caucasus also received coverage not only on television but also in the print media; most of the attention on television was focussed on economic recovery in the region, whereas newspapers were critical about the government's actions during the war. The frequencies at which the topics were mentioned are provided in Table 5.9. As seen, Channel One and Rossiia follow similar patterns in coverage, particularly with respect to discussion of Putin's activities or views on social issues, the economy, and foreign affairs. The topic of the economy also appears in coverage of other candidates more often than any other policy-related topic. Other than that topic, mostly personality characteristics of other candidates are reported. The high frequency of the topic of economic policies might be for any of the following three reasons: 1) the topic is important to the public; 2) as stated by one of the interviewed journalists, television sets the agenda and provokes national interest in the subject, so that newspapers must respond to that interest; and 3) the media agenda might be set by the campaign agendas. As was noticed in the previous section on campaign strategies, Putin's campaign mostly accentuated two groups of issues: social and economic. That pattern was mirrored in the media's agenda. However, it is difficult to establish a concrete link. It is not only that the ruling elite sets the agenda, telling the people what they should be interested in. If the results of opinion polls (Levada Centre 2012), which show that a majority of Russians are concerned with economic wellbeing, are taken seriously, then it is more likely that the ruling elite reflects those opinions and concerns and adjusts its policy platforms accordingly to receive higher approval ratings and, consequently, votes.

Table 5.8. Topics most frequently appearing on TV news

Channel One	Rossiia
- Increasing wages - Distributing financial benefits on Victory Day - Social development - Protecting the soldiers who participated in World War II - Covering travel fees for veterans who decide to participate in the parade - Allocating additional funds directed to completing construction of a rehabilitation centre for children - Putin's wife visits a children's hospital and shows interest in social problems - Increasing pensions and salaries - Improving the situation of orphans and children - Developing a system for extra-curricular activities for children - Improving the pension system - Funding of important social construction objects that must be completed - Improving and raising from zero the health care system, education, and energy sector in Chechnia	- Improving healthcare - Raising wages - Toughening control over allocation of budget finances directed toward paying wages - Conferring the title of Hero of Russia to military service members - Payments in honour of the Victory Day celebration - Inviting to the parade veterans not only from Russia but also from the CIS and Baltic States - Putin does not intend to leave war veterans or others on their own - Protect all the veterans of World War II - Raise the pension - Presidential decree on payment of an additional pension to veterans - Widows of veterans will receive minimum pensions - Preparing programs designed to help veterans - Putin ordered the allocation of an apartment in St. Petersburg to the widow of a General killed in Grozny - Creation of a civilised labour market - Defending the rights of working people - Trade unions will become an influential political force - Putin ordered that the conflict that transpired between the security and factory workers in a pharmaceuticals factory be resolved

Table 5.9. Topics and their frequencty by media outlet, 2000

Candidates	Categories	Novaia gazeta	Kommersant	Rossiia	Channel One
Putin	General rhetoric	-	3	-	7
	Policy issues	10	7	40	57
	Personality	11	2	6	7
Ziuganov	General rhetoric	-	-	-	-
	Policy issues	1	3	-	4
	Personality	1	1	1	2
Zhirinovskii	General rhetoric	-	-	-	-
	Policy issues	-	-	-	-
	Personality	-	1	2	-
Yavlinskii	General rhetoric	-	-	-	-
	Policy issues	-	1	2	1
	Personality	5	-	2	2

Framing

When analysing news coverage in more detail, one can observe that the same piece of news might be framed in either a positive or a negative light by the media. For example, when reporting about the war in Chechnia, national TV channels would usually touch upon issues such as improving the healthcare system, rebuilding the economy, and improving the education system after the war, or about the attacks by the terrorists, whereas the non-state newspaper—Novaia Gazeta—would devote most of its coverage of the Chechen war to casualties on both sides. The results of content analysis clearly illustrate this point.

Television: On both state channels, Channel One and Rossiia, Putin was broadcast as an active leader crisscrossing the country and solving the problems of "ordinary men." For example, television content broadcast about the Victory Day served well Putin's efforts to gain wider support.

Not only did he visit veteran soldiers in different regions but he also distributed financial benefits to the veterans of World War II and promised to cover the travel expenses of all the veterans in the CIS region who would like to participate in the Victory Day parade. The event benefitted Putin's campaign in several ways, making a bold official financial gesture, paying respect to veterans, and sending a message to the wider population that Putin is willing to protect Russians regardless of where they live, to strengthen the military, and not discriminate against veterans based on their current geographical location.

International Women's Day was another occasion that provided candidates an opportunity, this time to reach out to female voters. On the eve of this holiday, Putin paid a visit to the so-called women's capital of Russia, the city of Ivanovo. Putin presented state awards to ten women living in the city of Ivanovo and congratulated everyone with the upcoming holiday. Not only residents of Ivanovo were awarded; women in military service located in Chechnia received presents from Putin. These events were broadcast on state TV channel Rossiia.

Source: Rossiia - Vesti
Date: 07.03.2000
Olga Kokorekina

Today, Vladimir Putin visited Ivanovo. As recognised by the acting president, he wanted to go to the capital of Russian women on the eve of March 8. The Acting President went immediately from the airport to the meeting in the textile fabric factory.	Implication that Putin is a man of action
Business executives reported to the honoured guest about the workflow, not hiding problems/obstacles that they confront in achieving excellence.	Highlighting problems and an emphasis on problems not being hidden but addressed
Putin has promised full support and help to the textile fabric workers, but said that production workers must change their attitude to business, whereas local authorities must actively provide businesses tax benefits/exemptions.	Direct and personal promise of support by the acting president

The upcoming elections were not mentioned at all; however, Anatoly Chubais and actor Mikhail Boyarsky were seen in the hall.	Subtle reference to fairness of Putin's election campaign
The acting President admitted that visiting a textile fabric was only an excuse to come to Ivanovo. Putin presented state awards to 10 women living in the city of Ivanovo and congratulated everybody concerning the upcoming holiday.	Appeal to women

Compliments paid to Putin by women were also broadcast on the same channel. Personality traits such as perseverance, willpower, softness and an ability to be moved were also mentioned. Even his gait did not escape attention. Other candidates have also been covered, although perhaps in less detail. For example, Rossiia reported that Ziuganov came to congratulate women on this special occasion despite his illness.

Source: Rossiia - Vesti Source 06.03.2000 Vasiliy Kiknadze The leader of the Communists, Gennady Ziuganov, was absolutely unreachable by his electorate in the last few days.	Gennadii Ziuganov
Referring to the March draft, he found himself in ill health and even cancelled a series of pre-election meetings with representatives of science and the military. However, tonight Ziuganov and his wife are going to the Taganka Theatre. He explained that he could not deny women the pleasure of seeing him on the eve of the 8th of March.	
At the Taganka, communist supporters gathered today to congratulate the beautiful half of humanity.	
Gennady Ziuganov, the Communist Party leader, stated, "The woman – is the perfection. All the best that nature has created is inherent in women. That is why for Women's Day we dropped everything, forgot about sickness and came here for the celebration. We will have a good feast here…"	

In terms of foreign policy, Putin showed openness to cooperation with international organisations, even NATO. Rossiia broadcast excerpts from

Putin's interview with David Frost, a British journalist, in which Putin said that he considers Russia a part of European culture and cannot imagine his country apart from Europe and so-called civilised world. He said that Russia wants cooperation based on equality and mutual trust. Some of the topics that received broad coverage on TV were Putin's intention to address social issues, stabilise the economy, fight against corruption, and establish a "dictatorship" of the law. These issues were broadcast repeatedly both on Channel One and Rossiia.

Concerning personality traits, many, including other candidates for the presidential office, the director of the World Bank, political scientists, experts, and former and present politicians in Russia and abroad have expressed their opinions about Putin's character and his capabilities. On Channel One, for example, Ella Pamfilova declared her support and approval of Putin. She said that although she was suspicious in the beginning, Putin's modesty charmed her and she believes that he is going to work in the best interests of the country (Channel One, Novosti, 17 March 2000). Others (producer and director of the Mariinskii Theatre) noted during the interviews that the most important thing for Putin is the future destiny of the country, its people, and its culture (Channel One, Novosti, 14 February 2000). Boris Eltsin mentioned, "Putin takes the right direction and sticks to it; he is a man with an internal power, firm, resolute, and at the same time capable of understanding human feelings" (Channel One, Novosti, 23 February 2000). Rossiia reported that a political movement uniting Muslims in Russia – "Refah" – expressed its willingness to support Putin because he is the only one who has the qualities necessary to be Russia's leader. They expect that Putin will become a guarantor of social stability in Russia and peace in the North Caucasus (4 March 2000). The president of the World Bank commented that Putin provides the impression of a well-informed person, particularly concerning questions related to the economy. He highlighted that Putin is a very serious man with an impressive personality and felt that he is a man who can be trusted (Rossiia, Vesti, 15 March 2000). United States Secretary of State Madeleine

Albright was also quoted as commenting on Putin being a well-informed man and an interesting conversationalist. She also mentioned that he gave a very positive impression of an "open," "constructive," and "patriotic" person. Channel One (Novosti, 28 February 2000) has quoted Vladimir Putin saying that as a candidate, he has no moral ground to make promises that his government will not be able to fulfil. According to Putin, he cannot work that way, i.e., make promises and, after being elected, say, "Elections are over. Good-bye; now I have four years. I don't need anything else, and when the next elections come, I will make up another lie." Here again the emphasis is on Putin being a man of action and not of empty promises.

With respect to critical views expressed on state television, Rossiia broadcast a report about a demonstration that occurred on March 7th in Moscow. The organisers of the demonstration were calling for the electorate to vote against all, claiming that elections were not fair because citizens did not have sufficient viable choices from which to choose. However, the framing of the event was noteworthy. A few participants of the demonstration were questioned. One of them was a young student who said that she is dissatisfied that there is only one viable candidate at the moment and that she would like to have alternatives. She was presented as "Anna – student, who is not yet 18 and cannot participate in elections, but nevertheless calls to vote against all" (Rossiia, 7 March 2000). In general, people participating in the demonstration were described as "very few, and the number of pickets exceeds the number of people," and "when asked, some participants said that harsh life conditions make them take part in this demonstration" (as though they had been paid for their participation). Both Rossiia and Channel One reported similarly; the report capturesd critical views about the incumbent government or elections, but immediately following the criticism, the views were dismissed as irrelevant because the source is not sufficiently reliable.

Regardless, note that other candidates' policy platforms have also been discussed on television. For example, during the press overview, a publication by Komsomolskaia Pravda was presented. The publication presented Yavlinskii's letter, in which he set out the main paragraphs of his campaign, such as determining the productive interests of citizens, strengthening and developing civil society, the importance of the family institution, and property, which helps to accumulate and realise the potential of every individual and provides him an opportunity to be free.

Source: Rossiia - Vesti
Source 14.03.2000

"Komsomolskaia Pravda" published a letter of another presidential candidate – Grigorii Yavlinskii– in which he sets out the main points of his electoral programme. According to Yavlinskii, a democratic policy, which would tackle problems Russia faces, must first isolate genuine and productive interests of the people, strengthening the development of civil society. Yavlinskii believes that property allows you to collect and realise the potential of each individual and provides him the opportunity to be free. He also attaches great importance to the family and is convinced that the state must strengthen the institution of the family in every possible way.	Grigorii Yavlinskii/ Policy platform: Civil society Governance Property rights Economy Family Social issues

In addition, the TV channel Rossiia and to a lesser extent Channel One broadcast interviews with candidates and experts and broadcast excerpts from newspapers containing a critical evaluation of the fairness of presidential elections. Candidates mostly claimed that Putin received unfairly broad coverage on state TV as a prime minister and an interim president. As a response, Channel One transmitted a comment from Putin's political campaign staff stating that they refuse to use official airtime allocated to the candidates to level the playing field. According to the comments, because Vladimir Putin had sufficient opportunities to communicate with voters and present his political position, it would be unfair to use additional airtime (Novosti, 3 March 2000).

Print media: If television was mostly broadcasting positive remarks about Putin, his policies, and capabilities, the print media was more critical. For example, Novaia Gazeta published an article that listed and compared the praise, public congratulations, and greetings addressed to Putin and those addressed to Brezhnev. The article did not directly criticise but used irony to show that although times have changed, attitudes towards the leaders remained unchanged. Other articles published in Novaia Gazeta contained similar criticism of general attitudes towards the leaders (be that tsar, baron, the first secretary of the communist party, or a president) in the form of irony.

The criticism in Novaia Gazeta was mostly directed at the situation in Chechnia. The newspaper showed open support to Yavlinskii and was very critical about the North Caucasus, human rights, and media freedom issues under Putin's governance. Kommersant published several analytical articles critically assessing Putin's economic policy proposals. Ziuganov's policies were also discussed in the press, being occasionally framed negatively and other times in a neutral tone. The same was true for Yavlinskii.

Overall, it can be concluded that Putin did enjoy wider coverage in the media; however, other candidates' policy platforms and activities were discussed, printed, and broadcast. Critical remarks were noticed mostly in the print media, and the target of criticism was not only the opposition but also the incumbent candidate.

5.5. Presidential elections of 2008

Background

At the end of his second and, according to the constitution, his final term in the office, Putin announced that he would not abolish constitutional term limits and that he intended to step down by the expiration of his second term. However, in December 2007, he publicly endorsed his First Prime Minister Dmitrii Medvedev's candidacy for the presidential office, reassuring the public that Medvedev would keep the political course established by his predecessor, Putin. Moreover, it was announced that

Putin had accepted Medvedev's request to serve as prime minister were Medvedev to be elected. In 2005, Putin appointed Medvedev first Prime Minister. Medvedev had since been in charge of implementing various "national projects" aimed at tackling social and other issues. Previously, between 2000 and 2005, Medvedev held the Gazprom chairmanship.

Four candidates were nominated by their parties: Dmitrii Medvedev (United Russia), Gennadii Ziuganov (KPRF), Vladimir Zhirinovskii (LDPR), and Boris Nemcov (SPS [80]). The Democratic Party of Russia (DPR) supported Andrei Bogdanov's candidacy. In addition, a group supporting Mihail Kas'ianov's candidacy was registered. Consequently, on the 26th of December, the Central Electoral Committee registered Ziuganov and Zhirinovskii. Later in January, Medvedev received his registration. According to election rules, other potential candidates had to gather two million signatures of supporters within a few weeks. Among those candidates were Kas'ianov, Bogdanov, and Nemtsov. Nemtsov revoked his application in late December, claiming that only one candidate should represent the "democratic opposition" and that Kas'ianov should be that candidate. Another candidate from the opposition, Garri Kasparov, said that "United Civil Front group was repeatedly turned down in its attempts to rent halls for a meeting to nominate him as its candidate" (CRS 2008: 2). Both Kas'ianov and Bogdanov collected the necessary number of signatures; however, the CEC refused Kas'ianov's registration, arguing that 15.57% of his signatures were defective. A later recount showed that 13.38% defects were reported. In the case of Bogdanov, according to CEC, the number of defective signatures did not exceed the formal limit of 5%, hence, he has been registered as a candidate.

Long-term election observation mission run by ODIHR decided not to send the observers to monitor parliamentary elections of 2007 and presidential elections of 2008, as the observers were continuously denied entry visas. In addition, Russia established a limit on the number of

---

[80] Soiuz Pravih Sil

observers, claiming it can accept only 70, while during the parliamentary elections of 2003, 400 monitored the elections (European Council of foreign Relations 2007; Kommersant 2008). Moreover, "amendments to the electoral legislation in 2005 banned electoral observers from non-governmental organizations, permitting only representatives of the candidates and of media to observe voting" (CRS 2008: 3). The reasoning behind not letting the international observers and non-governmental organisations to monitor the elections might be an attempt to hide and increasing level of fraud committed on the election day itself, during tabulation and vote count. CEC refusal to register some members of opposition as candidates also signals that the regime has changed its strategy from subtle ways of influencing the voters (f.ex.: via the media) to less concealed ways of manipulating the electoral outcomes.

Table 5.10. Names and brief description of the candidates, 2008

Dmitrii Medvedev	Medvedev held the chairmanship of Gazprom beginning in 2000. In 2005, he was appointed Deputy Prime Minister by Putin and was tasked with implementing various "national projects" and addressing social service and other reforms. His candidacy for the presidential office was supported by incumbent president Vladimir Putin, and he was nominated by the parties United Russia, Fair Russia, Agrarian Party, Russian Ecological Party "The Greens" and Civilian Power.
Gennadii Ziuganov	Leader of the Communist Party of the Russian Federation and former presidential candidate; he ran for president in 1996, 2000, and 2008.
Vladimir Zhirinovskii	Deputy Speaker of the State Duma and leader of the Liberal Democratic Party of Russia. He ran for the presidency on three prior occasions: in 1991, 1996 and 2000.
Andrei Bogdanov	Leader of the Democratic Party of Russia.

Elections were held on 2 March 2008. In the end, the voters had to choose among four candidates – Medvedev, Ziuganov, Zhirinovskii, and Bogdanov. Medvedev gathered an overwhelming majority of votes – 70.3% support – winning the elections in the first round. Approximately 18% of votes were in support of Ziuganov. Zhirinovskii received 9.3%, and Bogdanov 1.3%.

Table 5.11. Election results, 2008

Candidates	Number of votes	Total Vote in Percentage
Dmitrii Medvedev	52,530,712	70.3
Gennadii Ziuganov	13,243,550	17.7
Vladimir Zhirinovskii	6,988,510	9.3
Andrei Bogdanov	968,344	1.3
Electorate	107,222,016	-
Invalid votes	1,015,533	0.9
Valid votes	73,731,116	68.8
Total votes	74,746,649	69.7

Source: CRS, 2008

Candidates' campaign strategies

During the electoral campaign of 2008, Medvedev used a strategy similar to the one used by Putin in 2000. He refused to participate in TV debates and did not use the free air time and space accorded to him by the electoral committee for promoting his candidacy. However, he was actively traveling across the country, controlling the execution of national projects focussed mostly on improvements in the social sphere, for example, by providing equipment to state medical centres and providing support for schools and hospitals. In terms of ideological orientation, the emphasis was on continuing the course taken by Putin, retaining the same team that was working and governing the country for the last eight years under the leadership of Vladimir Putin. Around election time, Putin published a programme, "Putin's Plan," a plan that the country would follow if Medvedev were elected. Some of the main ambitions of the plan were improving the health care system, improving education, providing better housing, increasing wages and pensions, improving the effectiveness of social services, ensuring citizens' safety and providing them legal protection (Plan Putina 2007).

According to Golos (2008), election reports indicate that Medvedev's campaign mostly used slogans such as "for stability and succession" and "continuity of Putin's course". These two topics received broad coverage on television. The fact that Medvedev's candidacy was endorsed by Putin was mostly described and presented as a positive phenomenon on television. The endorsement was also a recurring topic in the print media. Golos also states that the economic programme for the coming four years was based on four "I's" – institutions, infrastructure, innovations, and investments. To address these questions, he proposed to improve the quality of laws and their effectiveness, reduce taxes to stimulate innovations and partial investments in human capital, build powerful a financial system, modernise transport and energy infrastructure, and realise social development in the country (RIA Novosti, 26 February 2008).

Ziuganov's campaign became more active only in the beginning of February and followed the usual communist patterns—distribution of traditional communist newspapers and meetings against rising prices for grocery products and communal services (Nickol 2008). The main themes of Ziuganov's programme were nationalisation of natural resources and strategically important industries of the economy, changing the laws hindering the material wellbeing of citizens, improving infrastructure and agriculture, modernising production, cleaning of the electoral process, safeguarding that process against bureaucratic pressure, private capital and crime, focussing particularly on the military forces, and providing a high quality of education and medical care to the nation (RIA Novosti, 26 February 2008; KPRF 2008).

Zhirinovskii's campaign mostly used paid and free airtime on television provided to candidates and space in the print media. His programme was largely focussed on centralisation of power and some economic reforms related to the development of small and medium businesses (RIA Novosti, 26 February 2008; LDPR 2008). The proposals were quite vague and consisted of very broad ideas. Bogdanov's campaign went almost unnoticed (Nickol 2008). Some of his main policy proposals were related to creating closer economic and political links with the European Union, Russia's entry into the Schengen zone, increase of wages and pensions, reform of the education system and active participation in the Bologna process (RIA Novosti, 26 February 2008).

Results of content analysis

Golos (2008) reports that Medvedev dominated television. He received 76% of the television time devoted to candidates during the first two weeks of February 2008. Zhirinovskii received approximately 11% and Ziuganov approximately 9%. The least coverage was received by Bogdanov – only 3.8%.

Agenda setting

Television: TV news mostly covered events related to national projects, which were led by Medvedev. National projects primarily included social benefits to retired people, improving the military, building of new houses for young families, improving the health care system, and providing hospitals with new technologies. Although the tone was neutral and not too many positive adjectives were used, the general impression from the TV media report was very positive; the image of Medvedev was one of the "rescuer and supporter" of ordinary people. In the majority of cases, the fact that Medvedev was not completely independent of Putin's influence was described as a positive outcome. Issues of stability and continuity of the old order received extensive coverage.

A study of nationwide surveys by Colton and Hale (2009) shows that at least part of Putin's votes resulted from his personal appeal and from economic conditions. The study showed that Medvedev's popularity was also based on similar appeals. When media content of 2008 is analysed, at least on television channels, economic and social benefits, personal traits, and references to continuation of the previously led course were widely discussed.

Table 5.12. Topics and their frequency by media outlet, 2008

Candidates	Categories	gazeta.ru	lenta.ru	Novaiagazeta	Vedomosti	Kommersant	Rossiia	Channel One
Medvedev	General rhetoric	2	1	1	4	3	14	12
	Policy issues	103	9	14	34	57	103	79
	Personality	13	3	8	19	25	22	10
Ziuganov	General rhetoric	-	-	-	-	-	-	-
	Policy issues	-	-	-	2	2	-	4
	Personality	6	2	1	1	14	-	2
Zhirinovskii	General rhetoric	-	-	-	-	1	-	1
	Policy issues	1	2	-	2	-	1	2
	Personality	2	4	1	-	11	2	2
Bogdanov	General rhetoric	-	-	-	-	-	-	1
	Policy issues	-	-	-	-	-	-	-
	Personality	5	1	3	-	4	1	5

Print media and online media: Each of the four candidates' personal characteristics, his capabilities, and independence in decision making were discussed in the print media. However, concerning policy proposals, be they related to foreign affairs, social issues, economic policies, or governance, only Medvedev's views or actions were presented in the media. Ziuganov's social policy was mentioned twice in Vedomosti, and in

Kommersant, there was once mentioned that KPRF remains afloat because there is a demand by the Russian public for a party of this sort. Online media repeated the same patterns as the print media. Most discussed topics were related to candidates' personality traits. Any other topics were presented only in relation to Medvedev. The progress of "national projects" under Medvedev's supervision was covered in abundance.

The agenda related to elections, candidates, and policy received most of the attention. These areas are presented in Table 5.12. As seen, Medvedev was mentioned most often on almost every dimension, but particularly on policy issues. Two of his most debated and often addressed personal characteristics were his abilities and the fact that he is dependent upon Putin. Candidates other than Medvedev were almost ignored; they were mentioned and their policy platforms discussed only a few times. Moreover, it was largely their personal characterises that received media attention. Overall, the coverage was very unbalanced. Instead, the exact issues emphasised in the Medvedev campaign, i.e., economic stability, continuation, and social issues, dominated the media debate.

Framing

Television: Some scholars (Worcester 1991) argue that the publication of the polls predicting the electoral outcomes might also have influenced the election outcomes. Undecided voters might vote for the candidate supported by the majority. Robert Worcester's study shows that approximately 3% of voters in Britain are influenced by opinion polls. However, as McNair (2007) notes, arguments of this type are highly speculative, particularly considering how difficult it is to establish a connection between votes and media effects. Nevertheless, during the six weeks before the election day, opinion polls and forecasts about who was most likely to come to power were presented 65 times. Most of the predictions were presented not as opinion polls listing the names of all the candidates but rather as a statement – for example, "according to opinion polls, the majority will vote for Medvedev." Although value judgement (positive or negative) usually was not involved, a constant reminder that at least 70% of the population was willing to vote for Medvedev might have had an effect on voters.

Usually, candidates other than Medvedev did not receive much coverage; they were simply ignored. On television channels, opposition was mostly either mocked or presented as unreliable and incapable. For example, Bogdanov's candidacy did not receive much attention overall, but several references to the character of Bogdanov, emphasising his personality, his appearance, haircut, and personal web site, gave an impression of a very unserious candidate. This approach was also used when presenting others. The stories about Kas'ianov involved references to vote buying and signature fraud. Media reported the public fight between Zhirinovskii and Ziuganov's subordinate; the lawsuit between the two and finally a discussion of fines imposed on Ziuganov were presented in the media. However, the policy proposals and party platforms proposed by these candidates were not discussed. Even when Zhirinovskii was announcing his plans as a future president, the report did not give an impression of a serious candidate. Excerpts from coverage of television channels of non-Kremlin candidates are presented to illustrate an extreme form of belittling and ridiculing of a candidate.

About Bogdanov, the leader of the Democratic Party of Russia on television

However, Bogdanov never reached the court. He went to watch a football game and cheer for his favourite team. Andrei Bogdanov, leader of the Democratic Party of Russia, stated, "It is always a tradition to drink 50-70 grams before the match. I think it won't hurt any real man to do the same" (Channel One- News, 25.02.2008).	Negatively framed comments and reports on Andrei Bogdanov
Another presidential candidate – Andrei Bogdanov – conversed with foreign journalists. When asked about his extraordinary haircut, he said, "The important thing is not what is on the head but what is in the head." According to Bogdanov's words, in his head he has a good brain. The leader of the Democratic Party feels	Emphasis on ridiculousness of the candidate

that Russia should join NATO (Channel One - News, 12.02.2008).

A leader of the Democratic Party (DP), Andrey Bogdanov, was slightly worried about meeting journalists. He has moved the flag of the party to the centre of the hall. He has announced that he cannot be called a man from nowhere. Here is a photo made in 1991. He is at a meeting of the Democratic Party organised against the Belavezha Accords. Now, principle attention is not given to street protests but rather to Internet propaganda. The leader of the DP is on the net every night. Andrey Bogdanov stated, "I have had a blog for three years now. At that time, I could not even imagine I would lead a party and run for the presidential office. The blog is devoted to me and to my life. You can see for yourself my attendance of football matches" (Channel One - News, 31.01.2008).	Portrayal of the candidate as an unserious contender
According to RIA Novosti, on Wednesday, media outlets published reports about a brawl that allegedly occurred between representatives of presidential candidate Vladimir Zhirinovskii and Andrei Bogdanov after recording a televised debate on the channel "Star". According to the official website of the Russian Democratic Party, whose leader is Bogdanov, during the programme, Zhirinovskii repeatedly insulted Nikolai Bogdanov's confidant Gotz, who participated in the debate instead of the leader of the DP. According to the same source, at the end of the debates, Zhirinovskii ordered his security team to handle the opponent. Zhirinovsky's reaction to this message is not yet clear (Rossiia - Vesti, 22.03.2008).	Candidates' engagement in a fight

Print and online media: **Although discussion of policy proposals occurred in newspapers, discussions of candidates' personalities and personal characteristics prevailed. Only Medvedev's economic policy programme was presented and discussed. In the newspapers, there was critical discussion of these policies. The online media's coverage mostly retained a neutral tone.**

Personal characteristics of candidates, 2008

"Public Opinion Fund" (FOM – Fond Obsshestvennogo mneniia) attempted to draw portraits of candidates based on citizens' opinion about them. For instance, some Russians (8%) consider Gennadii Ziuganov a "blabber mouth" who cares only about his own well-being, and that is why he "talks much but does nothing" (Kommersant 22.02.2008).

Ziuganov's personality traits. Emphasis on his inability to act.

Ziuganov/Capability/Negative

In particular, the LDPR leader Vladimir Zhirinovskii showed unregistered land in the Saratov region and income of more than 12 million rubles in deposits. Leader of the DPR (Democratic Party of Russia) Andrei Bogdanov DWP did not submit information about the second apartment of his wife, and Communist Party leader Gennady Ziuganov failed to declare gifts worth 17 thousand Rubles (Kommersant 12.02.2008).

Report on Bogdanov and Zhirinovskii. Both are accused of not following the rule of the electoral commission concerning full disclosure of income and property during registration of their candidacy.

At the same time, according to opinion polls collected by "Levada-Center" among 1600 residents in 147 settlements in 53 regions of the country throughout the whole period of the electoral campaign, Vladimir Zhirinovskii has the highest anti-rating among Russian politicians. Forty-four per cent of those polled by "Levada-Center" in January said that in no circumstances would they vote for the leader of the LDPR. Thirty-three per cent are completely unsatisfied by Gennady Ziuganov. Twenty-five per cent said they would not vote for Andrey Bogdanov. Dmitry Medvedev has the lowest anti-ratings – 11% (Kommersant 22.02.2008).

Bogdanov/Zhirinovskii/Personality/Negative

Emphasise on trustworthiness and on approval by the population.

Ziuganov/Bogdanov/Zhirinovskii/Personality/not trustworthy – Negative

Medvedev/Personality/most trustworthy among four candidates – Positive

According to the prosecutor of the Yaroslavl region, Bogdanov's assistants were prosecuted for forging more than 300 signatures for Bogdanov. This accusation is combined with a case of fraud committed in Kas'anov's favour (Vedomosti 31.01.2008).

Candidate being accused of fraudulent activities

Bogdanov/Personality/Negative

5.6. Discussion: drawing comparisons

By the end of Yeltsin's second term in office, his popularity ratings had dwindled to 8% (Treisman 2010; Levada Center 2000). During his New Year speech on 31 December 1999, Yeltsin announced his resignation and named Vladimir Putin as his chosen successor for the presidential office. His early resignation served to move the elections from June to March. When the former director of the Federal Security Service, Vladimir Putin, assumed the position of Prime Minister in August 1999, his popularity rating was as low as two per cent, but by November, it had risen to 42%, reaching 62% after the Duma elections. By February 2000, public opinion polls showed that slightly less than 60% of the population supported Putin, twice as many as those who supported the KPRF leader Gennadii Ziuganov (approximately 20%), whereas the leader of "Yabloko" — Grigorii Yavlisnkii — received less than 10% support. Putin won in the March elections that, according to international election observers, were marked with numerous irregularities, securing a majority of votes in the first run-off election. Together with vagueness in legislation concerning financial disclosure requirements for candidates and the arbitrariness of their enforcement, biased media reporting of the campaign was outlined by international observers (Freedom House 2001; OCSE 2000; EIM 2000). The results of the media monitoring performed by the European Institute for the Media during the Russian presidential elections showed that Vladimir Putin dominated media coverage. Putin's success and high popularity ratings were attributed to different factors. Some claimed that economic recovery and stabilisation were key; others argued that Putin's ratings benefitted from the war in Chechnia and from the firm position he assumed in relation to the rest of the world. Regardless of the real causes of Putin's popularity, it was the media that broadcast news related to the Chechen war, to social benefits that people might receive because of economic growth and stability, and to Putin's vision of Russia in the international arena.

Framing: As Vitaly Silitski (2009) argues, in Russia, as in many other modern autocracies, rulers prefer "manufacturing consent" to using direct repression and force. One of the tools that Silitski mentions is the use of information and propaganda to discredit opponents. This case study shows that there is significant evidence of such usage – for example, ignoring the opposition, presenting them as incapable, ridiculing them, belittling their significance as politicians, and discrediting candidates as individuals on a personal level. To illustrate, during the 2000 pre-election campaign period, Ziuganov did receive negative coverage, both on television and in the print media. His policies were criticised but in a more serious manner. In 2000, Ziuganov's economic policies were mentioned either positively or negatively in four news excerpts, whereas his personality and capabilities were assessed five times. The picture is completely different in 2008, when economic policies are mentioned only twice, and personality traits 28 times. If negative coverage might contribute to popularity of a candidate, ridiculing and discrediting might have opposite effects.

In contrast to the 2008 elections, in 2000, candidates' policy platforms were presented and discussed in the media. Some critical comments towards Putin's leadership were transmitted on state television, and additional critical analyses were printed in the press. Interestingly, Putin in 2000 stressed the ideas of partnership with the USA, Europe, and international and transnational organisations. Fairness of elections is mentioned several times by Putin; he mentions that elections should be open for OSCE monitoring and attempts to justify the extra media coverage that he received by refusing to use the free air time distributed to candidates for the campaign.

The position of opposition candidates in 2000 is equally interesting when compared with media coverage of the 2008 elections. In the latter, the candidates were presented as less serious, and the coverage was mostly targeted at stories that would present them in a less competent light; they were significantly belittled. In 2000 coverage, the media seriously considered many candidates. Ziuganov presented his programme, and although a subtle sarcasm was used in describing his policy platform on television, the overall tone was serious. When the programme was referred to, comments were more of a critical character; the candidate was not merely ridiculed, belittled, dismissed, or simply ignored. Interviews with and about Yavlinskii were published in the newspapers.

Television: Comparing the framing of candidates and their policy platforms across media types and outlets shows that television has changed its framing tone most significantly. On both national channels, the amount of positive coverage of the incumbent candidate has increased remarkably. As seen in Table 5.13, in 2000, Channel One presented information about the incumbent candidate in a neutral tone (39 times) more often than in a positive tone (21 times). Even critical or, as coded here, negative points (5) were made. By 2008, no negative (0) coverage was presented and neutrality (2) almost disappeared, whereas a positive tone (81) prevailed overall. The results are slightly different on channel Rossiia; the number of times the incumbent candidate was mentioned in a negative (2) and neutral (30 times in 2000 and 23 times in 2008) light remained relatively unchanged in both election years. However, in comparison to 2000, in 2008 there was a ten-fold increase in the number of times the incumbent was positively framed. Coverage of candidates other than the incumbent has not changed. On television, the tone remained mostly negative or at best neutral.

Print media: Concerning the print media, cross-time comparisons can be made only for Kommersant and Novaia Gazeta because data for Vedomosti for 2000 are missing. As seen in Table 5.13, Novaia Gazeta remained critical of the government. In 2000, this newspaper openly supported Yavlinsky's candidacy; however, in 2008, only Medvedev was mentioned in a positive tone. This positivity is not necessarily due to pressure on the media but rather perhaps due to the absence of viable opposition that the newspaper deemed worthy of support. The picture is very different at Kommersant. In 2008, all of the candidates were mentioned more often than in 2000; however, they were mostly platforms. presented in a negative or neutral tone. Among the opposition and other candidates, Zhirinovskii and Ziuganov were most frequently discussed; theyeach were mentioned ten to twenty times, mostly negatively. In 2000, Kommersant did not mention

Putin frequently, and even when he was mentioned, the tone of coverage was either neutral or negative. In 2008, Medvedev was praised 42 times, he or his policy proposals were criticised 23 times, and the reporting remained neutral 17 times. In 2008, Vedomosti did present both negative and positive sides of the incumbent, although the positive framing still prevailed.

Table 5.13. Framing across media types and outlets

Media	Framing	Putin 2000	Medvedev 2008	Ziuganov 2000	Ziuganov 2008	Zhirinovskii 2000	Zhirinovskii 2008	Yavlinskii 2000	Bogdanov 2008
Television									
Channel One	Positive	21	87	0	2	0	3	0	0
	Negative	5	0	4	1	0	1	2	5
	Neutral	39	2	2	3	0	0	1	0
Rossiia	Positive	13	100	0	0	0	0	2	0
	Negative	2	2	1	0	2	2	0	1
	Neutral	30	23	0	0	0	1	2	0
Print media									
NovaiaGazeta	Positive	4	3	0	0	0	0	5	0
	Negative	10	14	2	1	0	1	0	3
	Neutral	2	5	0	0	0	0	0	0
Kommersant	Positive	0	42	0	6	0	1	0	0
	Negative	6	23	2	8	1	9	0	3
	Neutral	3	17	2	4	0	2	1	1
Vedomosti	Positive	No data	28	No data	0	No data	0	No data	0
	Negative	No data	9	No data	1	No data	0	No data	1
	Neutral	No data	16	No data	2	No data	2	No data	0
Online media									
gazeta.ru	Positive	No data	17	No data	0	No data	0	No data	0
	Negative	No data	9	No data	6	No data	2	No data	3
	Neutral	No data	90	No data	0	No data	1	No data	2
lenta.ru	Positive	No data	1	No data	0	No data	0	No data	0
	Negative	No data	2	No data	2	No data	4	No data	1
	Neutral	No data	9	No data	0	No data	2	No data	0

Online media: Reporting on both online media outlets was quite neutral. gazeta.ru had more reports of candidates than lenta.ru in general, and most of them were neutral, the statement about neutrality also applies to lenta.ru.

Agenda setting In 2000, some of the most frequently mentioned topics were social issues, restoring order, economic growth, and fighting corruption. Most of these topics also received high frequencies of mentions in 2008. However, topics such as social issues and economic growth were added to stability, continuity of the previous course, and rule of law.

Concerning times each candidate was mentioned in the media, the results appear similar for both years, with only minor differences. The number of times the candidates were mentioned did not change, the opposition did not receive less coverage, and the incumbent elite candidate's name was not mentioned more often in 2008. This result signifies that the principle difference was in the tone of coverage and in the framing of events, candidates, and their policy

Table 5.14. Number of times each candidate was mentioned in the media, 2000

	Print media	Broadcast media
	- Kommersant - Novaia Gazeta	- Channel One - Rossiia
Putin	824 in 146	1928 in 545
Ziuganov	139 in 54	281 in 105
Zhirinovskii	40 in 25	157 in 60
Yavlinskii	54 in 29	142 in 66

Note: *Times mentioned in number of documents
**Numbers are based on search results within the media outlets selected for this analysis
***Names were searched for only in the nominative case. However, because the same method was used to search for each name, the results are comparable.

Table 5.15. Number of times each candidate was mentioned in the media, 2008

	Print media		Broadcast media	Online media
	- Kommersant - NovaiaGazeta	- Kommersant - Vedomosti - NovaiaGazeta	- Channel One - Rossiia	- gazeta.ru - lenta.ru
Medvedev	1198 in 254	1826 in 396	1687 in 389	1791 in 488
Ziuganov	144 in 55	246 in 87	201 in 89	291 in 100
Zhirinovskiii	59 in 35	82 in 51	134 in 76	144 in 63
Bogdanov	118 in 49	152 in 75	147 in 70	240 in 89

Note: *Times mentioned in number of documents
**To provide a more even comparison between 2000 and 2008, I included separately how often the candidates were mentioned in "Kommersant" and "NovaiaGazeta."

5.7. Conclusions

This chapter presented an analysis of news content, presence and extent of content bias, agendas, and framing during the election campaigns. Based on the table presented in the research design part, a short summary of findings of this chapter is provided in Table 5.16. The table summarises some of the main differences in campaign coverages of 2000 and 2008, primarily focusing on two main points: framing and agenda setting. The content analysis of more than 2000 news reports published/broadcast during the 2000 and 2008 elections shows that content bias was present in both cases; however, the nature of the bias differed significantly. In 2000, the bias was less frequent and less obvious compared with 2008. Some popular media outlets were more often critical of government policies and more open in supporting candidates other than the ruling elite's candidate.

Table 5.16. Effects of media manipulations on news content

Effects	List of indicators	Year- 2000	Year-2008
Content bias or Editorial slant	a. Framing b. Agenda	Content bias was present in both cases. However, its extent differed significantly. In 2000, the bias was less frequent and less obvious compared with 2008.	
		Framing	
	1. Tone used in presenting each candidate in the media: - Positive - Negative - Neutral 2. Tone used in presenting policy programme presented by each candidate: - Positive - Negative - Neutral	1. Presentation of the candidates: a. The opposition: - Receives coverage - Programs of candidates other than the incumbent candidate are presented and critically discussed - Some candidates are openly supported by newspapers b. The incumbent is presented as - Able - A man of actions and not words - Saviour of the nation - Caring yet tough - One who is able to restore Russia's position in the world 2. Policies: - Presented in critical, positive, and neutral ways. Depending upon the media outlet and the candidate, policies are either discussed critically or provided positive or neutral coverage.	1. Presentation of the candidates: a. The opposition is - Ridiculed - Belittled - Not taken seriously b. The incumbent is presented as - The one who is capable of maintaining stability and economic growth in the country - Able - A man of action - A man who is able to and will ensure continuity of the course set by his predecessor 2. Policies: - Rarely addressed. If they are, they are mostly the incumbent elite candidate's policies and are presented predominantly in a positive or at worst in a neutral light.

		Agenda setting	
	3. Number of times each candidate was mentioned 4. Number of times each candidate's policy programme was discussed 5. Most frequently mentioned policy topics by the candidates	3. Candidates mentioned, see section 5.4.3 and table 5.14. 4. Frequency of policy platforms mentioned 5. Policy topics: - Social issues - Restoring order - Economic growth - Fighting corruption	3. Candidates mentioned, see section 5.5.3 and Table 5.15. 4. Frequency of policy platforms mentioned 5. Policy topics: - Social issues - Stability - Continuity - Economic growth - Rule of law
Self-censorship		—	—
Priming		- War in Chechnya - Social issues - Economic development - Stability	- Social issues - Economic development

Candidates and their policies were framed differently in the two cases. In 2000, opposition candidates were criticised, and their programs were critically discussed. In 2008, this attitude changed; the opposition was no longer taken seriously. It was ridiculed, belittled, or accused of being incapable. Concerning the representation of the ruling elite's candidate, a similar strategy of framing was used in both years. Putin was presented as able, a man of action, saviour of the nation, caring yet tough, and able to restore Russia's position in the world. Later, in 2008, Medvedev was presented in a similar light but with promises of continuing the course laid by his predecessor. He was also presented as forward looking, modern, and capable of maintaining stability and economic growth in the country.

As seen in Table 5.16, which presents a detailed cross-media comparison, the topics most often mentioned in the news were related to social issues, restoring order, economic growth, and fighting corruption. In 2008, topics such as stability and continuity were added to social issues receiving most of the attention, followed by economic growth and rule of law. It would not be correct to say that the principle agenda was set by the ruling elite, even in 2008. More likely, the broader issues in the news were those with which citizens most concerned themselves. Opinion polls often show that for Russians, economic stability and social guarantees matter (Levada Center 2012). Treisman's (2010) research even shows that the president's approval rate correlates with Russian's perceptions of economic wellbeing in the country. Every speech of a candidate mentioned at least once the idea of improving social policies. However, only the candidates representing the ruling elite demonstrated the idea with action, e.g., Medvedev travelled across the country implementing different national projects. Later, this importance of actions rather than words was emphasised on state television.

Concerning the tone of coverage across various media outlets, note that in all of the cases, the candidate from the incumbent elite received much more coverage than did any other candidate. However, print and online media outlets were able to maintain some neutrality in reporting, with online media and Novaia Gazeta doing so considerably more. The latter has not changed its tone of coverage. However, Kommersant became more positive when discussing the incumbent candidate. In the case of Vedomosti, the comparison is not possible. However, in 2008, coverage was mostly positive (28) but not exclusively so; the newspaper also published critical views (9), and some of the reports were neutral (16). Overall, the analysis shows that primarily television was affected by media manipulations. Considering that a majority of the population receives information of current political events from television, these results are not surprising. Television being under the state's control had a significant effect on news content, indicating that that the ownership structure has a large effect on news content. The same might be true although to a much lesser degree with Kommersant, whose owner has close ties with the incumbent elite. In the case of opposition newspaper Novaia Gazeta, the effects of some media manipulation strategies might yet occur. As the editor of the politics department of this newspaper noted during my interview, "new laws regulating the source of finance of news organisations might hinder their independence." If the outlet no longer has an opportunity to be financed by foreign grants, it might resort to either state or business groups for financial support, which might later give such groups leverage to influence the content.

Overall, comparing the media coverage of campaigns at two different points in time supports the argument that expansion of media manipulation strategies used by the elite and discussed in Chapter 4 did have an effect on media content, particularly with respect to the framing of events, candidates, and their policies. This link between media manipulation strategies and media content is further discussed in the Conclusions.

Conclusions

Aim of the study

As it was noted in the Introduction, this research was aimed to examine in depth the media manipulation strategies that the incumbent elite uses to skew media coverage in favour of its candidate and the effects that these strategies have on news content during the presidential campaign periods in competitive and hegemonic types of electoral authoritarian regimes. Based on a comparative case study of Russia in 2000 and 2008, this study illustrated the internal mechanisms according to which these regimes work. In this, last concluding chapter I summarise the primary findings of my research, which was based on document analysis, interviews conducted with media professionals, and content analysis of news media during the Russian presidential election campaigns in 2000 — when the regime was competitive authoritarian — and in 2008 — when the regime became more authoritarian, sharing many characteristics with hegemonic authoritarian regimes.

In Chapter 1, I have argued that there is a disagreement in the literature on hybrid regimes concerning the operationalisation of these regimes. Taking the example of post-Soviet states, I have illustrated that neither country experts nor comparative politics scholars are able to agree on how this or that regime in the region is to be categorised. A similar disagreement is present in regime data sets; the same country case seems to be classified into different regime categories, depending on the data set used. I have also argued that hybrid regimes as such are durable, have their own regime-specific characteristics, and thus should be studied as a separate regime species. Thus, concepts such as "competitive" and "hegemonic" authoritarian regimes are useful; however, when scholars attempt to devise measurements, the issue becomes somewhat confusing. This issue of measurements has been raised by many scholars (Bogaards 2009). Measurement errors in the coding of competitive authoritarianism per se have also been widely discussed in more recent articles by Bardall (2015) and Helle (2015). Some clarity is also needed in conceptualisation. Levitsky and Way (2010) show how competitive authoritarian regimes are different from full autocracies and democracies. However, they do not discuss competitive regimes in the context of other hybrid regimes, nor do they show the existing specific differences among them, which adds confusion to regime classification by making regimes as different as Russia in 2008 and Turkmenistan fall into the same category of full authoritarian regimes.

In the regime categorisation, which I develop in this work, Russia in 2000 is a clear case of competitive authoritarianism: a) there is broad adult suffrage—any Russian citizen above the age of 18 has the right to vote; b) the elected government is not restricted by any unelected "tutelary" powers; c) competitive multi-party elections occur—eleven candidates competed during the elections of 2000; d) there is the presence of media pluralism; and e) there is an unfairness of competition—the electoral competition is not entirely fair but instead is skewed in favour of the incumbent candidate.

As noted above, Russia in 2008 does not fit the description of full authoritarianism as defined by Levitsky and Way (2010), even though they classify it as such. They claim that, in full authoritarian regimes, at least one of the following characteristics should be present: a) "major opposition parties and/or candidates are routinely excluded—either formally or effectively—from competing in elections for the national executive; b) large-scale falsification of electoral results makes voting effectively meaningless; c) repression is so severe that major civic and opposition groups cannot operate in the public arena; thus, much of the opposition is underground, in prison, or in exile[81]" (p. 365). In the case of Russia in 2008, although some candidates were denied registration, major opposition parties were not excluded; in addition, the scale of falsification was not as high as to make the elections meaningless, which can be confirmed by opinion polls favouring the candidate who won. It is, thus, not justified to equate the Russian regime was equated to regimes such as Uzbekistan and Turkmenistan, where the incumbent candidate repeatedly wins the elections with at least 97% of votes; no freedom of the press exists; and both civic and political forms of opposition are severely repressed (Freedom House 1999-2015). As noted in Chapter 1, according to Schedler (2013), hegemonic regimes fall into a category of regimes in which the opposition does not stand a chance of winning elections but the elections are minimally competitive (parties and candidates outside of the ruling elite are allowed to win votes and seats — in the case of Russia 2008, they have even been granted free air time on national television), minimally open (the repression of dissidents is selective and intermittent), and minimally pluralistic (opposition parties are allowed to participate in elections, as the KPRF did in 2008).

This work aims to enrich our understanding of electoral authoritarian regimes, to solve some of the measurement problems, to illustrate the differences and to draw clearer boundaries between the competitive and hegemonic sub-types of electoral authoritarian regime. To do so, I argue that it is vital to use both qualitative and quantitative data. The book presents a detailed comparative case study to specify the boundaries between the sub-types of electoral authoritarianism, and it makes use of the literature on electoral fraud / manipulation / integrity to observe the differences in the types of manipulation strategies used in each of these regimes. Based on quantitative data analysis, a longitudinal, comparative, in-depth case study, and both qualitative and quantitative media content analysis, the book reveals some of the mechanisms of control and

---

[81] For details, see Chapter 1.

manipulation strategies used by the ruling elite to stay in power in competitive and hegemonic authoritarian regimes. A comparative case study of Russia in 2000, when it was considered competitive authoritarian, and Russia in 2008, when it was considered hegemonic authoritarian, not only demonstrates the inner working of these two regimes but also shows how they differ from each other in the methods that they use to manipulate elections.

To summarise the methods and findings, *first,* by using data sets on electoral fraud, I differentiated between competitive and hegemonic authoritarian regimes. This preliminary quantitative analysis indicated that, in the case of hegemonic regimes, the strategies used by the ruling elite are less disguised. Fraud is mostly committed on election day, during tabulation and vote counting, and through electoral administration. By contrast, in competitive authoritarian regimes, the manipulation is more subtle, and it mostly manifests itself in the media coverage of political events. In other words, a battery of the most frequently used manipulation techniques is slightly different in hegemonic regimes. In competitive regimes, the incumbent elite takes precautionary measures before election day. The manipulation of the voting act is more widespread in hegemonic regimes, whereas competitive regimes prefer the manipulation of institutional design and vote choice. The differences are observable, and further research could make use of electoral fraud data sets to build better justified and less fuzzy boundaries between the two.

Second, taking the example of the Russian media, I show that the extent of media control and content bias is much lower when the regime is competitive. Although the media are skewed in favour of the ruling elite's candidate, there is still an open discussion of other candidates and their policy platforms. The number of regulations restricting media freedom is lower. By the time that the regime becomes more authoritarian, the ownership structure of principle media outlets changes, the regulatory framework becomes more constraining, and the number of cases in which journalists are threatened and detained by the police increases significantly, in addition to the number of charges against the media.

The case study also shows that there are certain characteristics of regimes that make them work in a certain manner and that these characteristics are observable also when examining the manner in which the incumbent elite and the media interact. For instance, in electoral authoritarian regimes, in general, the boundaries between the state, the ruling elite, and business are faded, and democratic institutions are weak. This situation is particularly observable in the example of a) the control that the ruling elite exerts over state-owned television; and b) the control over media through the loyalty and crony ownership of media outlets. Another specificity of this regime is uncertainty. No one actually knows how to act, what is allowed, and what is not. Thus, to be on the safe side, any media professional must think twice before publishing anything controversial. Because of vague regulations, journalists may not be completely confident in what to report on, what they are allowed to talk about, and what they are not. The rules are unclear, which leaves space to keep the media within a certain frame without directly pressuring it. The extent of uncertainty and the boundaries may differ in the two sub-types, but the general logic remains.

The media has the potential to shape opinions, and it is widely used to manipulate public opinion in non-democracies. In electoral authoritarian regimes, in which the outcomes of elections depend not only on vote buying but also repression, and tossing the election results, the ruling elite is keen to use the media to construct positive views of the favoured candidate. To do so, various tools are used, for instance, journalist intimidation, rewards or punishments for media outlets either by cutting or increasing financial assistance, and the introduction of laws regulating the activities of media outlets. The case studies in this book demonstrate in detail what strategies and mechanism are used in a competitive authoritarian regime (i.e., Russia in 2000) and in a hegemonic regime (i.e., Russia 2008).

Media manipulations in competitive vs. hegemonic regimes

My research shows that, in competitive authoritarian regimes, the extent of media manipulation is generally lower. The list of practices presented in the Table 6.1 may seem equally long in both cases, but some of the manipulations (blackmail, bartering, the selective collection of debts) were related to weak institutionalisation during the period when Russia was building a new system after the collapse of the Soviet Union. Over time, the manipulation strategies became more centralised; legal ways of constraining media freedom have increased, whereas practices such as bartering and blackmail have decreased. One of the strategies used during both periods was control of the media via ownership or financial subsidies. This particular strategy has the most durable, effective, and systematic influence on the media. It makes it possible to control the media from the top, making it easier to dictate the rules. Control through ownership was used in both 2000 and 2008; however, it was used in two different ways. In 2000, if the ruling elite wanted to have the media on its side, then it had to ask the owners or financiers of any given media outlet. At the time, the main television channels belonged to media moguls or oligarchs. When the interests of these oligarchs coincided with those of the ruling elite, media support could be provided. This was the case in the 2000 elections. The main opponent of the incumbent was the communist party candidate, who was inclined to renationalise certain industries of the economy, which was not in the interest of the oligarchs, who made their fortune during the privatisation of the early 1990s. Given that the state could not afford to fully finance the federal channels, it was largely dependent on business groups. On the one hand, this situation ensured some pluralism; on the other hand, at crucial moments such as elections, the media still supported the candidate representing the ruling elite. However, these arrangements had changed by the time of the 2008 elections, when the oligarchs no longer had that much power. By 2008, the media was controlled in two different ways. Either the most popular media outlets were nationalised and the ruling elite was able to exert direct control over them, or the ruling elite had placed its cronies or those dependent on it in charge of the principal media outlets. Regulating the legal framework in which the media had to operate also entails similar characteristics. The effect of this strategy is equally durable and systematic. However, with the help of this strategy, the media can only be tamed; some type of censorship or filtering on the flow of information can be established, but it is not effective in regard to dictating or shaping the content of the news itself.

Considering some specificities of the manipulation strategies, it seems that, to influence the media on a large scale, strategies such as ownership, the legal framework, access to information, and co-optation are the most effective. By contrast, threats against the media, control over office facilities, the destruction of media outlets' property or video tapes, blackmail, interference with the printing and distribution process of newspapers, access to information, and co-optation are used on a lower scale, mostly on the level of local governments. They also have a lower impact on the media content and are directed at one case at a time, having a short-term effect.

These strategies are used in both regimes but in different proportions; most importantly, in competitive regimes, there are some constraints on the incumbent that are financial or institutional or that perhaps even entail a fear of vertical accountability. Thus, the media is manipulated only to the extent that doing so is possible with the available resources, for example, making deals with large business and media owners as opposed to confiscating their assets. Less institutionalised methods are used to force some media into self-censorship (e.g., targeting certain media outlets or journalists) rather than creating an effective legal framework, which would ensure general compliance. The list of manipulation strategies is presented in Table 6.1. The sub-types of the mechanisms of influence are divided into two groups: general—strategies that can be used in any electoral regime; and specific—strategies that are mostly unique to the case of Russia and its period of national rebuilding after the collapse of the previous system.

Table 6.1. *Media manipulation in competitive vs. hegemonic regimes*

Mechanisms of influence	Russia 2000 - Competitive authoritarianism	Russia 2008 - Hegemonic authoritarianism
	Sub-types	Sub-types

Misuse of state resources	*General:*
	- Ownership:
	  . Direct state-ownership
	  . Partial state-ownership
	  . Crony ownership
	- The media's source of financing:
	  - State subsidies/Selective funding
	  - Financial rewards for compliance and fulfilling agreements/orders of larger businesses and/or state actors
	- Personal ties with
	  - Owners of media outlets
	  - Media distribution channels
	  - Owners of facilities rented by media outlets
	  - Businesses on whose financial support a media outlet depends (sponsorships, advertisement)
	- Control over distribution channels; ex. state postal services, broadcast frequencies, etc.
	- Direct or indirect control over facilities rented by media outlets and thus an opportunity to manipulate the terms and conditions of lease
	- Cooptation
	- Control over office facilities
	- Control over access to information
	-
	Case-specific:
	- Blackmail
	- Barter deals
	- Selective recovery of debts
		General:
		- Ownership:
		  . Higher levels of direct ownership and partial ownership
		  . Ownership via state companies
		  . Crony ownership
		- Limiting the media's source of financing:
		  . State subsidies
		  . Advertisement
		  . Foreign funds
		- Ensuring loyalty of media professionals by cooptation
		- Control over distribution channels; ex. state postal services, broadcast frequencies, etc.
		- State or crony ownership of printing facilities
		- Control over access to information

	Russia 2000 - Competitive authoritarianism	Russia 2008 - Hegemonic authoritarianism
Mechanisms of influence	Sub-types	Sub-types
Legal constraints	*General:* - The state controls the issuance of the broadcast license *Case-specific:* - Superfluity of rules - Selective use of rules	*General:* - Media law amendments banning any television or video information on acts of terror, except information allowed for publication by law enforcement agencies - Law against extremist activities prohibiting the dissemination of information supporting "extremist activities" - Legislation allowing government authorities to close print or broadcast media outlets that spread "biased" political commentary *Case-specific:* - Establishment of *RosKomNadzor*
Other ways of ensuring compliance	*General:* - Coercion	*General:* - Coercion

Media content in competitive vs. hegemonic regimes

The effects of all of these media manipulation strategies are reflected in the media content. The incumbent can force the state-run media to introduce a certain content bias in its reporting, forcing journalists and media organisations into self-censorship. Content bias — identified by examining the agenda and framing across different media types and outlets — is present in both cases but in different forms. The summary of the results is provided in Table 6.2.

Agenda: In the case of Russia, when the competitive and the hegemonic regimes are compared, during the hegemonic regime, the number of times that the candidates were noted did not change, the opposition did not receive less coverage, and the incumbent's name was not noted more frequently when the more authoritarian regime was in place. Hence, the principle difference is not the frequency with which the candidates are noted but instead in the tone of the coverage, that is, the framing of events, candidates, and their policy platforms.

The topics most often noted in the news were related to social issues, restoring order, economic growth, and the fight against corruption. In 2008, topics such as stability and continuity were added to social issues, receiving most of the attention, followed by economic growth and the rule of law. Perhaps the principle agenda was not set by the ruling elite even in 2008. It is likely that the broader issues that were in the news were those with which the citizens themselves were most concerned. Each of the candidates noted the idea of improving social policies and economic growth at least once. However, only the candidates representing the ruling elite showed it in action. Subsequently, the importance of action over rhetoric was emphasised on state television, which signifies that all of the candidates similarly play on the general sentiments of the population but the ruling elite has more resources to do so in a manner that the citizens find compelling.

Framing: The candidates and their policies were framed in a different manner in the two cases. In 2000, bias was less frequent and less obvious compared to 2008. Some popular media outlets were more frequently critical of government policies and more open in supporting candidates other than the individual representing the ruling elite. The opposition candidates were criticised, and their programmes were critically discussed. However, with the turn to a more authoritarian regime, this situation has changed: the opposition is no longer taken seriously, and it is ridiculed, belittled or deemed incapable (see Table 6.2). The difference between competitive and hegemonic regimes lies not only in the extent and the types of manipulations but also in the content of the media. The number of times that a candidate or his policy platform is noted in the media may not change; however, the framing is significantly different in these two regime types. This difference can only be identified by using a qualitative approach. Table 6.2 shows the differences in the framing and the agenda.

Evidently, the agenda and the issues that have been primed did not change much; however, the tone and the approach used in the coverage of the candidates and their policy platforms did.

These changes in framing also differ depending on the type of media. On television, the effects are more obvious. As the regime acquires more authoritarian patterns, television becomes more positively biased in favour of the incumbent elite. The frequency of reports that use a neutral tone decreases or simply drops to zero. Some print and online media outlets may maintain neutrality. In the case of Russia, an opposition newspaper has retained its critical and neutral tone in its reporting, whereas a newspaper owned by a large business owner whose business prospers due to its connections to the ruling elite has changed its coverage from neutral to more positive and has increased the frequency of reports on the incumbent candidate. In the case of a purely business community-targeted newspaper, the content is skewed in favour of the incumbent; however, some critical and neutral reporting still persists. The online media has maintained neutrality, even in 2008; however, this could be because, in 2008, the online media was not yet tightly controlled by the state or because the ruling elite mostly targets the average Russian population, which receives most information on political events from television.

In this work, I have analysed the news content of three principal newspapers for certain population groups (the business community, the intellectuals, the opposition). The framing in these newspapers is different from that on television: in contrast to television, in 2008, the framing of the incumbent candidate is still not exclusively, and in some cases not even predominantly, positive; indeed, both negative and neutral types of coverage of events are present. Further research is necessary to reveal the reasons behind the existence of these islands of pluralism, albeit ever so small, in this hegemonic regime. Whether the survival of some independent print media falls into the grand strategy of the ruler or for some reason has not yet been addressed is difficult to say. However, considering the new regulations imposed on the media in recent years, such as the limitations on foreign media ownership[82], regulating online publications within the same framework as the traditional media and restrictions on foreign grants for the financing of any media outlet (in one of the interviews, the editor of Novaia Gazeta expressed his worries about the possible negative effects of this regulation on the future independence of this opposition newspaper) — it may be assumed that the full effects of the media manipulation strategies remain to be seen. What can be said with some confidence is that, since 2008, when the regime slid to hegemonic authoritarianism, the media manipulation strategies have been taken to another level, from targeting certain outlets to creating a new, more restrictive regulatory framework with which every media outlet in the country must comply.

Regarding the frames used to present the candidates and their policies, they may certainly vary depending on the context, perceptions of voters, and the preferences of the ruling elite, in addition to the type of media outlet, the outlet's editorial line, and its target audience, and they also may depend on the presence of viable opposition candidates. Thus, further research is necessary on whether ridiculing, belittling, or describing the opposition as incapable is specific to the single case of Russia or can be observed in other cases of hegemonic regimes. As noted in Chapter 2, in competitive regimes, the media is one of the most crucial levers that the regime uses; however, hegemonic regimes employ a broader array of strategies to stay in power (for details, see Table 2.8). In addition to media manipulations, they pressure opposition (as noted in Table 2.8: candidate intimidation/obstruction), which may lead to diminishing the opposition's importance in general, which may partly explain the media's increasingly negative framing of opposition candidates; or, considering that, in hegemonic regimes, the level of electoral authorities' independence is lower, opposition candidates are sometimes denied registration, as was the

---

[82] The law going into effect in January 2016. Pearson and Dow Jones, partial foreign owners of Vedomosti already had to sell their shares in this business newspaper.

case in 2008 with Mikhail Kas'ianov, who allegedly was not able to collect 2 million valid signatures in support of his candidacy.

Table 6.2. Content bias in competitive vs. hegemonic regimes

Russia in 2000 - Competitive authoritarianism	Russia in 2008 - Hegemonic authoritarianism
Framing: The opposition: - Programmes of candidates other than the incumbent candidate are critically discussed The incumbent is presented as: - Able - A man of actions and not words - The saviour of the nation - Caring but tough - One who is able to restore Russia's position in the world	**Framing:** The opposition is: - Ridiculed - Belittled - Not taken seriously The incumbent is presented as: - The one who is capable of maintaining the stability and economic growth in the country - Able - A man of action - A man who is able and who will ensure the continuity of the course set by his predecessor
Agenda setting: - Social issues - Restoring the order - Economic growth - The fight against corruption	**Agenda setting:** *General:* - Social issues - Economic growth - The rule of law *Case-specific:* - Continuity - Stability
Priming: *General:* - War/conflicts - Social issues - Economic development - Stability *Case-specific:* - The war in Chechnia	**Priming:** *General:* - Social issues - Economic development

Summary of the findings

To summarise, using both quantitative and qualitative approaches to data analysis, this work demonstrates the principle as well as the more subtle differences between competitive and hegemonic regimes. In Chapter 4, I argue that the extent of media manipulations and even the types of these manipulation strategies differ depending on the regime type. In competitive regimes, less centralised and less ubiquitously effective strategies are used, and most of them aim at a single target (a single media outlet or a media professional). In the case of hegemonic regimes, the strategies are more observable, more institutionalised, more targeted at the media in general (e.g., laws and the regulatory framework) and more centralised (e.g., the ownership structure). Additionally, the extent of the manipulations is different. In competitive regimes, the manipulations are subtle and do not always determine the outcome, i.e., media coverage favouring the incumbent. The differences between these two regimes types are also present in terms of the effects or the content bias. As demonstrated in Chapter 5, in competitive regimes, opposition candidates and their policy platforms are presented and discussed; the extent and the tone of the coverage differ from one media outlet to another, depending on the outlet's editorial line and ownership structure; however, although it is overall biased the discussion occurs. With a hegemonic regime in place, the opposition is no longer taken seriously; it is ignored, belittled, or ridiculed. Instead of policy platforms, the personal characteristics of the candidates are presented in the least appealing and the least informative manner. It could be argued that this type of coverage can be explained by the absence of a viable opposition in hegemonic regimes. For example, in Russia, during the 2000 elections, an opposition candidate, Grigory Yavlinskii, participated in elections and even received open support in the independent press; however, in 2008, the leader of the opposition coalition "The Other Russia," Mikhail Kas'ianov, was denied registration as a candidate. Nevertheless, the restrictions placed on the opposition are only one facet of the explanation. As in the case of Russia, even the same opposition candidates received different coverage in the 2000 and 2008 elections. In 2000, Ziuganov was criticised for certain policies, their viability, and Russia's need for them; in 2008, his candidacy was mostly framed as incapable and outdated. The framing also varies depending on the media type. Although the incumbent candidate is noted much more frequently than any other candidate, the media in a competitive regime provides some neutral reporting. Even on television, the incumbent receives both negative and neutral coverage. However, as the regime becomes more authoritarian, television promotes a positive image of the incumbent and a less appealing image of any other candidate; it may equally be the case that, even in hegemonic regimes, some islands of neutral or critical media remain or some online media outlets as is the case with "Novaia Gazeta" in Russia. However, 1) only in the case of opposition newspapers is the incumbent criticised more often than he is noted in a neutral or positive tone; 2) most popular online media outlets keep a neutral tone, avoiding any negative reports; 3) even when the negative coverage or neutral tone is maintained, the debate centres on the incumbent; and 4) the print and online media have a much smaller target audience and are less accessible than television, which means that their content is disseminated only among small population groups.

Other cases of electoral authoritarian regimes

The "media effects in electoral process" model proposed in this work is not specific to Russia; it can be further used in studying other cases of electoral authoritarian regimes. The list of manipulations may vary slightly depending on the context and the historical development of institutions in each particular case; however, the underlying logic remains the same. In competitive regimes, the ruling elite uses more subtle methods of influencing the electoral process. In hegemonic regimes, not only are the manipulation strategies employed before the election day, but also some fraud is committed on the election day itself. Additionally, in hegemonic regimes, the extent of the manipulations is higher. Concerning the media, a similar logic prevails. The main difference is in the extent of the constraints placed on the media, with the media content varying accordingly. In competitive regimes candidates, other than the individual representing the ruling elite receive some coverage in the media, although the coverage is skewed in favour of the incumbent. However, in hegemonic regimes, the incumbent candidate dominates the media, whereas the opponents are belittled, ridiculed, or ignored altogether.

Media manipulation strategies similar to those discussed in this work can be observed in the case of hybrid regimes, which lie beyond the scope of this work. For instance, in Latin America, in countries such as Venezuela[83] and Mexico[84], television broadcast is highly concentrated. In Mexico, two companies, "Televisa" and "Television Azteca", control approximately 71% of the national television market. As Hughes and Lawson argue (2005: 13), "[m]arket concentration is typically the result of media owners' collusive relations with political elites, be they the autocrats of previous years or today's elected leaders". Additionally, exactly as in the case of Russia, because of this collusion, even private media companies are more careful in their political reporting. The boundaries between media owners and editors are not well built, which lets the owners dismiss anyone whose reporting is offensive to the owners and their allies, political or otherwise. Another obstacle to a free media in these countries is the threats and pressure exerted on media professionals. The media is threatened not only by politicians and government official but also by non-state actors,

---

[83] The case of Venezuela has been widely studied. Diamond (2002) referred to it as an ambiguous case, whereas Mainwaring (2012), Levitsky and Loxton (2013) defined the regime under Hugo Chavez as competitive authoritarian.

[84] Mexico is another case of a hybrid regime. The Polity IV and Freedom House scores attributed to the Mexican regime yet again demonstrate the existing disagreement between them. Since 2005, Polity IV gives a score of 8, where 10 stands for democracy and -10 for autocracy. By contrast, Freedom House rates it as "partly free", assigning it a score of 3 (1 and 2 being "free," 5, 6, and 7 being "not free") on both the political rights and the civil liberties dimensions.

which certainly discourages investigative journalism, or worse, results in systematic self-censorship. Barriers such as the legal climate, e.g., the criminal defamation laws protecting public officials, and limited access to government information are also present in the countries of Latin America.

Such cases are present in Southeast Asia as well. For example, in Malaysia[85], although the majority of the media is privately owned, the government seeks to ensure media compliance and a certain bias in favour of the government by using various measures, such as legislative mechanisms and the ownership structure. Among other laws, Abbot (2011) notes a law allowing the police to arrest anyone whose actions may be considered in "any manner prejudicial to the security of Malaysia" (Abbot 2011: 14). Detention may last up to sixty days, after which a person can be further detained for a longer period of time. The concentration of the media in the hands of a few companies closely linked to the state is another method by which the government ensures a pro-government bias. Abbot (2011) also notes some cultural and environmental causes of a constrained media; however, they are country-specific. He notes that the continuous pressure exerted on the media and the legislations that have been in place for decades have created a culture of self-censorship that prevents even privately owned newspapers from publishing controversial or highly critical reports. Manipulation strategies that are similar in nature have also been employed throughout the post-Soviet region, for example, in competitive authoritarian Ukraine under Kuchma (Dyczok 2006) and in hegemonic Kazakhstan (Schatz 2009; Richter 2008).

These examples illustrate that media manipulation, the effects of manipulations on the news content, and the internal mechanisms according to which the electoral authoritarian regimes function are not exclusively specific to Russia. Some insights that were revealed in this work can be

---

[85] The regime in Malaysia was evaluated differently by scholars; for example, Abbot (2011) claimed that it is electoral authoritarian; Means (1996) considers it soft authoritarian; and in a 1993 article by Case, it was even identified as semi-democratic. Despite these disagreements, the regime is essentially hybrid.

applied to better understand competitive and hegemonic authoritarian regimes, create clearer boundaries between these two regime sub-types, and constitute a step forward in creating a more precise operationalisation of electoral authoritarian regimes.

References

Abbot, Jason. 2011. "Electoral Authoritarianism and Print Media in Malaysia: Measuring Political Bias and Analyzing its Cause," *Asian Affairs: An American Review* 38 (1): 1-38.

Adachi, Yuko. 2015. Dynamics of State—Business Relations and The Evolution of Capitalism in Russia in an Age of Globalization. In Toshiaki Hirai (eds.) *Capitalism and the World Economy: The Light and Shadow of Globalization.* London: Routledge.

Akhrarkhodjaeva, Nozima. 2012. "Die Medienlandschaft Kasachstans: Verschwinden die letzten Biotope der Pressefreiheit?," *Zentralasien-Analysen* 59 (30 November): 10-16.

Aksartova, Sada, Floriana Fossato, Anna Kachkaeva, and Grigory Libergal. 2003. "Television in the Russian Federation: Organizational Structure, Programme Production and Audience," a report for The European Audiovisual Observatory.

Allina-Pisano, Jessica. 2010. "Social Contracts and Authoritarian Projects in Post-Soviet Space: The Use of Administrative Resource," *Communist and Post-Communist Studies* 43: 373-382.

Allison, Olivia. 2006. "Selective Enforcement and Irresponsibility: Central Asia's Shrinking Space for Independent Media," *Central Asia Survey* 25 (1-2): 93-114.

Alvarez, Michael and Thad E. Hall. 2006. "Controlling Democracy: The Principal agent problems in election administration," *Policy Studies Journal* 34 (4): 491-510.

Alvarez, Michael, Lonna Atkenson, and Thad E. Hall. 2012. *Confirming Elections: Creating Confidence and Integrity through Election Auditing.* New York: Palgrave Macmillan.

Alvarez, Michael, Thad E. Hall, and Susan D. Hyde. 2008. *Election Fraud: Detecting and Deterring Electoral Manipulation.* Washington, DC: Brookings Institution Press.

Anceschi, Luca. 2011. Reinforcing authoritarianism through media control: the case of post-Soviet Turkmenistan. In Freeman, E. and Shafer, R. (eds.) *After the Czars and Commissars: Journalism in Authoritarian Post-Soviet Central Asia.* Series: Eurasion political economy and public policy study series. East Lansing, MI: Michigan State University, pp. 59-77.

Arutunyan, Anna. 2009. *The Media in Russia.* New York: Open University Press.

Azhgikhina, N. 2007. "The Struggle for Press Freedom in Russia: Reflections of a Russian Journalist," *Europe-Asia Studies* 59 (8): 1245-62.

Baran, Stanley J. and Dennis K. Davis. 2010. *Mass Communication Theory. Foundations, Ferment, and Future*, 6th ed. Wadsworth: Cengage Learning.

Bardall, Gabrielle. 2016. "Coding Competitive Authoritarianism," *Zeitschrift für Vergleichende Politikwissenschaft* 10 (1): 19-46.

Baron, David. 2006. "Persistent Media Bias," *Journal of Public Economics* 90: 1-36.

BBC News. August 1, 2014. Russia enacts "draconian" law for bloggers and online media. Retrieved from http://www.bbc.com/news/technology-28583669

Beck, Thorsten, George Clarke, Alberto Groff, Philip Keefer, and Patrick Walsh. 2001. "New Tools in Comparative Political Economy: The Database of Political Institutions," *World Bank Economic Review* 15 (1): 165-176.

Becker, Jonathan. 2004. "Lessons from Russia—a Neo-Authoritarian Media System," *European Journal of Communication* 19 (2): 139-163.

Belin, Laura. 2002. "The Rise and Fall of Russia's NTV," *Stanford Journal of International Law* 38 (19): 19-42.

Belin, Laura. 2004. Politics and the Mass Media under Putin. In Cameron Ross (ed.) Russian Politics under Putin. Manchester: Manchester University Press, pp. 133-151.

Bennett, Lance and Shanto Iyengar. 2008. "A New Era of Minimal Effects? The Changing Foundations of Political Communication," *Journal of Communication* 58: 707-731.

Beumers, Birgit, Stephen Hutchings and Natalia Rulyova. 2009. *The Post-Soviet Russian Media: Conflicting Signals*. Hoboken: Taylor and Francis.

Beumers, Birgit, Stephen Hutchings and Natalia Rulyova. 2009. *The Post-Soviet Russian Media: Conflicting Signals*. Hoboken: Taylor and Francis.

Birch, Sarah. 2007. "Electoral Systems and Electoral Misconduct," *Comparative Political Studies*, 40 (12): 1533-56.

Birch, Sarah. 2011. *Electoral Malpractice*. Oxford: Oxford University Press.

Bland, Gary, Andrew Green and Toby Moore. 2013. "Measuring the Quality of Election Administration," *Democratization* 20 (2): 358-377.

Blumer, Herbert and Philip M Hauser. 1933. *Movies, Delinquency, and Crime, Motion Pictures and Youth*. London: Macmillan and Co.

Blumer, Herbert. 1933. *Movies and Conduct*. New York: Macmillan and Co.

Blumler, Jay G. and Michael Gurevitch. 1995. *The Crisis of Public Communication Communication and Society*. London: Routledge.

Bogaards, Matthijs. 2009. "How to classify hybrid regimes? Defective Democracy and Electoral Authoritarianism," *Democratization* 16 (2): 399-423.

Bogaards, Matthijs. 2013. Multi-Party Elections in Africa: Attribute of Authoritarianism and Driver of Democracy. Paper to be presented at the Annual Meeting of the American Political Science Association (APSA) in Chicago, August 29 – September 1, 2013.

Boyatzis, Richard. 1998. *Transforming qualitative information*. Thousand Oaks etc.: Sage, 29-52.

Braguinsky, Serguey. 2009. "Postcommunist Oligarchs in Russia: Quantitative Analysis," *Journal of Law and Economics* 52 (2): 307-349.

Bremmer Ian and Charap Samuel. 2007. "The Siloviki in Putin's Russia: Who They Are and What They Want," *The Washington Quarterly* 30 (1): 83-92.

Brewer, Paul R., Joseph Graf and Lars Willnat. 2003. "Priming or Framing: Media Influence on Attitudes toward Foreign Countries," *Gazette* 65 (6): 493-508.

Brooker, Paul. 2000. *Non-Democratic Regimes. Theory, Government and Politics*. New York: St. Martin's Press.

Brown, Jeff. 1995. "Mass Media in Transition in Central Asia," *Gazette* 54, 249-265.

Brownlee, Jason. 2009. "Harbinger of Democracy: Competitive Elections before the end of authoritarianism." In Steffan I. Lindberg (ed.) *Democratization by Elections: A New Mode of Transition*. Baltimore: Johns Hopkins University Press, pp. 128-147.

Brownlee, Jason. 2009. "Portents of Pluralism: How Hybrid Regimes Affect Democratic Transitions," *American Journal of Political Science* 53 (3): 515-532.

Brumberg, Daniel. 2002. "The Trap of Liberalized Autocracy," *Journal of Democracy* 13 (4): 56–68.

Bryant, Jennings and Mary Beth Oliver. 2009. *Media Effects. Advances in Theory and Research*, 3rd ed. New York and London: Routledge.

BTI. 2010. Transformation Index 2010. Political Management in International Comparison. Retrieved from http://www.bti2010.bertelsmann-transformation-index.de/fileadmin/pdf/Anlagen_BTI_2010/BTI_2010__Brochure_E_web.pdf

Bunce, Valerie and Sharon Wolchik. 2005. "Favorable Conditions and Electoral Revolutions," *Journal of Democracy* 17 (4): 5-18.

Bunce, Valerie and Sharon Wolchik. 2010. "Defeating Dictators: Electoral Change and Stability in Competitive Authoritarian Regimes," *World Politics* 62 (1): 43-86.

Bunce, Valerie. 2003. "Rethinking Recent Democratization: Lessons from the Postcommunist Experience," *World Politics* 55 (2): 167-192.

Burrett, T. 2009. "The End of Independent Television? Elite Conflict and the Reconstruction of the Russian Television Landscape." In Beumers, B. et al. (eds.) *The Post-Soviet Russian Media: Conflicting Signals*. Abingdon: Routledge, 71–86.

Burrett, Tina. 2014. "Reaffirming Russia's Remote Control: Exploring Kremlin Influence On Television Coverage Of Russian-Japanese Relations And The Southern Kuril Islands Territorial Dispute," *Demokratizatsiya: The Journal Of Post-Soviet Democratization* 22 (3): 359-381.

Buxton, Julia. 1999. "Venezuela: degenerative democracy." In Burnell, Peter J. and Peter Calvert (ed.) *The Resilience of Democracy: Persistent Practice, Durable Idea*. Portland, Oregon: Frank Cass, 246-270.

Calingaert, Daniel. 2006. "Election Rigging and How to Fight It," *Journal of Democracy* 17 (3): 138-151.

Carothers, Thomas. 2002. "The End of the Transition Paradigm," *Journal of Democracy* 13 (1): 5-21.

Case, William. 1993. "Semi-Democracy in Malaysia: Withstanding the Pressures for Regime Change," *Pacific Affairs* 66 (2): 183-205.

Chad, Vickery and Erica Shein. 2012. "Assessing Electoral Fraud in New Democracies: Refining the Vocabulary," International Foundation for Electoral Systems (IFES) White Papers, May 2012. Retrieved from http://www.ifes.org/~/media/Files/Publications/White%20PaperReport/2012/Assessing_Electoral_Fraud_Series_Vickery_Shein.pdf

Chehabi, Houchang E. and Linz, Juan. 1998. *Sultanistic Regimes*. Baltimore and London: John Hopkins University.

Christians, Clifford G. 2009. *Normative Theories of the Media: Journalism in Democratic Societies The History of Communication*. Urbana: University of Illinois Press.

Cohen, Bernard. 1963. *The Press and Foreign Policy*. Princeton, NJ: Princeton University Press.

Collier, David and Robert Adcock. 1999. "Democracy and Dichotomies: A Pragmatic Approach to Choices about Concepts," *Annual Review of Political Science* 2: 537-65.

Collier, Paul. 2009. "The Dictator's Handbook. Why is Democracy Failing Even as Elections Proliferate? A Thought Experiment Sheds New Light on Why Ageing Autocrats Remain so Hard to Dislodge," *Foreign Policy*, September 30. Retrieved from http://foreignpolicy.com/2009/09/30/the-dictators-handbook/

Collins, Allan and Elizabeth Loftus. 1975. "A Spreading-Activation Theory of Semantic Processing," *Psychological Review* 82 (6): 407-428.

Colton, Timothy and Michael McFaul. 2003. *Popular Choice and Managed Democracy. The Russian Elections of 1999 and 2000*. Washington DC: Brookings Institution Press.

Colton, Timothy J. and Henry E. Hale. 2009. "The Putin Vote: Presidential Electorates in a Hybrid Regime," *Slavic Review* 68 (3): 473-503.

Coppedge, Michael. 1993. "Parties and Society in Mexico and Venezuela: Why Competition Matters," *Comparative Politics* 25 (3): 253-274.

Coulloudon, Virginie. 1998. "Elite Groups in Russia," *Demokratizatsiya* 6 (Summer): 535-49.

Croissant, Aurel and Wolfgang Merkel. 2004. "Consolidated or Defective Democracy? Problems of Regime Change," *Democratization* 11 (5): 156-179.

CRS. 2008. CRS Report for Congress. Russia's March 2008 Presidential Election: Outcomes and Implications. Retrieved from http://fpc.state.gov/documents/organization/103693.pdf

CSPP. 1996-2004. Centre for the Study of Public Policy University of Strathclyde. Russia Votes. Results of Presidential Elections 1999-2004. Retrieved from http://www.russiavotes.org/president/presidency_96-04.php

Dahl, Robert. 1997. *Polyarchy: Participation and Opposition*. New Haven, CT: Yale University Press.

Davis-Roberts, Avery and David J. Carroll. 2010. "Using International Law to Assess Elections," *Democratization* 17 (3): 416-441.

De Smaele, Hedwig. 2007. "Mass Media and the Information Climate in Russia," *Europe-Asia Studies* 59 (8): 1299-1313.

De Vaus, David. 2001. *Research Design in Social Research*. SAGE Publications, London.

Denscombe, Martyn. 2007. *The Good Research Guide for Small-scale Social Research Projects*. 3rd.ed. Open University Press. Berkshire, England.

Diamond, Larry. 1996. "Is the Third Wave Over?" *Journal of Democracy* 7(3): 20-37.

Diamond, Larry. 2002. "Thinking About Hybrid Regimes," *Journal of Democracy* 13 (2): 21-35.

Domke, David, David P. Fan, Michael Fibison, Dhavan V. Shah, Steven S. Smith and Mark D. Watts. 1997. "News Media, Candidates and Issues, and Public Opinion in the 1996 Presidential Campaign," *Journalism and Mass Communication Quarterly* 74 (4): 718-737.

Domke, David, Dhavan V. Shah and Daniel Wackman. 1998. "Media Priming Effects: Accessibility, Association, and Activation," *International Journal of Public Opinion Research* 10 (1), 51-74.

Dunn, John A. 2014. "Lottizzazione Russian Style: Russia's Two-tier Media System," *Europe-Asia Studies* 66 (9): 1425-1451.

Dunn, John. A. 2009. "Where Did It All Go Wrong? Russian Television in the Putin Era." In Beumers, B. et al. (eds.) *The Post-Soviet Russian Media: Conflicting Signals*. Abingdon: Routledge, 42–55.

Dyczok, Marta. 2006. "Was Kuchma's Censorship Effective? Mass Media in Ukraine before 2004," *Europe-Asia Studies* 58 (2): 215-238.

Eckman, Joakim. 2009. "Political Participation and Regime Stability: A Framework for Analyzing Hybrid Regimes," *International Political Sceince Review* 30 (1): 7-31.

Economist. 2010. Fraud and Election: Going Postal, May 6. Retrieved from http://www.economist.com/node/16076117

Economist Index of Democracy. 2010. Democracy Index 2010. A report from the Economist Intell https://graphics.eiu.com/PDF/Democracy_Index_2010_web.pdf

Egorov, Geogry, Sergei Guriev, and Konstantin Sonin. 2009. "Why Resource-poor Dictators Allow Freer Media: A Theory and Evidence from Panel Data," *American Political Science Review* 103 (4): 645-68.

EIM. 1996. The European Institute for the Media Reports. Russia 1996 Presidential elections. Retrieved from http://www.media-politics.com/EIM%20reports/Russia%201996.pdf

EIM. 2000. Monitoring the Media Coverage of the March 2000 Presidential Elections in Russia, Final Report, August, 2000.

Elkit, Jorgen and Andrew Reynolds. 2005. "A Framework for the Systematic Study of Election Quality," *Democratization* 12 (2): 147-162.

Elklit, Jorgen and Andrew Reynolds. 2002. "The Impact of Election Administration on the Legitimacy of Emerging Democracies: A New Comparative Politics Research Agenda," *Commonwealth and Comparative Politics* 40 (2): 86-119.

Elklit, Jorgen and Andrew Reynolds. 2005a. "Judging elections and election management quality by process," *Representation* 41 (3): 189-207.

Enikolopov, R., M. Petrova and E. Zhuravskaya. 2011. "Media and Political Persuasion: Evidence from Russia," *American Economic Review* 101 (7): 3253-3285.

Entman, Robert. 1989. "How the Media Affect What People Think: An Information Processing Approach," *Journal of Politics* 51 (2): 347-370.

Entman, Robert. 2007. "Framing Bias: Media in the Distribution of Power," *Journal of Communication* 57 (1): 163-173.

European Commission for Democracy Through Law. 2002. "Code of good practice in electoral matters. Guidelines and explanatory report," adopted by the Venice Commission at its 52nd session. Venice, October 18-19. Retrieved from http://www.venice.coe.int/webforms/documents/default.aspx?pdffile=CDL-AD%282002%29023rev-e

European Council on Foreign Relations. 2007. Observing Russia's Elections," commentary by Nicu Popescu, 2 December. Retrieved from http://www.ecfr.eu/article/commentary_observing_russias_elections/

Eveland, William. 2003. "A "Mix of Attributes" Approach to the Study of Media Effects and New Communication Technologies," *Journal of Communication* (September): 395-410.

Fearon, James and David Laitin. 2003. "Ethnicity, Insurgency, and Civil War," *American Political Science Review* 97 (1): 75-90.

Fish, Steven. 2005. *Democracy Derailed in Russia: The Failure of Open Politics*. Cambridge: Cambridge University Press.

Fish, Steven. 2006. "Creative Constitutions: How Do Parliamentary Powers Shapes the Electoral Arena?" In Andreas Schedler (ed.) *Electoral Authoritarianism: The Dynamics of Unfree Competition*. Boulder: Lynne Rienner Publishers, 181-197.

Forbes. 2012. Alisher Usmanov: Milliardi i Chelovecheskiye Otnosheniya, April 23. Retrieved from http://www.forbes.ru/sobytiya/lyudi/81454-alisher-usmanov-milliardy-i-chelovecheskie-otnosheniya?page=0,2

References

Forbes. 2013. Milliarder Lebedev Vozglavit Byuro Rassledovaniy "Novoy Gazeti", October 12. Retrieved from http://www.forbes.ru/news/246122-lebedev-vozglavit-otdel-rassledovanii-novoi-gazety

Fossato, Floriana. 2006. "Vladimir Putin and the Russian Television 'Family'," *The Russia Papers/Les Cahiers Russie,* Paris: CeRI Sciences Po.

Fox, Sean and Kristian Hoelscher. 2011. "Political Order, Development and Social Violence: A Cross-Country Study," Paper presented at the annual meeting of the International Studies Association Annual Conference "Global Governance: Political Authority in Transition," Le Centre Sheraton Montreal Hotel, Montreal, Quebec, Canada, Mar 16. Retrieved from http://www.allacademic.com/meta/p499199_index.html

Freedom House. 2005. Freedom in the World, Report on Russia. Retrieved from https://freedomhouse.org/report/freedom-world/2005/russia

Freedom House. 2014. Freedom in the World, Country Ratings. Retrieved from https://www.freedomhouse.org/sites/default/files/Country%20Status%20%26%20Ratings%20Overview%2C%201973-2014.pdf

Freedom House. 2016. Freedom House Freedom in the World Report: Mexico. Retrieved from https://freedomhouse.org/report/freedom-world/2016/mexico

Gandhi, Jennifer and James R.Vreeland. 2004. *Political Institutions and Civil War: Unpacking Anocracy.* Emory University, manuscript.

Gandhi, Jennifer. 2015. "Elections and Political Regimes," *Government and Opposition* 50 (3): 446-468.

Gasiorowski, Mark J.1996. "An Overview of the Political Regime Change Dataset," *Comparative Political Studies* 29 (4): 469-483.

Geddes, Barbara. 1999. "What Do We Know About Democraztization After Twenty Years?" *Annual Review of Political Science* 2 (June): 115-144.

Gehlbach, Scott. 2010. "Reflections on Putin and the Media," *Post-Soviet Affairs* 26 (1): 77-87.

Gel'man, Vladimir. 2008. "Out of Frying Pan, into the Fire? Post-Soviet Regime Changes in Comparative Perspective," *International Political Science Review* 29 (2): 157-180.

Gentzkow, Matthew and Jesse M. Shapiro. 2005. "Media Bias and Reputation," Working Paper 11664, National Bureau of Economic Research, September.

Glasnost Defense Foundation. 2008. Sluzhba Monitoringa Fonda Zasshiti Glasnosti. Materiali Monitoringa. Retrieved from http://www.gdf.ru/monitoring

Golos. 2008. Zayavleniye No.2 Assotsiatsii "Golos" po Rezultatam Dolgosrochnogo Nablyudeniya Hoda Izbiratelnoy Kampanii Prezidenta RF 2 Marta 2008 Goda. Etap Agitatsionnoy Kampanii. February 28, 2008. Retrieved from http://archive.golos.org/asset/75

Golosov, Grigorii. 2010. "Contemporary Regional Politics in Russia: A Chronicle of Degradation," *Russian Analytical Digest.* Institutions in Russia 77 (April 26): 10-13.

Goode, J. Paul. 2010. "Redefining Russia: Hybrid Regimes, Fieldwork, and Russian Politics," *Perspectives on Politics* 8 (4): 1055-1075.

Goode, Paul. 2010. "Redefining Russia: Hybrid Regimes, Fieldwork, and Russian Politics," *Perspectives on Politics* 8 (4): 1055-1075.

Gross, Kimberly and Lisa D'Ambrosio. 2004. "Framing Emotional Response," *Political Psychology* 25 (1): 1-29.

Gudkov, Lev. 2015. "Kogo Rossijane schitajut Svoimi Druz'jami, a Kogo—'Vragami'" – "Whom Do Russians Consider Friends and Foes," *Novoje Vremja*, June 12. Retrieved from http://nv.ua/opinion/Gudkov/kogo-Rossiia ne-schitayut-svoimi-druzyami-a-kogo-vragami-52794.html

Guillermo, A. O'Donell. 2008. "Delegative Democracy," *Journal of Democracy* 5 (1): 55-69.

Guliyev, Farid. 2005. "Post-Soviet Azerbaijan: Transition to Sultanistic Semiauthoritarianism? An Attempt at Conceptualization," *Demokratizatsiya: The Journal of Post-Soviet Democratization* 13 (3): 393-436.

Guliyev, Farid. 2011. "Personal rule, Neopatrimonialism, and Regime Typologies: Integrating Dahlian and Weberian Approaches to Regime Studies," *Democratization* 18 (3): 575-601.

Guriev, Sergei and Andrei Rachinsky. 2005. "The Role of Oligarchs in Russian Capitalism," *Journal of Economic Perspectives* 19: 131-150.

Guriev, Sergei. Rachinsky Andrei. 2004. Ownership concentration in Russian Industry Retrieved from www.cefir.ru/download.php?id=136

Hafez, Kai. 2010. "Journalism Ethics Revisited: A Comparison of Ethics Codes in Europe, North Africa, the Middle East, and Muslim Asia," *Political Communication* 19 (2): 225-250.

Hahn, Gordon. 2004. "Managed Democracy? Building Stealth Authoritarianism in St. Petersburg," *Demokratizatsiya* 12 (2): 195–231.

Hale, Henry E. 2010. "Eurasian Polities as Hybrid Regimes: The Case of Putin's Russia," *Journal of Eurasian Studies* 1: 33-41.

Hale, Henry E. 2011. "Hybrid Regimes: When Democracy and Autocracy Mix." In Nathan Brown (ed.) *Dynamics of Democratization: Dictatorship, Development, and Diffusion*. Baltimore: Johns Hopkins University Press.

Hale, Henry. 2005. "Regime Cycles: Democracy, Autocracy, and Revolution in Post-Soviet Eurasia," *World Politics* 58 (1): 133-65.

Hale, Henry. 2010. "Eurasian Polities as Hybrid Regimes: The Case of Putin's Russia," *Journal of Eurasian Studies* 1 (1): 33-41.

Hallin, Daniel C. and Paolo Mancini. 2004. *Comparing Media Systems : Three Models of Media and Politics Communication, Society, and Politics*. Cambridge: Cambridge University Press.

Hallin, Daniel C. and Paolo Mancini. 2012. *Comparing Media Systems Beyond the Western World Communication, Society and Politics.* Cambridge: Cambridge University Press.

Hanley, Eric, Natasha Yershova and Richard Anderson. 1995. "Russia—Old Wine in a new Bottle? The Circulation and Reproduction of Russian Elites, 1983 - 1993," *Theory and Society* 24: 639-668.

Hansen, Anders. 2000. Claims-making in the Brent Star Controversy. In Stuart Allan, Barbara Adam, Cynthia Carter (ed.) *Environmental Risks and the Media.* London: Routledge.

Hardy, Jonathan. 2008. *Western Media Systems.* Communication and Society. London: Routledge.

Hartlyn, Jonathan, Jennifer McCoy and Thomas Mustillo. 2008. "Electoral Governance Matters. Explaining the Quality of Elections in Contemporary Latin America," *Comparative Political Studies* 41 (1): 73-98.

Hartlyn, Jonathan. 1994. "Crisis-Ridden Elections (Again) in the Dominican Republic: Neopatrimonialism, Presidentialism, and Weak Electoral Oversight," *Journal of International Studies and World Affairs* 36 (4): 91-144.

Hassner, Pierre. 2008. "Russia's Transition to Autocracy," *Journal of Democracy* 19 (2): 5-15.

Hegre, Havard, Tanja Ellingsen, Scott Gates, and Nils Petter Gleditsch. 2001. "Toward a Democratic Civil Peace? Democracy, Political Change, and Civil War, 1816-1992," *American Political Science Review* 95 (1): 33-48.

Helle, Svein-Erik. 2016. "Defining the Playing Field. A Framework for Analysing Fariness in Access to Resources, Media and the Law," *Zeitschrift für Vergleichende Politikwissenschaft* 10 (1): 47-78.

Herman, Edward S. and Noam Chomsky. 1998. *Manufacturing Consent: The Political Economy of the Mass Media.* New York, NY: Pantheon Books.

Higley, John, Jan Pakulski, Wlodzimierz Wesolowski. 1998. *Postcommunist Elites and Democracy in Eastern Europe.* London: Palgrave Macmillan.

Holbert, Lance R., Kelly Garrett and Laurel Gleason. 2010. "A New Era of Minimal Effects? A response to Bennett and Iyengar," *Journal of Communication* 60: 15-34.

Howard, Mark. M. and Philip, G. Roessler. 2006. "Liberalizing Electoral Outcomes in Competitive Authoritarian Regimes," *American Journal of Political Science* 50 (2): 365-381.

Hughes, Sallie and Chappell Lawson. 2005. "The Barriers to Media Opening in Latin America," *Political Communication* 22 (1): 9-25.

Interfax. January, 2016. Novosti Podmoskov'ya. Stabil'nost i Socialnye Garantii stali dlya Rossiia n Vazhnee, chem Bor'ba s Prestupnost'yu - Opros.

Iyengar, Shanto, Mark Peters and Donald Kinder. 1982. "Experimental Demonstrations of the 'Not-So-Minimal' Consequences of Television News Programs," *American Political Science Review* 76 (4): 848-858.

Jasperson, Amy. E., Dhavan. V. Shah, Mark Watts, Ronald J. Faber and David P. Fan. 1998. "Framing and the Public Agenda: Media Effects on the Importance of the Federal Budget Deficit," *Political Communication* 15 (2): 205-224.

Jordan, Gans-Morse. 2004. "Searching for Transitologists: Contemporary Theories of Post-Communist Transitions and the Myth of a Dominant Paradigm," *Post-Soviet Affairs* 20 (4): 320-349.

Junisbai, Barbara (2011). Oligarchs and Ownership: The Role of Financial-Industrial Groups in Controlling Kazakhstan's "Independent Media." In Eric Freedman and Richard Shafer (eds.) *After the Czars and Commissars*. Michigan: Michigan University Press.

Kaid, Lynda Lee and Anne Johnston. 1991. "Negative Versus Positive Television Advertising in U.S. Presidential Campaigns, 1960–1988," *Journal of Communication* 41 (3): 53-064.

Karl, Terry Lynn. 1990. "Dilemmas of Democratization in Latin America," *Comparative Politics* 23 (1): 1-21.

Karl, Terry Lynn. 1995. "The Hybrid Regimes of Central America," *Journal of Democracy* 6 (3): 72-86.

Kaya, Ruchan and Michael Bernhard. 2013. "Are Elections Mechanisms of Authoritarian Stability or Democratization? Evidence from Postcommunist Eurasia," *Perspectives on Politics* 11 (3): 734-754. DOI:10.1017/S1537592713002119.

Kazimova, Arifa. 2011. "Media in Azerbaijan: The Ruling Family Dominates TV, the Opposition Has Some Papers," *Caucasus Analytical Digest* 25 (18 March): 4-7.

Kelley, Judith. 2009. "D-Minus Elections: The Politics and Norms of International Election Observation," *International Organization* 63, 765-787.

Kenzior, Sarah. 2010. "A Reporter Without Borders. Interner Politics and State Violence in Uzbekistan," *Problems of Post-Communism* 57 (1): 40-50.

Klapper, Joseph T. 1960. *The Effects of Mass Communication Foundations of Communications Research*. New York: Free Press.

Kleinnijenhuis, Jan and Edwald Rietberg. 1995. "Parties, Media, the Public and the Economy: Patterns of Societal Agenda-Setting," *European Journal of Political Research: Official Journal of the European Consortium for Political Research* 28 (1): 95-118.

Koikkalainen, Katja. 2007. "The Local and the International Business Journalism: Structures and Practices," *Europe-Asia Studies* 59 (8): 1315-1329.

Koltsova, Olessia. 2001. "News Production in Contemporary Russia: Practices of Power," *European Journal of Communication* 16 (3): 315-335.

Koltsova, Olessia. 2006. *News Media and Power in Russia*. Routledge, Taylor and Francis Group.

Kommersant. 25 Feb, 2000. Otkritoye Pis'mo Vladimira Putina k Rossiiskim Izbiratelyam. Retrieved from http://www.kommersant.ru/doc/141144

Kommersant. 2008. "Europe Gives up Russia. OSCE Decided not to Monitor the State Duma Elections." Retrieved from http://www.kommersant.com/pda/doc.asp?id=826514

Kommerstant. 2010. 13 September. Gruppa YeSN, Company profile. Retrieved from http://www.kommersant.ru/doc/1503280

Konig, Ruben Peter and Karsten Renckstorf. 2009. *Meaningful Media: Communication Research on the Social Construction of Reality.* Nijmegen: Tandem Felix.

KPRF. 1999. "Programma Vosstanovleniya i Razvitiya Ekonomiki Agropromishlennogo Kompleksa Rossii," Moskva, ITRK. Accessed at The Collection of Documents Produced by Russian Political Parties and Organizations, held by the Research Centre for Easteuropean Studies at the University of Bremen, Germany.

KPRF. 2008. "Programma Kommunisticheskoy Partii Rossiiskoi Federatsii," Moskva. Accessed at The Collection of Documents Produced by Russian Political Parties and Organizations, held by the Research Centre for Easteuropean Studies at the University of Bremen, Germany.

Krippendorff, Klaus. 2004. "Reliability in Content Analysis - Some Common Misconceptions and Recommendations," *Human Communication Research* 30 (3): 411-433.

Krippendorff, Klaus. 2004. *Content Analysis: An Introduction to Its Methodology,* 2nd (ed.) Thousand Oaks: SAGE.

Kryshtanovskaya, Olga and Stephen White. 1996. "From Soviet Nomenklatura to Russian Elite," *Europe-Asia Studies* 48 (5): 711-733.

Kryshtanovskaya, Olga and Stephen White. 2005. "The Rise of the Russian Business Elite," *Communist and Post-Communist Studies* 38 (3): 293-307.

Kryshtanovskaya, Olga and White Stephen. 2005. "Inside the Putin Court: A Research Note," *Europe-Asia Studies* 57 (7): 1065-1075.

Kryshtanovskayaa, Olga and Stephen White. 2011. "Can Medvedev Change Sistema?: Informal Networks and Public Administration in Russia." In Vadim Kononenko, Arkady Moshes (eds.) *Russia as a network state : what works in Russia when state institutions do not?* New York, NY : Palgrave Macmillan

Lane, David, Cameron Ross, Jan Pakulski, John Higley, W. Weselowski. 1998. The Russian Political Elites, 1991–95: Recruitment and Renewal. In John Higley, Jan Pakulski, and Wlodzimierz Wesolowski (eds.) *Post Communist Elites in Eastern Europe.* London: Macmillan, 34-66.

Lane, David. and Cameron Ross. 1999. *From Communism to Capitalism: Ruling Elites from Gorbachev to Yeltsin.* New York: St. Martin's Press.

Lang, Gladys Engel and Kurt Lang. 1981. "Watergate: An Exploration of the Agenda-Building Process," *Mass Communication Review Yearbook* 2, 447-468.

Lang, Kurt and Gladys Engel Lang. 1966. The Mass Media and Voting. In Bernard Berelson and Morris Janowitz (eds.) *Reader in Public Opinion and Communication*, 2nd ed. New York: Free Press.

Lasswell, Harold D. 1935. *World Politics and Personal Insecurity*. New York: Whittlesey House.

Lawrence, Regina G. 2000. "Game-Framing the Issues: Tracking the Strategy Frame in Public Policy News," *Political Communication* 17 (2): 93-114.

Lazarsfeld, Paul F., Bernard Berelson and Hazel Gaudet. 1944. *The People's Choice: How the Voter Makes up His Mind in a Presidential Campaign*. New York: Duelle.

Lazitski, Olga. 2013. "Media Endarkenment: A Comparative Analysis of 2012 Election Coverage in the United States and Russia," *American Behavioral Scientist* 58 (7): 898-927.

LDPR. 2008. Uspokoyu Vseh! Programma Kandidata v Prezidenti Rossii V.V. Zhirinovskogo, Moskva. Accessed at The Collection of Documents Produced by Russian Political Parties and Organizations, held by the Research Centre for Easteuropean Studies at the University of Bremen, Germany.

Ledeneva Alena. 2012. "Cronies, Economic Crime and Capitalism in Putin's Sistema," *International Affairs* 88 (1): 149-157.

Lehoucq, Fabrice (2003). "Electoral Fraud: Causes, Types, and Consequences," *Annual Review of Political Science* 6: 233-256.

Lehoucq, Fabrice and Ivan Molina. 2002. *Stuffing the Ballot Box: Fraud, Electoral Reform, and Democratization in Costa Rica*. Cambridge: Cambridge University Press.

Lenta.ru. 2012. Usmanov, Alisher. Vladelec Izdatel'skogo Doma "Kommerstan'" i Kompanii "Mediaholding." Retrieved from https://lenta.ru/lib/14164974/, 24 October, 2015.

Levada Center. 2009. Russian Public Opinion – March 2008 – March 2009. Retrieved from http://www.levada.ru/old/sites/default/files/levada_2008_eng.pdf

Levada Center. 2012. Annual Russian Public Opinion – 2012-213. Retrieved from http://www.levada.ru/sites/default/files/2012_eng.pdf

Levada Centre. 2015. "Putin's approval ratings." Retrieved from http://www.levada.ru/eng/indexes-0

Levitsky, S. and L. A. Way. 2002. "The Rise of Competitive Authoritarianism," *Journal of Democracy* 13 (2): 51-65.

Levitsky, Steven and James Loxton. 2013. "Populism and competitive authoritarianism in the Andes," *Democratization* 20 (1): 107-136.

Levitsky, Steven and Lucan A. Way. 2010. *Competitive Authoritarianism: Hybrid Regimes after the Cold War Problems of International Politics*. Cambridge: Cambridge University Press.

Lindberg, Staffan I. 2009. *Democratization by Elections: A New Mode of Transition.* Baltimore: Johns Hopkins University Press.

Lindberg, Staffan. 2004. Code book for data set on Elections and Democracy in Africa 1989-2003. Retrieved from http://users.clas.ufl.edu/sil/downloads/demo_elect_africa_fileinfo.pdf

Lindberg, Staffan. 2009. "The power of elections in africa revisited," In Staffan I. Lindberg (eds.) *Democritization by Elections: A New Mode of Transition.* Baltimore: Johns Hopkins University Press, 25-46.

Lipman Maria. and Michal McFaul. 2001. "'Managed Democracy' in Russia: Putin and the Press," *The Harvard International Journal of Press/Politics* 6, 117-128.

Lipman, Maria. 2009. "Media Manipulation and Political Control in Russian," Carnegie Moscow Center, Russian and Eurasia Programme: REP PP 09/01

Lipman, Masha and Michael McFaul. 2003. The Media and Political Development. In Stephen Wegren and Dale Herspring (eds.) *After Putin's Russia: Past Imperfect, Future Uncertain.* Lanham: Rowman and Littlefield.

Lipman, Masha. 2014. "Russia's Nongovernmental Media Under Assault," *Demokratizatsiya* 22 (2): 179-190.

Lippmann, Walter. 1922. "The World Outside and the Pictures in Our Heads," *Public opinion* 4, 1-22.

Lopez-Pintor, Rafael. 2011. "Assessing Electoral Fraud in New Democracies. A Basic Conceptual Framework," IFES Conference Paper, February 16-19, 2011, Sao Paulo, Brazil.

Mainwaring, Scott. 2012. "From Representative Democracy to Participatory Competitive Authoritarianism: Hugo Chávez and Venezuelan Politics," *Perspectives on Politics* 10 (4): 955-967.

Mansfield, Edward and Jack Snyder. 2002. "Democratic Transitions, Institutional Strength, and War," *International Organization* 56 (2): 297–337.

Mansfield, Edward and Jack Snyder. 2005. *Electing to Fight. Why Emerging Democracies Go to War.* Cambridge, MA: MIT Press.

Marcuse, Herbert. 1964. *One-Dimensional Man: Studies in the Ideology of Advanced Industrial Society.* Boston: Beacon.

Marlino, Leonardo. 2009. "Are there Hybrid Regimes? Or are They Just an Optical Illusion?" *European Political Science Review* 1 (2): 273-296.

Marshall, Monty G. and Keith Jaggers. 2002. Polity IV Project: Political Regime Characteristics and Transitions, 1800-2002.

McCombs, Maxwell and Amy Reynolds. 2009. "How the News Shapes our Civic Agenda." In Jennings Bryant and Mary Beth Oliver (eds.) *Media Effects: Advances in Theory and Research.* New York: Routlegde.

McCombs, Maxwell and David Weaver. 1985. "Toward a Merger of Gratifications and Agenda-Setting Research." In Karl Erik Resengren, Lawrence A. Wenner and Philip Palmgreen, P. (ed.) *Media Gratifications Research: Current Perspectives*. Beverly Hills, CA.: Sage.

McCombs, Maxwell and Donald Shaw. 1972. "The Agenda-Setting Function of Mass Media," *The Public Opinion Quarterly* 36 (2): 176-187.

McCombs, Maxwell, Donald Shaw and David Weaver. 1997. *Communication and Democracy: Exploring the Intellectual Frontiers in Agenda-Setting Theory*. Mahwah, New Jersey: Lawrence Erlbaum Associates Inc., Publishers.

McCombs, Maxwell, Juan Pablo Llamas, Esteban Lopez-Escobar and Federico Rey. 1998. "Candidate Images in Spanish Elections: Second-Level Agenda-Setting Effects," *Journalism and Mass Communication Quarterly* 74 (4): 703-717.

McCoy, Jennifer L. and Jonathan Hartlyn. 2009. "The relative powerlessness of elections in latin america." In Staffan I. Lindberg (ed.) *Democritization by Elections: A New Mode of Transition*. Baltimore: Johns Hopkins University Press, pp. 47-76.

McDonald, Ronald H. 1972. "Electoral Fraud and Regime Controls in Latin," *The Western Political Quarterly* 25 (1): 81-93.

McFaul, Michael and Timothy Colton. 2003. *Popular Choice and Managed Democracy: The Russian Elections of 1999 and 2000*. The Brookings Institution Press. Washington, D.C.

McFaul, Michal. 2005. "Transitions from Postcommunism," *Journal of Democracy* 16 (3): 5-19.

McNair, Brian. 1991. *Glasnost, Perestroika and the Soviet Media*. London and New York: Routledge.

McNair, Brian. 1994. "Media in Post-Soviet Russia: An Overview," *European Journal of Communication* 9 (2): 115-135.

McNair, Brian. 2007. *An Introduction to Political Communication*. London: Routledge, Taylor and Francis Group.

McQuail, Denis. 1992. *Mass Communication Theory: An Introduction*. London: Sage Publ.

McQuail, Denis. 1999. *Media Performance: Mass Communication and the Public Interest*. London: Sage Publ.

McQuail, Denis. 2010. *McQuail's Mass Communication Theory*, 6th ed. London: Sage Publications.

Means, Gordon P. 1996. "Soft Authoritarianism in Malaysia and Singapore," *Journal of Democracy* 7 (4): 103-117.

Merkel, Wolfgang. 2004. "Embedded and Defective Democracies," *Democratization* 11 (5): 33-58.

Mickiewicz, Ellen. 1997. *Changing Channels: Television and the Struggle for Power in Russia*. Revised and Expanded Paperback Edition. Durham, NC: Duke University Press.

References

Mickiewicz, Ellen. 2005. "Excavating Concealed Tradeoffs: How Russians Watch the News," *Political Communication* 22: 355-380.

Mickiewicz, Ellen. 2006. "The Election News Story on Russian Television: A World Apart from Viewers," *Slavic Review* (Spring): 1-23.

Mickiewicz, Ellen. 2008. *Television, Power, and the Public in Russia.* London: Cambridge University Press.

Monroe, Price. 1995. "Low, Force, and the Russia Media," *Cardozo Arts and Entertainment Law Journal* 13: 795-846.

Morse, Yonatan. 2012. "The Era of Electoral Authoritarianism," *World Politics* 64 (1): 161-198.

Mozaffar, Shaheen and Andreas Schedler. 2002. "The Comparative Study of Electoral Governance – Introduction," *International Political Science Review* 23 (1): 5-27.

MSI. 2009. "Russia Media Sustainability Index." Retrieved from https://www.irex.org/sites/default/files/EE_MSI_09_russ_Russia.pdf

Munck, Gerardo L. and Jay Verkuilen. 2002. "Conceptualizing and Measuring Democracy: Evaluating Alternative Indices," *Comparative Political Studies* 35 (1): 5-34.

Myagkov, Mikhail, Peter C. Ordeshook and Dimitry Shakin. 2005. "Fraud or Fairytales: Russia and Ukraine's Electoral Experience," *Post-Soviet Affairs* 21 (2): 91-131.

Nelson, Thomas. E., Rosalee A. Clawson and Zoe M. Oxley. 1997. "Media Framing of a Civil Liberties Conflict and Its Effect on Tolerance," *American Political Science Review* 91 (3): 567-583.

Nerone, John C. and William E. Berry. 1995. *Last Rights: Revisiting Four Theories of the Press The History of Communication.* Urbana: University of Illinois Press.

Neuman, Russell and Lauren Guggenheim. 2011. "The Evolution of Media Effects Theory: A Six-stage Model of Communicative Research," *Communication Theory* 21: 169-196.

Nickol, Jim. 2008. CRS Report for Congress, "Russia's March 2008 Presidential Election: Outcome and Implications." Retrieved from http://fpc.state.gov/documents/organization/103693.pdf

Nikolai Petrov, Masha Lipman and Henry E. Hale. 2010. "Overmanaged Democracy in Russia: Governance Implications of Hybrid Regimes," *Carnegie Papers Russia and Eurasia Program* No. 106, February.

Noelle-Neumann, Elisabeth. 1983. "The Effect of Media on Media Effects Research," *Journal of Communication* (Summer): 157-165.

Norris, Pippa. 2014. *Why Electoral Integrity Matters.* New York: Cambridge University Press.

O'Donnell, Guillermo. 1994. "Delegative Democracy," *Journal of Democracy* 5 (1): 55-69.

Oates, Sarah and Laura Roselle. 2000. "Russian Elections and TV News. Comparison of Campaign News on State-Controlled and Commercial Television Channels," *Press/Politics* 5 (2): 30-51.

Oates, Sarah. 2006. *Television, Democracy, and Elections in Russia*. London: Routledge.

Olson, Mancur. 1971. *The Logic of Collective Action: Public Goods and the Theory of Groups*. Cambridge Harvard University Press.

Orttung, Robert W. 2010. "Understanding Recent Developments in Russia's Political System," *Russian Analitical Digest*. Institutions in Russia 77 (April 26): 6-9.

OSCE. 2000. ODIHR Election Observation. Russian Federation, Presidential Election, Final Report, March 26, 2000.

Ottaway, Marina. 2003. *Democracy Challenged: The Rise of Semi-Authoritarianism*. Washington. DC: Carnegie Endowment for International Peace.

Parenti, Michael. 1993. *Inventing Reality: The Politics of the News Media*. New York: St. Martin's Press.

Pasti, Svetlana. 2005. "Two Generations of Contemporary Russian Journalists," *European Journal of Communication* 20 (1): 89-115.

Pastor, Robert. 2007. "The Role of Electoral Administration in Democratic Transitions: Implications for Policy and Research," *Democratization* 6 (4): 1-27.

Patton, Michael Quinn. 2010. *Qualitative Research and Evaluation Methods*. 3rd. ed. Thousand Oaks: Sage.

Pearce, Katy and Sarah Kendzior. 2012. "Networked Authoritarianism and Social Media in Azerbaijan," *Journal of Communication* 62 (2): 283-298.

Pearce, Katy. 2014. "Two Can Play at That Game: Social Media Opportunities in Azerbaijan for Government and Opposition," *Demokratizatsiya* 22: 39-66.

Peeler, John. 2009. *Building Democracy in Latin America*, 3rd ed. Boulder: Lynne Rienner Publishers.

Peterson, Ruth and Louis L. Thurstone. 1933. *Motion Pictures and the Social Attitudes of Children: A Payne Fund Study*. New York: Macmillan and Co.

Petrov, Nikolai, Masha Lipman and Henry E. Hale. 2010. "Overmanaged Democracy in Russia: Governance Implications of Hybrid Regimes," Carnegie Papers Russia and Eurasia Program 106, February.

Plan Putina. 2007. "Plan Putina. Kratkiy Spravochnik Putevoditel'." Accessed at The Collection of Documents Produced by Russian Political Parties and Organizations, held by the Research Centre for Easteuropean Studies at the University of Bremen, Germany.

Polit-Gramota. 2013. Politologiya 14 March. Retrieved from http://polit-gramota.ru/bez-rubriki/politologiya-5/1866

Polity IV. 2010. Polity IV Country Report: Mexico. Retrieved from http://www.systemicpeace.org/polity/Mexico2010.pdf

Polsby, Nelson W. 1980. "The News Media as an Alternative to Party in the Presidential Selection Process," Political parties in the Eighties, 50-66.

Przeworski, Adam, Michael Alvarez, Jose A. Cheibub, and Fernando Limongi. 2000. *Democracy and development*. Cambridge: Cambridge University Press.

Radio Svoboda. 26 Feb, 2016. Kakoy Bila Predvibornaya Kampaniya Dmitriya Medvedeva. Retrieved from http://www.svoboda.org/content/transcript/436662.html

Radnitz, Scott. 2010. "The Color of Money: Privatization, Dispersion, and the Post-Soviet 'Revolutions'," *Comparative Politics* 42 (2): 127-146.

Renz, Bettina. 2006. "Putin's Militocracy? An alternative interpretation of Siloviki in contemporary Russian politics," *Europe-Asia Studies* 58 (6): 903-924.

RFERL September 3, 2007. "Russia: 'Nezavisimaia Gazeta' Is Worth Watching Again." Retrieved from http://www.rferl.org/content/article/1078496.html

RIA Novosti. 26 Feb, 2008. "Predvibornaya Programma Andreya Bogdanova." Retrieved from http://ria.ru/spravka/20080226/100054951.html

RIA Novosti. 26 Feb, 2008. "Predvibornaya programma Dmitriy Medvedeva." Retrieved from http://ria.ru/spravka/20080226/100066207.html

RIA Novosti. 26 Feb, 2008. "Predvibornaya Programma Gennadiia Ziuganova." Retrieved from http://ria.ru/spravka/20080226/100061680.html

RIA Novosti. 26 Feb, 2008. "Predvibornaya Programma Vladimira Zhirinovskogo." Retrieved from http://ria.ru/spravka/20080226/100055236.html

Richter, Andrei. 2008. "Post-Soviet Perspective on Censorship and Freedom of the Media," *The International Communication Gazette* 70 (5): 307-324.

Rigby, T. H. 1999. "New Top Elites for Old in Russian Politics," *British Journal of Political Science* 29 (2): 323-343.

Rivera, Sharon Werning and David W. Rivera. 2006. "The Russian Elite under Putin: Militocratic or Bourgeois?" *Post-Soviet Affairs* 22 (2): 125-144.

Rivera, Sharon Werning. 2000. "Elites in Post-Communist Russia: A Changing of the Guard?" *Europe-Asia Studies* 52 (3): 413–432.

Roessler, Philip G. and Marc M. Howard. 2009. "Post-Cold war political regimes: when do elections matter?" In by Staffan I. Lindberg (ed.) *Democritization by Elections: A New Mode of Transition*. Baltimore: Johns Hopkins University Press, pp. 101-127.

Rollberg, Peter. 2014. "Peter the Great, Statism, and Axiological Continuity in Contemporary Russian Television," *Demokratizatsiya* 22(2): 335-355.

Ross, Cameron. 2005."Federalism and Electoral Authoritarianism under Putin," *Demokratizatsiya: The Journal of Post-Soviet Democratization* 13 (3): 347–72;

Rossiiskaia Gazeta. 18 Feb, 2000. "Vladimir Zhirinovsky. Pochemu Ya - Kandidat v prezidenti Rossii." Retrieved from http://www.agitclub.ru/vybory/put/put2000/putinn213.htm

Rossiiskaia Gazeta. 22 March, 2000. "Strategiya Proriva. Prezidentskaya Programma (2000-2004) Grigoriya Yavlinskogo." Retrieved from http://www.agitclub.ru/vybory/put/put2000/putinn212.htm

Roudakova, Natalia. 2009. "Journalism as "Prostitution": Understanding Russia's Reactions to Anna Politkovskaya's Murder," *Political Communication* 26: 412-429.

Sartori, Giovanni. 1970. "Concept misinformation in comparative politics," *American Political Science Review* LXIV (4), 1033–1053.

Schatz, Edward. 2009. "The Soft Authoritarian Tool Kit: Agenda-Setting Power in Kazakhstan and Kyrgyzstan," *Comparative Politics* 41 (2): 203-222.

Schedler, Aadreas. 2006. *Electoral Authoritarianism: The Dynamics of Unfree Competition*. Boulder: Lynne Rienner Publishers.

Schedler, Aadreas. 2013. *The Politics of Uncertainty: Sustaining and Subverting Electoral Authoritarianism*. Oxford: Oxford University Press.

Schedler, Andreas. 2002. "The Menu of Manipulation," *Journal of Democracy* 13 (2): 36-50.

Scheufele, Dietram. 1999. "Framing as a Theory of Media Effects," *Journal of Communication* (Winter): 103-122.

Schimpfossl, Elisabeth and Yablokov, Ilya. 2014. "Coercion or Conformism? Censorship and Self-Censorship among Russian Media Personalities and Reporters in the 2010s," *Demokratizatsiya* 295-311.

Schlesinger, Philip. 1987. *Putting "Reality" Together: BBC News*. New York: Methuen.

Schmitter, Philippe and Terry Lynn Karl. 1991. "What Democracy Is … and Is Not," *Journal of Democracy* 2(3): 75-88.

Schreier, Margrit. 2012. *Qualitative Content Analysis in Practice*. Los Angeles: Sage.

Seymour-Ure, Colin. 1974. *The Political Impact of Mass Media*. Communication and Society 4. Beverly Hills, Calif: Sage Publications.

Shafer, Michael. 1994. *Winners and Losers: How Sectors Shape the Developmental Prospects of States*. Ithaca and London: Cornell University Press.

Shafer, Richard and Eric Freedman. 2003. "Obstacles to the Professionalization of Mass Media in Post-Soviet Central Asia: A Case Study of Uzbekistan," *Journalism Studies* 4 (1): 91-103.

Shaw, Donald and Maxwell McCombs. 1977. *The Emergence of American Political Issues: The Agenda-Setting Function of the Press*. St. Paul: West.

Shevtsova, Lilia. 2009. "The Return of Personalized Power," *Journal of Democracy* 20 (2): 61–5.

Shlapentokh, Vladimir. 2004. "Wealth Versus Political Power: the Russian Case," *Communist and Post-Communist Studies* 37, 135-160.

Sidorov, Dmitriy. 2015. "Kak Delayut TV-propagandu: Chetire Svidetel'stva," *Colta.ru*. Retrieved from http://www.colta.ru/articles/society/8163

Siebert, Fredrick Seaton, Theodore Peterson and Wilbur Schramm. 1956. *Four Theories of the Press: The Authoritarian, Libertarian, Social Responsibility, and Soviet Communist Concepts of What the Press Should Be and Do.* Urbana, Ill.: University of Illinois Press.

Silitski, Vitali. 2009. "Reading Russia: Tools of Autocracy," *Journal of Democracy* 20 (2): 42-46.

Spencer, Douglas M. and Zachary S. Markovitz. 2010. "Long Lines at Polling Stations? Observations from an Election Day Field Study," *Election Law Journal* 9 (1): 3-17.

Staun J. 2007. "Siloviki Versus Liberal-Technocrats. The Fight for Russia and Its Foreign Policy," DIIS Report, Copenhagen.

Stoker, Gerry. 1998. "Governance as Theory: Five Propositions," International Social Science Journal 50 (155): 17-28.

Street, John. 2001. *Mass Media, Politics and Democracy.* Basingstoke: Palgrave.

Takens, Janet, Wouter van Atteveldt, Anita van Hoof and Jan Kleinnijenhuis. 2013. "Media Logic in Election Campaign Coverage," *European Journal of Communication* 28 (3): 277-293.

Tan, Netina. 2013. "Manipulating Electoral laws in Singapore," *Electoral Studies* 32, 632-643.

Tankard, J., Hendrickson, L., Silberman, J., Bliss, K., and Ghanem, S. 1991. Media frames: Approaches to Conceptualization and Measurement. Paper presented to the Association for Education in Journalism and Mass Communication, Boston.

The Telegraph. March, 2016. Alexander Mamut Profile: Probably the Most Powerful Oligarch You Have Heard of. Retrieved from: http://www.telegraph.co.uk/finance/newsbysector/epic/hmv/8303237/Alexander-Mamut-profile-probably-the-most-powerful-oligarch-you-have-never-heard-of.html

The Moscow Times. 2001. Norwegians Sign Deal for $10M Press, 20 June. Retrieved from http://www.themoscowtimes.com/sitemap/free/2001/6/article/norwegians-sign-deal-for-10m-press/253009.html

Thussu, Daya Kishan. 2009. *News as Entertainment: The Rise of Global Infotainment.* Los Angeles: SAGE Publ.

TNS Gallup. Danniye Issledovaniy Auditorii SMI. Retrieved from http://www.tns-global.ru/services/media/media-audience/dannye_issledovaniy_auditorii_smi/

Transparency International. 2015. Corruption Perceptions Index. Retrieved from http://www.transparency.org/research/cpi/overview

Treisman, Daniel. 2007. "Putin's Solovarchs," *Orbis* 51 (1): 141-153.

Treisman, Daniel. 2010. "Is Russia Cursed by Oil," *Journal of International Affairs* 63 (2): 85-102.

Treisman, Daniel. 2011. "Presidential Popularity in a Hybrid Regime: Russia under Yeltsin and Putin," *American Journal of Political Science* 55 (3); 590–609.

United Nations. 2005. "Declaration of principles for international election observation and code of conduct for international election observers," October 27, New York. Retrieved from https://www.ndi.org/files/1923_declaration_102705.pdf

Van Ham, Carolien (2015). "Getting elections right? Measuring electoral integrity," *Democratization* 22 (4): 714-737. DOI: 10.1080/13510347.2013.877447.

Vartanova, Elena. 2011. "The Russian Media Model in the Context of Post-Soviet Dynamics." In Daniel Hallin and Paolo Mancini (eds.) *Comparing Media Systems Beyond the Western World*. Cambridge: Cambridge University Press.

Vedomosti. 2014. U Rambler Snovo Noviy Direktor. 21 April. Retrieved from http://www.vedomosti.ru/newspaper/articles/2014/04/21/u-rambler-snova-novyj-direktor

Voltmer, Katrin. 2000. "Constructing Political Reality in Russia: Izvestiya — Between Old and New Journalistic Practices," *European Journal of Communication* 15 (4): 469-500.

Voltmer, Katrin. 2007. *Mass Media and Political Communication in New Democracies*. (Repr. ed.) Routledge/Ecpr Studies in European Political Science. London: Routledge.

Voltmer, Katrin. 2013. *The Media in Transitional Democracies. Contemporary Political Communication*. Cambridge: Polity.

Vulchanov, Nikolai and Anders Eriksson. 2010. "Report on Figure Based Management of Possible Election Fraud," adopted by the Council for Democratic Election at its 35th meeting (Venice, 16 December 2010) and by the Venice Commission at its 85th Plenary Session (Venice, 17-18 December 2010). Retrieved from http://www.venice.coe.int/webforms/documents/default.aspx?pdffile=CDL-AD%282010%29043-e=

Walker, Christopher and Robert Orttung. 2014. "Breaking the News: The Role of State-Run Media," *Journal of Democracy* 25 (1): 71-85.

Wantchekon, Leonard. 2003. "Clientelism and Voting Behavior: Evidence from a Field Experiment in Benin," *World Politics* 55, 399-422.

Way, Lucan. 2008. "The Real Causes of the Color Revolutions," *Journal of Democracy* 19 (3): 55-69.

Weaver, David. 2007. "Thoughts on Agenda Setting, Framing, and Priming," *Journal of Communication* 57 (1): 142-147.

Wheatley, Jonathan and Christoph Zuercher. 2008. "On the Origin and Consolidation of Hybrid Regimes. The State of Democracy in the Caucasus," *Taiwan Journal of Democracy* 4 (1): 1-31.

White, Stephen and Ian McAllister. 2003. "Politics and the Media in Post-Communist Russia," *Politics* 23(1): 31-37.

White, Stephen and Ian McAllister. 2006. "Politics and the Media in Post-Communist Russia," In Voltmer, Katrin, (ed.)*Mass Media and Political Communication in New Democracies*. Series: Routledge/ECPR studies in European Political Science (42). Routledge, London.

White, Stephen, Sarah Oates and Ian McAllister. 2005. "Media Effects and Russian Elections, 1999-2000," *British Journal of Political Science* 35, 191-208.

White, Stephen. 2008. *Media, Culture and Society in Putin's Russia.* New York: Palgrave Macmillan.

Wigell, Mikael. 2008. "Mapping 'Hybrid Regimes': Regime Types and Concepts in Comparative Politics," *Democratization* 15 (2): 230–50.

Woong Rhee, June. 1997. "Strategy and Issue Frames in Election Campaign Coverage: A Social Cognitive Account of Framing Effects," *Journal of Communication* 47 (3): 26-48.

World Bank. 2015. Data on GDP Growth. Retrieved from http://data.worldbank.org/indicator/NY.GDP.MKTP.KD.ZG?page=3

World Bank. 2015. Data on Inflation. Retrieved from http://data.worldbank.org/indicator/NY.GDP.DEFL.KD.ZG/countries?page=3

Wu, Wei, David Weaver, Owen V. Johnson. 1996. "Professional Roles of Russian and U.S. Journalists: A Comparative Study," *Journal of Mass Communication Quarterly* 73 (3): 534-548.

Yabloko. 1999. "Programmnih Podhod k Reformam v Rossii," by Alyoshin, D., Novikov A., Ul'yanov A. Accessed at The Collection of Documents Produced by Russian Political Parties and Organizations, held by the Research Centre for Easteuropean Studies at the University of Bremen, Germany.

Zakaria, Fareed. 1997. "The Rise of Illiberal Democracy," *Foreign Affairs* 76 (6): 22-43.

Zasurskii, Ivan. 2004. *Media and Power in Post-Soviet Russia.* New York: M.E. Sharpe, Inc.

Ziblatt, Daniel. 2006. "How did Europe Democratize?" *World Politics* 58 (2): 311-338.

Ziblatt, Daniel. 2009. "Shaping Democratic Practice and the Causes of Electoral Fraud: The case of Nineteenth-Century Germany," *American Political Science Review* 103 (1): 1-21.

Zinicker, Heidrun. 2007. Democracy, Diversity, and Conflict. Regime-Hybridity and Violent Ceivil Societies in Fragmented Societies—Conceptual Considerations. Cornell University, Peace Studies Program, Occasional Paper, 30-5.

SOVIET AND POST-SOVIET POLITICS AND SOCIETY

Edited by Dr. Andreas Umland

ISSN 1614-3515

1   *Андреас Умланд (ред.)*
    Воплощение Европейской
    конвенции по правам человека в
    России
    Философские, юридические и
    эмпирические исследования
    ISBN 3-89821-387-0

2   *Christian Wipperfürth*
    Russland – ein vertrauenswürdiger
    Partner?
    Grundlagen, Hintergründe und Praxis
    gegenwärtiger russischer Außenpolitik
    Mit einem Vorwort von Heinz Timmermann
    ISBN 3-89821-401-X

3   *Manja Hussner*
    Die Übernahme internationalen Rechts
    in die russische und deutsche
    Rechtsordnung
    Eine vergleichende Analyse zur
    Völkerrechtsfreundlichkeit der Verfassungen
    der Russländischen Föderation und der
    Bundesrepublik Deutschland
    Mit einem Vorwort von Rainer Arnold
    ISBN 3-89821-438-9

4   *Matthew Tejada*
    Bulgaria's Democratic Consolidation
    and the Kozloduy Nuclear Power Plant
    (KNPP)
    The Unattainability of Closure
    With a foreword by Richard J. Crampton
    ISBN 3-89821-439-7

5   *Марк Григорьевич Меерович*
    Квадратные метры, определяющие
    сознание
    Государственная жилищная политика в
    СССР. 1921 – 1941 гг
    ISBN 3-89821-474-5

6   *Andrei P. Tsygankov, Pavel
    A.Tsygankov (Eds.)*
    New Directions in Russian
    International Studies
    ISBN 3-89821-422-2

7   *Марк Григорьевич Меерович*
    Как власть народ к труду приучала
    Жилище в СССР – средство управления
    людьми. 1917 – 1941 гг.
    С предисловием Елены Осокиной
    ISBN 3-89821-495-8

8   *David J. Galbreath*
    Nation-Building and Minority Politics
    in Post-Socialist States
    Interests, Influence and Identities in Estonia
    and Latvia
    With a foreword by David J. Smith
    ISBN 3-89821-467-2

9   *Алексей Юрьевич Безугольный*
    Народы Кавказа в Вооруженных
    силах СССР в годы Великой
    Отечественной войны 1941-1945 гг.
    С предисловием Николая Бугая
    ISBN 3-89821-475-3

10 *Вячеслав Лихачев и Владимир
    Прибыловский (ред.)*
    Русское Национальное Единство,
    1990-2000. В 2-х томах
    ISBN 3-89821-523-7

11 *Николай Бугай (ред.)*
    Народы стран Балтии в условиях
    сталинизма (1940-е – 1950-е годы)
    Документированная история
    ISBN 3-89821-525-3

12 *Ingmar Bredies (Hrsg.)*
    Zur Anatomie der Orange Revolution
    in der Ukraine
    Wechsel des Elitenregimes oder Triumph des
    Parlamentarismus?
    ISBN 3-89821-524-5

13 *Anastasia V. Mitrofanova*
    The Politicization of Russian
    Orthodoxy
    Actors and Ideas
    With a foreword by William C. Gay
    ISBN 3-89821-481-8

14 Nathan D. Larson
    Alexander Solzhenitsyn and the
    Russo-Jewish Question
    ISBN 3-89821-483-4

15 Guido Houben
    Kulturpolitik und Ethnizität
    Staatliche Kunstförderung im Russland der
    neunziger Jahre
    Mit einem Vorwort von Gert Weisskirchen
    ISBN 3-89821-542-3

16 Leonid Luks
    Der russische „Sonderweg"?
    Aufsätze zur neuesten Geschichte Russlands
    im europäischen Kontext
    ISBN 3-89821-496-6

17 Евгений Мороз
    История «Мёртвой воды» – от
    страшной сказки к большой
    политике
    Политическое неоязычество в
    постсоветской России
    ISBN 3-89821-551-2

18 Александр Верховский и Галина
    Кожевникова (ред.)
    Этническая и религиозная
    интолерантность в российских СМИ
    Результаты мониторинга 2001-2004 гг.
    ISBN 3-89821-569-5

19 Christian Ganzer
    Sowjetisches Erbe und ukrainische
    Nation
    Das Museum der Geschichte des Zaporoger
    Kosakentums auf der Insel Chortycja
    Mit einem Vorwort von Frank Golczewski
    ISBN 3-89821-504-0

20 Эльза-Баир Гучинова
    Помнить нельзя забыть
    Антропология депортационной травмы
    калмыков
    С предисловием Кэролайн Хамфри
    ISBN 3-89821-506-7

21 Юлия Лидерман
    Мотивы «проверки» и «испытания»
    в постсоветской культуре
    Советское прошлое в российском
    кинематографе 1990-х годов
    С предисловием Евгения Марголита
    ISBN 3-89821-511-3

22 Tanya Lokshina, Ray Thomas, Mary
    Mayer (Eds.)
    The Imposition of a Fake Political
    Settlement in the Northern Caucasus
    The 2003 Chechen Presidential Election
    ISBN 3-89821-436-2

23 Timothy McCajor Hall, Rosie Read
    (Eds.)
    Changes in the Heart of Europe
    Recent Ethnographies of Czechs, Slovaks,
    Roma, and Sorbs
    With an afterword by Zdeněk Salzmann
    ISBN 3-89821-606-3

24 Christian Autengruber
    Die politischen Parteien in Bulgarien
    und Rumänien
    Eine vergleichende Analyse seit Beginn der
    90er Jahre
    Mit einem Vorwort von Dorothée de Nève
    ISBN 3-89821-476-1

25 Annette Freyberg-Inan with Radu
    Cristescu
    The Ghosts in Our Classrooms, or:
    John Dewey Meets Ceauşescu
    The Promise and the Failures of Civic
    Education in Romania
    ISBN 3-89821-416-8

26 John B. Dunlop
    The 2002 Dubrovka and 2004 Beslan
    Hostage Crises
    A Critique of Russian Counter-Terrorism
    With a foreword by Donald N. Jensen
    ISBN 3-89821-608-X

27 Peter Koller
    Das touristische Potenzial von
    Kam''janec'–Podil's'kyj
    Eine fremdenverkehrsgeographische
    Untersuchung der Zukunftsperspektiven und
    Maßnahmenplanung zur
    Destinationsentwicklung des „ukrainischen
    Rothenburg"
    Mit einem Vorwort von Kristiane Klemm
    ISBN 3-89821-640-3

28 Françoise Daucé, Elisabeth Sieca-
    Kozlowski (Eds.)
    Dedovshchina in the Post-Soviet
    Military
    Hazing of Russian Army Conscripts in a
    Comparative Perspective
    With a foreword by Dale Herspring
    ISBN 3-89821-616-0

29 *Florian Strasser*
Zivilgesellschaftliche Einflüsse auf die Orange Revolution
Die gewaltlose Massenbewegung und die ukrainische Wahlkrise 2004
Mit einem Vorwort von Egbert Jahn
ISBN 3-89821-648-9

30 *Rebecca S. Katz*
The Georgian Regime Crisis of 2003-2004
A Case Study in Post-Soviet Media Representation of Politics, Crime and Corruption
ISBN 3-89821-413-3

31 *Vladimir Kantor*
Willkür oder Freiheit
Beiträge zur russischen Geschichtsphilosophie
Ediert von Dagmar Herrmann sowie mit einem Vorwort versehen von Leonid Luks
ISBN 3-89821-589-X

32 *Laura A. Victoir*
The Russian Land Estate Today
A Case Study of Cultural Politics in Post-Soviet Russia
With a foreword by Priscilla Roosevelt
ISBN 3-89821-426-5

33 *Ivan Katchanovski*
Cleft Countries
Regional Political Divisions and Cultures in Post-Soviet Ukraine and Moldova
With a foreword by Francis Fukuyama
ISBN 3-89821-558-X

34 *Florian Mühlfried*
Postsowjetische Feiern
Das Georgische Bankett im Wandel
Mit einem Vorwort von Kevin Tuite
ISBN 3-89821-601-2

35 *Roger Griffin, Werner Loh, Andreas Umland (Eds.)*
Fascism Past and Present, West and East
An International Debate on Concepts and Cases in the Comparative Study of the Extreme Right
With an afterword by Walter Laqueur
ISBN 3-89821-674-8

36 *Sebastian Schlegel*
Der „Weiße Archipel"
Sowjetische Atomstädte 1945-1991
Mit einem Geleitwort von Thomas Bohn
ISBN 3-89821-679-9

37 *Vyacheslav Likhachev*
Political Anti-Semitism in Post-Soviet Russia
Actors and Ideas in 1991-2003
Edited and translated from Russian by Eugene Veklerov
ISBN 3-89821-529-6

38 *Josette Baer (Ed.)*
Preparing Liberty in Central Europe
Political Texts from the Spring of Nations 1848 to the Spring of Prague 1968
With a foreword by Zdeněk V. David
ISBN 3-89821-546-6

39 *Михаил Лукьянов*
Российский консерватизм и реформа, 1907-1914
С предисловием Марка Д. Стейнберга
ISBN 3-89821-503-2

40 *Nicola Melloni*
Market Without Economy
The 1998 Russian Financial Crisis
With a foreword by Eiji Furukawa
ISBN 3-89821-407-9

41 *Dmitrij Chmelnizki*
Die Architektur Stalins
Bd. 1: Studien zu Ideologie und Stil
Bd. 2: Bilddokumentation
Mit einem Vorwort von Bruno Flierl
ISBN 3-89821-515-6

42 *Katja Yafimava*
Post-Soviet Russian-Belarussian Relationships
The Role of Gas Transit Pipelines
With a foreword by Jonathan P. Stern
ISBN 3-89821-655-1

43 *Boris Chavkin*
Verflechtungen der deutschen und russischen Zeitgeschichte
Aufsätze und Archivfunde zu den Beziehungen Deutschlands und der Sowjetunion von 1917 bis 1991
Ediert von Markus Edlinger sowie mit einem Vorwort versehen von Leonid Luks
ISBN 3-89821-756-5

44 Anastasija Grynenko in Zusammenarbeit mit Claudia Dathe
Die Terminologie des Gerichtswesens der Ukraine und Deutschlands im Vergleich
Eine übersetzungswissenschaftliche Analyse juristischer Fachbegriffe im Deutschen, Ukrainischen und Russischen
Mit einem Vorwort von Ulrich Hartmann
ISBN 3-89821-691-8

45 Anton Burkov
The Impact of the European Convention on Human Rights on Russian Law
Legislation and Application in 1996-2006
With a foreword by Françoise Hampson
ISBN 978-3-89821-639-5

46 Stina Torjesen, Indra Overland (Eds.)
International Election Observers in Post-Soviet Azerbaijan
Geopolitical Pawns or Agents of Change?
ISBN 978-3-89821-743-9

47 Taras Kuzio
Ukraine – Crimea – Russia
Triangle of Conflict
ISBN 978-3-89821-761-3

48 Claudia Šabić
"Ich erinnere mich nicht, aber L'viv!"
Zur Funktion kultureller Faktoren für die Institutionalisierung und Entwicklung einer ukrainischen Region
Mit einem Vorwort von Melanie Tatur
ISBN 978-3-89821-752-1

49 Marlies Bilz
Tatarstan in der Transformation
Nationaler Diskurs und Politische Praxis 1988-1994
Mit einem Vorwort von Frank Golczewski
ISBN 978-3-89821-722-4

50 Марлен Ларюэль (ред.)
Современные интерпретации русского национализма
ISBN 978-3-89821-795-8

51 Sonja Schüler
Die ethnische Dimension der Armut
Roma im postsozialistischen Rumänien
Mit einem Vorwort von Anton Sterbling
ISBN 978-3-89821-776-3

52 Галина Кожевникова
Радикальный национализм в России и противодействие ему
Сборник докладов Центра «Сова» за 2004-2007 гг.
С предисловием Александра Верховского
ISBN 978-3-89821-721-7

53 Галина Кожевникова и Владимир Прибыловский
Российская власть в биографиях I
Высшие должностные лица РФ в 2004 г.
ISBN 978-3-89821-796-5

54 Галина Кожевникова и Владимир Прибыловский
Российская власть в биографиях II
Члены Правительства РФ в 2004 г.
ISBN 978-3-89821-797-2

55 Галина Кожевникова и Владимир Прибыловский
Российская власть в биографиях III
Руководители федеральных служб и агентств РФ в 2004 г.
ISBN 978-3-89821-798-9

56 Ileana Petroniu
Privatisierung in Transformationsökonomien
Determinanten der Restrukturierungs-Bereitschaft am Beispiel Polens, Rumäniens und der Ukraine
Mit einem Vorwort von Rainer W. Schäfer
ISBN 978-3-89821-790-3

57 Christian Wipperfürth
Russland und seine GUS-Nachbarn
Hintergründe, aktuelle Entwicklungen und Konflikte in einer ressourcenreichen Region
ISBN 978-3-89821-801-6

58 Togzhan Kassenova
From Antagonism to Partnership
The Uneasy Path of the U.S.-Russian Cooperative Threat Reduction
With a foreword by Christoph Bluth
ISBN 978-3-89821-707-1

59 Alexander Höllwerth
Das sakrale eurasische Imperium des Aleksandr Dugin
Eine Diskursanalyse zum postsowjetischen russischen Rechtsextremismus
Mit einem Vorwort von Dirk Uffelmann
ISBN 978-3-89821-813-9

60 Олег Рябов
    «Россия-Матушка»
    Национализм, гендер и война в России XX
    века
    С предисловием Елены Гощило
    ISBN 978-3-89821-487-2

61 Ivan Maistrenko
    Borot'bism
    A Chapter in the History of the Ukrainian
    Revolution
    With a new introduction by Chris Ford
    Translated by George S. N. Luckyj with the
    assistance of Ivan L. Rudnytsky
    ISBN 978-3-89821-697-5

62 Maryna Romanets
    Anamorphosic Texts and
    Reconfigured Visions
    Improvised Traditions in Contemporary
    Ukrainian and Irish Literature
    ISBN 978-3-89821-576-3

63 Paul D'Anieri and Taras Kuzio (Eds.)
    Aspects of the Orange Revolution I
    Democratization and Elections in Post-
    Communist Ukraine
    ISBN 978-3-89821-698-2

64 Bohdan Harasymiw in collaboration
    with Oleh S. Ilnytzkyj (Eds.)
    Aspects of the Orange Revolution II
    Information and Manipulation Strategies in
    the 2004 Ukrainian Presidential Elections
    ISBN 978-3-89821-699-9

65 Ingmar Bredies, Andreas Umland and
    Valentin Yakushik (Eds.)
    Aspects of the Orange Revolution III
    The Context and Dynamics of the 2004
    Ukrainian Presidential Elections
    ISBN 978-3-89821-803-0

66 Ingmar Bredies, Andreas Umland and
    Valentin Yakushik (Eds.)
    Aspects of the Orange Revolution IV
    Foreign Assistance and Civic Action in the
    2004 Ukrainian Presidential Elections
    ISBN 978-3-89821-808-5

67 Ingmar Bredies, Andreas Umland and
    Valentin Yakushik (Eds.)
    Aspects of the Orange Revolution V
    Institutional Observation Reports on the 2004
    Ukrainian Presidential Elections
    ISBN 978-3-89821-809-2

68 Taras Kuzio (Ed.)
    Aspects of the Orange Revolution VI
    Post-Communist Democratic Revolutions in
    Comparative Perspective
    ISBN 978-3-89821-820-7

69 Tim Bohse
    Autoritarismus statt Selbstverwaltung
    Die Transformation der kommunalen Politik
    in der Stadt Kaliningrad 1990-2005
    Mit einem Geleitwort von Stefan Troebst
    ISBN 978-3-89821-782-8

70 David Rupp
    Die Rußländische Föderation und die
    russischsprachige Minderheit in
    Lettland
    Eine Fallstudie zur Anwaltspolitik Moskaus
    gegenüber den russophonen Minderheiten im
    „Nahen Ausland" von 1991 bis 2002
    Mit einem Vorwort von Helmut Wagner
    ISBN 978-3-89821-778-1

71 Taras Kuzio
    Theoretical and Comparative
    Perspectives on Nationalism
    New Directions in Cross-Cultural and Post-
    Communist Studies
    With a foreword by Paul Robert Magocsi
    ISBN 978-3-89821-815-3

72 Christine Teichmann
    Die Hochschultransformation im
    heutigen Osteuropa
    Kontinuität und Wandel bei der Entwicklung
    des postkommunistischen Universitätswesens
    Mit einem Vorwort von Oskar Anweiler
    ISBN 978-3-89821-842-9

73 Julia Kusznir
    Der politische Einfluss von
    Wirtschaftseliten in russischen
    Regionen
    Eine Analyse am Beispiel der Erdöl- und
    Erdgasindustrie, 1992-2005
    Mit einem Vorwort von Wolfgang Eichwede
    ISBN 978-3-89821-821-4

74 Alena Vysotskaya
    Russland, Belarus und die EU-
    Osterweiterung
    Zur Minderheitenfrage und zum Problem der
    Freizügigkeit des Personenverkehrs
    Mit einem Vorwort von Katlijn Malfliet
    ISBN 978-3-89821-822-1

75 Heiko Pleines (Hrsg.)
    Corporate Governance in post-
    sozialistischen Volkswirtschaften
    ISBN 978-3-89821-766-8

76 Stefan Ihrig
    Wer sind die Moldawier?
    Rumänismus versus Moldowanismus in
    Historiographie und Schulbüchern der
    Republik Moldova, 1991-2006
    Mit einem Vorwort von Holm Sundhaussen
    ISBN 978-3-89821-466-7

77 Galina Kozhevnikova in collaboration
    with Alexander Verkhovsky and
    Eugene Veklerov
    Ultra-Nationalism and Hate Crimes in
    Contemporary Russia
    The 2004-2006 Annual Reports of Moscow's
    SOVA Center
    With a foreword by Stephen D. Shenfield
    ISBN 978-3-89821-868-9

78 Florian Küchler
    The Role of the European Union in
    Moldova's Transnistria Conflict
    With a foreword by Christopher Hill
    ISBN 978-3-89821-850-4

79 Bernd Rechel
    The Long Way Back to Europe
    Minority Protection in Bulgaria
    With a foreword by Richard Crampton
    ISBN 978-3-89821-863-4

80 Peter W. Rodgers
    Nation, Region and History in Post-
    Communist Transitions
    Identity Politics in Ukraine, 1991-2006
    With a foreword by Vera Tolz
    ISBN 978-3-89821-903-7

81 Stephanie Solywoda
    The Life and Work of
    Semen L. Frank
    A Study of Russian Religious Philosophy
    With a foreword by Philip Walters
    ISBN 978-3-89821-457-5

82 Vera Sokolova
    Cultural Politics of Ethnicity
    Discourses on Roma in Communist
    Czechoslovakia
    ISBN 978-3-89821-864-1

83 Natalya Shevchik Ketenci
    Kazakhstani Enterprises in Transition
    The Role of Historical Regional Development
    in Kazakhstan's Post-Soviet Economic
    Transformation
    ISBN 978-3-89821-831-3

84 Martin Malek, Anna Schor-
    Tschudnowskaja (Hrsg.)
    Europa im Tschetschenienkrieg
    Zwischen politischer Ohnmacht und
    Gleichgültigkeit
    Mit einem Vorwort von Lipchan Basajewa
    ISBN 978-3-89821-676-0

85 Stefan Meister
    Das postsowjetische Universitätswesen
    zwischen nationalem und
    internationalem Wandel
    Die Entwicklung der regionalen Hochschule
    in Russland als Gradmesser der
    Systemtransformation
    Mit einem Vorwort von Joan DeBardeleben
    ISBN 978-3-89821-891-7

86 Konstantin Sheiko in collaboration
    with Stephen Brown
    Nationalist Imaginings of the
    Russian Past
    Anatolii Fomenko and the Rise of Alternative
    History in Post-Communist Russia
    With a foreword by Donald Ostrowski
    ISBN 978-3-89821-915-0

87 Sabine Jenni
    Wie stark ist das „Einige Russland"?
    Zur Parteibindung der Eliten und zum
    Wahlerfolg der Machtpartei
    im Dezember 2007
    Mit einem Vorwort von Klaus Armingeon
    ISBN 978-3-89821-961-7

88 Thomas Borén
    Meeting-Places of Transformation
    Urban Identity, Spatial Representations and
    Local Politics in Post-Soviet St Petersburg
    ISBN 978-3-89821-739-2

89 Aygul Ashirova
    Stalinismus und Stalin-Kult in
    Zentralasien
    Turkmenistan 1924-1953
    Mit einem Vorwort von Leonid Luks
    ISBN 978-3-89821-987-7

90   *Leonid Luks*
     Freiheit oder imperiale Größe?
     Essays zu einem russischen Dilemma
     ISBN 978-3-8382-0011-8

91   *Christopher Gilley*
     The 'Change of Signposts' in the
     Ukrainian Emigration
     A Contribution to the History of
     Sovietophilism in the 1920s
     With a foreword by Frank Golczewski
     ISBN 978-3-89821-965-5

92   *Philipp Casula, Jeronim Perovic
     (Eds.)*
     Identities and Politics
     During the Putin Presidency
     The Discursive Foundations of Russia's
     Stability
     With a foreword by Heiko Haumann
     ISBN 978-3-8382-0015-6

93   *Marcel Viëtor*
     Europa und die Frage
     nach seinen Grenzen im Osten
     Zur Konstruktion ‚europäischer Identität' in
     Geschichte und Gegenwart
     Mit einem Vorwort von Albrecht Lehmann
     ISBN 978-3-8382-0045-3

94   *Ben Hellman, Andrei Rogachevskii*
     Filming the Unfilmable
     Casper Wrede's 'One Day in the Life
     of Ivan Denisovich'
     Second, Revised and Expanded Edition
     ISBN 978-3-8382-0044-6

95   *Eva Fuchslocher*
     Vaterland, Sprache, Glaube
     Orthodoxie und Nationenbildung
     am Beispiel Georgiens
     Mit einem Vorwort von Christina von Braun
     ISBN 978-3-89821-884-9

96   *Vladimir Kantor*
     Das Westlertum und der Weg
     Russlands
     Zur Entwicklung der russischen Literatur und
     Philosophie
     Ediert von Dagmar Herrmann
     Mit einem Beitrag von Nikolaus Lobkowicz
     ISBN 978-3-8382-0102-3

97   *Kamran Musayev*
     Die postsowjetische Transformation
     im Baltikum und Südkaukasus
     Eine vergleichende Untersuchung der
     politischen Entwicklung Lettlands und
     Aserbaidschans 1985-2009
     Mit einem Vorwort von Leonid Luks
     Ediert von Sandro Henschel
     ISBN 978-3-8382-0103-0

98   *Tatiana Zhurzhenko*
     Borderlands into Bordered Lands
     Geopolitics of Identity in Post-Soviet Ukraine
     With a foreword by Dieter Segert
     ISBN 978-3-8382-0042-2

99   *Кирилл Галушко, Лидия Смола
     (ред.)*
     Пределы падения – варианты
     украинского будущего
     Аналитико-прогностические исследования
     ISBN 978-3-8382-0148-1

100 *Michael Minkenberg (ed.)*
     Historical Legacies and the Radical
     Right in Post-Cold War Central and
     Eastern Europe
     With an afterword by Sabrina P. Ramet
     ISBN 978-3-8382-0124-5

101 *David-Emil Wickström*
     Rocking St. Petersburg
     Transcultural Flows and Identity Politics in
     the St. Petersburg Popular Music Scene
     With a foreword by Yngvar B. Steinholt
     Second, Revised and Expanded Edition
     ISBN 978-3-8382-0100-9

102 *Eva Zabka*
     Eine neue „Zeit der Wirren"?
     Der spät- und postsowjetische Systemwandel
     1985-2000 im Spiegel russischer
     gesellschaftspolitischer Diskurse
     Mit einem Vorwort von Margareta Mommsen
     ISBN 978-3-8382-0161-0

103 *Ulrike Ziemer*
     Ethnic Belonging, Gender and
     Cultural Practices
     Youth Identitites in Contemporary Russia
     With a foreword by Anoop Nayak
     ISBN 978-3-8382-0152-8

104   Ksenia Chepikova
      ‚Einiges Russland' - eine zweite
      KPdSU?
      Aspekte der Identitätskonstruktion einer
      postsowjetischen „Partei der Macht"
      Mit einem Vorwort von Torsten Oppelland
      ISBN 978-3-8382-0311-9

105   Леонид Люкс
      Западничество или евразийство?
      Демократия или идеократия?
      Сборник статей об исторических дилеммах
      России
      С предисловием Владимира Кантора
      ISBN 978-3-8382-0211-2

106   Anna Dost
      Das russische Verfassungsrecht auf dem
      Weg zum Föderalismus und zurück
      Zum Konflikt von Rechtsnormen und
      -wirklichkeit in der Russländischen Föderation
      von 1991 bis 2009
      Mit einem Vorwort von Alexander Blankenagel
      ISBN 978-3-8382-0292-1

107   Philipp Herzog
      Sozialistische Völkerfreundschaft,
      nationaler Widerstand oder harmloser
      Zeitvertreib?
      Zur politischen Funktion der Volkskunst
      im sowjetischen Estland
      Mit einem Vorwort von Andreas Kappeler
      ISBN 978-3-8382-0216-7

108   Marlène Laruelle (ed.)
      Russian Nationalism, Foreign Policy,
      and Identity Debates in Putin's Russia
      New Ideological Patterns after the Orange
      Revolution
      ISBN 978-3-8382-0325-6

109   Michail Logvinov
      Russlands Kampf gegen den
      internationalen Terrorismus
      Eine kritische Bestandsaufnahme des
      Bekämpfungsansatzes
      Mit einem Geleitwort von
      Hans-Henning Schröder
      und einem Vorwort von Eckhard Jesse
      ISBN 978-3-8382-0329-4

110   John B. Dunlop
      The Moscow Bombings
      of September 1999
      Examinations of Russian Terrorist Attacks
      at the Onset of Vladimir Putin's Rule
      Second, Revised and Expanded Edition
      ISBN 978-3-8382-0388-1

111   Андрей А. Ковалёв
      Свидетельство из-за кулис
      российской политики I
      Можно ли делать добро из зла?
      (Воспоминания и размышления о
      последних советских и первых
      послесоветских годах)
      With a foreword by Peter Reddaway
      ISBN 978-3-8382-0302-7

112   Андрей А. Ковалёв
      Свидетельство из-за кулис
      российской политики II
      Угроза для себя и окружающих
      (Наблюдения и предостережения
      относительно происходящего после 2000 г.)
      ISBN 978-3-8382-0303-4

113   Bernd Kappenberg
      Zeichen setzen für Europa
      Der Gebrauch europäischer lateinischer
      Sonderzeichen in der deutschen Öffentlichkeit
      Mit einem Vorwort von Peter Schlobinski
      ISBN 978-3-89821-749-1

114   Ivo Mijnssen
      The Quest for an Ideal Youth in
      Putin's Russia I
      Back to Our Future! History, Modernity, and
      Patriotism according to *Nashi*, 2005-2013
      With a foreword by Jeronim Perović
      Second, Revised and Expanded Edition
      ISBN 978-3-8382-0368-3

115   Jussi Lassila
      The Quest for an Ideal Youth in
      Putin's Russia II
      The Search for Distinctive Conformism in the
      Political Communication of *Nashi*, 2005-2009
      With a foreword by Kirill Postoutenko
      Second, Revised and Expanded Edition
      ISBN 978-3-8382-0415-4

116   Valerio Trabandt
      Neue Nachbarn, gute Nachbarschaft?
      Die EU als internationaler Akteur am Beispiel
      ihrer Demokratieförderung in Belarus und der
      Ukraine 2004-2009
      Mit einem Vorwort von Jutta Joachim
      ISBN 978-3-8382-0437-6

117 *Fabian Pfeiffer*
Estlands Außen- und Sicherheitspolitik I
Der estnische Atlantizismus nach der
wiedererlangten Unabhängigkeit 1991-2004
Mit einem Vorwort von Helmut Hubel
ISBN 978-3-8382-0127-6

118 *Jana Podßuweit*
Estlands Außen- und Sicherheitspolitik II
Handlungsoptionen eines Kleinstaates im
Rahmen seiner EU-Mitgliedschaft (2004-2008)
Mit einem Vorwort von Helmut Hubel
ISBN 978-3-8382-0440-6

119 *Karin Pointner*
Estlands Außen- und Sicherheitspolitik III
Eine gedächtnispolitische Analyse estnischer
Entwicklungskooperation 2006-2010
Mit einem Vorwort von Karin Liebhart
ISBN 978-3-8382-0435-2

120 *Ruslana Vovk*
Die Offenheit der ukrainischen
Verfassung für das Völkerrecht und
die europäische Integration
Mit einem Vorwort von Alexander
Blankenagel
ISBN 978-3-8382-0481-9

121 *Mykhaylo Banakh*
Die Relevanz der Zivilgesellschaft
bei den postkommunistischen
Transformationsprozessen in mittel-
und osteuropäischen Ländern
Das Beispiel der spät- und postsowjetischen
Ukraine 1986-2009
Mit einem Vorwort von Gerhard Simon
ISBN 978-3-8382-0499-4

122 *Michael Moser*
Language Policy and the Discourse on
Languages in Ukraine under President
Viktor Yanukovych (25 February
2010–28 October 2012)
ISBN 978-3-8382-0497-0 (Paperback edition)
ISBN 978-3-8382-0507-6 (Hardcover edition)

123 *Nicole Krome*
Russischer Netzwerkkapitalismus
Restrukturierungsprozesse in der
Russischen Föderation am Beispiel des
Luftfahrtunternehmens "Aviasta"
Mit einem Vorwort von Petra Stykow
ISBN 978-3-8382-0534-2

124 *David R. Marples*
'Our Glorious Past'
Lukashenka's Belarus and
the Great Patriotic War
ISBN 978-3-8382-0574-8 (Paperback edition)
ISBN 978-3-8382-0675-2 (Hardcover edition)

125 *Ulf Walther*
Russlands "neuer Adel"
Die Macht des Geheimdienstes von
Gorbatschow bis Putin
Mit einem Vorwort von Hans-Georg Wieck
ISBN 978-3-8382-0584-7

126 *Simon Geissbühler (Hrsg.)*
Kiew – Revolution 3.0
Der Euromaidan 2013/14 und die
Zukunftsperspektiven der Ukraine
ISBN 978-3-8382-0581-6 (Paperback edition)
ISBN 978-3-8382-0681-3 (Hardcover edition)

127 *Andrey Makarychev*
Russia and the EU
in a Multipolar World
Discourses, Identities, Norms
With a foreword by Klaus Segbers
ISBN 978-3-8382-0629-5

128 *Roland Scharff*
Kasachstan als postsowjetischer
Wohlfahrtsstaat
Die Transformation des sozialen
Schutzsystems
Mit einem Vorwort von Joachim Ahrens
ISBN 978-3-8382-0622-6

129 *Katja Grupp*
Bild Lücke Deutschland
Kaliningrader Studierende sprechen über
Deutschland
Mit einem Vorwort von Martin Schulz
ISBN 978-3-8382-0552-6

130 *Konstantin Sheiko, Stephen Brown*
History as Therapy
Alternative History and Nationalist
Imaginings in Russia, 1991-2014
ISBN 978-3-8382-0665-3

131 *Elisa Kriza*
Alexander Solzhenitsyn: Cold War
Icon, Gulag Author, Russian
Nationalist?
A Study of the Western Reception of his
Literary Writings, Historical Interpretations,
and Political Ideas
With a foreword by Andrei Rogatchevski
ISBN 978-3-8382-0589-2 (Paperback edition)
ISBN 978-3-8382-0690-5 (Hardcover edition)

132 Serghei Golunov
The Elephant in the Room
Corruption and Cheating in Russian Universities
ISBN 978-3-8382-0570-0

133 Manja Hussner, Rainer Arnold (Hgg.)
Verfassungsgerichtsbarkeit in Zentralasien I
Sammlung von Verfassungstexten
ISBN 978-3-8382-0595-3

134 Nikolay Mitrokhin
Die "Russische Partei"
Die Bewegung der russischen Nationalisten in der UdSSR 1953-1985
Aus dem Russischen übertragen von einem Übersetzerteam unter der Leitung von Larisa Schippel
ISBN 978-3-8382-0024-8

135 Manja Hussner, Rainer Arnold (Hgg.)
Verfassungsgerichtsbarkeit in Zentralasien II
Sammlung von Verfassungstexten
ISBN 978-3-8382-0597-7

136 Manfred Zeller
Das sowjetische Fieber
Fußballfans im poststalinistischen Vielvölkerreich
Mit einem Vorwort von Nikolaus Katzer
ISBN 978-3-8382-0757-5

137 Kristin Schreiter
Stellung und Entwicklungspotential zivilgesellschaftlicher Gruppen in Russland
Menschenrechtsorganisationen im Vergleich
ISBN 978-3-8382-0673-8

138 David R. Marples, Frederick V. Mills (eds.)
Ukraine's Euromaidan
Analyses of a Civil Revolution
ISBN 978-3-8382-0660-8

139 Bernd Kappenberg
Setting Signs for Europe
Why Diacritics Matter for European Integration
With a foreword by Peter Schlobinski
ISBN 978-3-8382-0663-9

140 René Lenz
Internationalisierung, Kooperation und Transfer
Externe bildungspolitische Akteure in der Russischen Föderation
Mit einem Vorwort von Frank Ettrich
ISBN 978-3-8382-0751-3

141 Juri Plusnin, Yana Zausaeva, Natalia Zhidkevich, Artemy Pozanenko
Wandering Workers
Mores, Behavior, Way of Life, and Political Status of Domestic Russian Labor Migrants
Translated by Julia Kazantseva
ISBN 978-3-8382-0653-0

142 Matthew Kott, David J. Smith (eds.)
Latvia – A Work in Progress?
100 Years of State- and Nation-building
ISBN 978-3-8382-0648-6

143 Инна Чувычкина (ред.)
Экспортные нефте- и газопроводы на постсоветском пространстве
Анализ трубопроводной политики в свете теории международных отношений
ISBN 978-3-8382-0822-0

144 Johann Zajaczkowski
Russland – eine pragmatische Großmacht?
Eine rollentheoretische Untersuchung russischer Außenpolitik am Beispiel der Zusammenarbeit mit den USA nach 9/11 und des Georgienkrieges von 2008
Mit einem Vorwort von Siegfried Schieder
ISBN 978-3-8382-0837-4

145 Boris Popivanov
Changing Images of the Left in Bulgaria
The Challenge of Post-Communism in the Early 21st Century
ISBN 978-3-8382-0667-7

146 Lenka Krátká
A History of the Czechoslovak Ocean Shipping Company 1948-1989
How a Small, Landlocked Country Ran Maritime Business During the Cold War
ISBN 978-3-8382-0666-0

147 Alexander Sergunin
Explaining Russian Foreign Policy Behavior
Theory and Practice
ISBN 978-3-8382-0752-0

148 Darya Malyutina
     Migrant Friendships in a Super-Diverse City
     Russian-Speakers and their Social Relationships in London in the 21st Century
     With a foreword by Claire Dwyer
     ISBN 978-3-8382-0652-3

149 Alexander Sergunin, Valery Konyshev
     Russia in the Arctic
     Hard or Soft Power?
     ISBN 978-3-8382-0753-7

150 John J. Maresca
     Helsinki Revisited
     A Key U.S. Negotiator's Memoirs on the Development of the CSCE into the OSCE
     With a foreword by Hafiz Pashayev
     ISBN 978-3-8382-0852-7

151 Jardar Østbø
     The New Third Rome
     Readings of a Russian Nationalist Myth
     With a foreword by Pål Kolstø
     ISBN 978-3-8382-0870-1

152 Simon Kordonsky
     Socio-Economic Foundations of the Russian Post-Soviet Regime
     The Resource-Based Economy and Estate-Based Social Structure of Contemporary Russia
     With a foreword by Svetlana Barsukova
     ISBN 978-3-8382-0775-9

153 Duncan Leitch
     Assisting Reform in Post-Communist Ukraine 2000–2012
     The Illusions of Donors and the Disillusion of Beneficiaries
     With a foreword by Kataryna Wolczuk
     ISBN 978-3-8382-0844-2

154 Abel Polese
     Limits of a Post-Soviet State
     How Informality Replaces, Renegotiates, and Reshapes Governance in Contemporary Ukraine
     With a foreword by Colin Williams
     ISBN 978-3-8382-0845-9

155 Mikhail Suslov (ed.)
     Digital Orthodoxy in the Post-Soviet World
     The Russian Orthodox Church and Web 2.0
     With a foreword by Father Cyril Hovorun
     ISBN 978-3-8382-0871-8

156 Leonid Luks
     Zwei „Sonderwege"? Russisch-deutsche Parallelen und Kontraste (1917-2014)
     Vergleichende Essays
     ISBN 978-3-8382-0823-7

157 Vladimir V. Karacharovskiy, Ovsey I. Shkaratan, Gordey A. Yastrebov
     Towards a New Russian Work Culture
     Can Western Companies and Expatriates Change Russian Society?
     With a foreword by Elena N. Danilova
     Translated by Julia Kazantseva
     ISBN 978-3-8382-0902-9

158 Edmund Griffiths
     Aleksandr Prokhanov and Post-Soviet Esotericism
     ISBN 978-3-8382-0903-6

159 Timm Beichelt, Susann Worschech (eds.)
     Transnational Ukraine?
     Networks and Ties that Influence(d) Contemporary Ukraine
     ISBN 978-3-8382-0944-9

160 Mieste Hotopp-Riecke
     Die Tataren der Krim zwischen Assimilation und Selbstbehauptung
     Der Aufbau des krimtatarischen Bildungswesens nach Deportation und Heimkehr (1990-2005)
     Mit einem Vorwort von Swetlana Czerwonnaja
     ISBN 978-3-89821-940-2

161 Olga Bertelsen (ed.)
     Revolution and War in Contemporary Ukraine
     The Challenge of Change
     ISBN 978-3-8382-1016-2

162 Natalya Ryabinska
     Ukraine's Post-Communist Mass Media
     Between Capture and Commercialization
     With a foreword by Marta Dyczok
     ISBN 978-3-8382-1011-7

163   *Alexandra Cotofana,*
      James M. Nyce (eds.)
      Religion and Magic in Socialist and
      Post-Socialist Contexts
      Historic and Ethnographic Case Studies of
      Orthodoxy, Heterodoxy, and Alternative
      Spirituality
      With a foreword by Patrick L. Michelson
      ISBN 978-3-8382-0989-0

164   *Nozima Akhrarkhodjaeva*
      The Instrumentalisation of Mass
      Media in Electoral Authoritarian
      Regimes
      Evidence from Russia's Presidential Election
      Campaigns of 2000 and 2008
      ISBN 978-3-8382-1013-1

ibidem-Verlag

Melchiorstr. 15

D-70439 Stuttgart

info@ibidem-verlag.de

www.ibidem-verlag.de
www.ibidem.eu
www.edition-noema.de
www.autorenbetreuung.de